Understanding Education

Understanding Education

A Sociological Perspective

Sharon Gewirtz and Alan Cribb

polity

KH

First published in 2009 by Polity Press

Polity Press
65 Bridge Street
Cambridge CB2 1UR, UK

Polity Press
350 Main Street
Malden, MA 02148, USA

ISBN-13: 978-0-7456-3344-2
ISBN-13: 978-0-7456-3345-9 (pb)

A catalogue record for this book is available from the British Library.

Typeset in 10.5 on 12 pt Plantin
by Servis Filmsetting Ltd, Stockport, Cheshire
Printed and bound by MPG Books Group, UK

The publisher has used its best endeavours to ensure that the URLs for
external websites referred to in this book are correct and active at the time of
going to press. However, the publisher has no responsibility for the websites
and can make no guarantee that a site will remain live or that the content is or
will remain appropriate.

Every effort has been made to trace all copyright holders, but if any have been
inadvertently overlooked the publisher will be pleased to include any necessary
credits in any subsequent reprint or edition.

For further information on Polity, visit our website: www.politybooks.com

10/07/10

Contents

Preface

Both sociology and education are seemingly defined by rifts. In the sixty or so years since sociology of education has been a recognized academic domain the fault lines and fractures which constitute its internal conversation have multiplied. This means that anyone coming to the field for the first time has not only to grapple with a large set of substantive topics – equality and inequality, knowledge and the curriculum, educational politics and policy, etc. – but they also have to do so through the medium of innumerable theoretical and methodological contests. What is more, over the past thirty years the addition of poststructuralist perspectives to what was already a multi-layered set of disputes has highlighted problems about the nature of sociological knowledge. In particular, these currents have justifiably challenged the authority of sweeping sociological generalizations and have at the same time raised doubts about the point of sociological analysis. In this climate even experienced scholars frequently feel uncertain about the nature of 'the game they are playing'. For these reasons we think that another text which simply maps the substantive field and sets out the many available alternative readings would be of little help. Rather what is needed – and what we are offering here – is a text which is designed actively to 'make sense' of the sociology of education and the disputes that make it up and which includes an explicit discussion of sociological purposes and their relation to social values.

As we shall see, as well as offering a rich set of sometimes competing descriptions and explanations of educational and social relations, institutions and structures, the sociology of education has made a very important contribution to the understanding of social and educational values and how they are produced, allocated and experienced. In

other words, sociology has both descriptive/explanatory and normative agendas.[1] In this book we review and discuss a broad range of
work in the sociology of education that contributes to both of these
agendas and which, we would argue, illuminates the interdependency
of the two. In crude terms, if we are interested in how social and educational institutions and processes work, we need to decide what processes and institutions to look at and what to look for, and in order to
do that we need to have a view about which processes and institutions
matter and why. Similarly, if our values incline us to believe that there
is something wrong with some educational institution or process, and
that therefore it should be changed, we need to have an understanding of why things are the way they are and of how things might be
changed, and this is totally dependent on adequate descriptions and
explanations of social and educational phenomena.

In this book we want to argue that the normative agenda in the
sociology of education has in some ways been relatively neglected.
That is to say, whilst the increasingly complex and theoretically
sophisticated work that has been undertaken by sociologists in education has been rightly celebrated, much less attention has been paid
to the normative dimension of such work. There are arguably two
main reasons for this neglect. First, the normative dimension of work
in sociology of education is very often implicit and is often arguably
treated either as part of the background to, or as a side effect of, the
main descriptive/explanatory function of sociology. Second, many
sociologists for very good reasons are sceptical about the extent to
which it is their business to be making value judgements about the
phenomena that they study or recommendations for action. Whilst we
accept that these are good reasons for this scepticism, we also think it
is important to bring the normative agenda of sociology of education
into the light. Specifically, we would argue that contemporary work
in sociology of education illuminates the many 'goods' and 'harms'
with which education is entangled and thereby makes an important
contribution to the understanding of educational values, which needs
recognition and in itself deserves celebrating. In addition, we would
argue that the debate about the proper level of engagement of sociologists with value judgements and policy recommendations itself
needs to be seen as a central problematic for the field. There are
some sociologists who are ready to embrace the ethical and political
nature of their work explicitly, and even to make recommendations
about what should be done. Others see their work differently and, in
particular, are wary about the 'contaminating' effects of these kinds
of engagement with value. In this book we will argue that both of

these positions have a lot going for them, and we will endeavour to steer a course between them.

The book is divided into three parts. Part I (chapters 1–3) provides a general introduction to the field of sociology of education. Part II (chapters 4–7) focuses on four important themes – social reproduction, knowledge and the curriculum, identity, and teachers' work. Part III (chapter 8) pulls together our conclusions. Two strands run throughout. First, we introduce, open up and discuss a range of competing approaches, theories and explanatory accounts in the sociology of education and do so by discussing examples of sociological writing. Second, we develop our argument about the importance of the normative dimension of sociological work and of the interdependence of normative and descriptive/explanatory dimensions. This second strand is increasingly foregrounded as the book progresses and is the main focus of chapter 8, where we set out our own view about the tension between being engaged with and being wary of the normative agenda.

The focus of specific chapters is as follows. In chapter 1 we introduce the concerns of sociology of education and the potential contribution that sociology has to make to understanding education by focusing on five examples of recent writing in the field. Our aim is to provide a gentle entry point to the discipline, to begin to illustrate the contestability of education and of its nature, purposes and effects, and also thereby to indicate the way in which sociology of education has a preoccupation with value questions, particularly those around educational and social inequality.

Chapters 2 and 3 provide a more substantial introduction to sociology of education by reviewing the most influential theoretical approaches in the field through a focus on 'classic' texts. In chapter 2 we foreground the theme of structure and agency through a consideration of structural functionalism, symbolic interactionism, Marxism and work in the 'new sociology of education', specifically that of Bernstein and Bourdieu. Through its discussion of Marxism and the 'new sociology of education', this chapter also introduces the critical current that runs through a good deal of work in the sociology of education.

This idea of critique provides the main theme for chapter 3, in which we consider a range of work from other critical traditions, namely feminism, critical race theory and poststructuralism. Almost by definition, critical currents in the sociology of education have a strong normative agenda, and thus chapters 2 and 3 considered together provide more detailed illustrations of the richness and complexity of both the normative and the descriptive/explanatory agendas in the sociology of education and the ways in which the two agendas are intertwined.

The chapters in part II revisit some of the central substantive themes introduced in part I and, in so doing, seek to pull together some of the major contributions that sociological work has made to understanding these themes. In chapter 4 we consider the role of education in the reproduction of social and educational advantage. We begin part II with this chapter because it is in the theme of social inequality that the normative dimension is predominantly manifest in the work of sociologists, both implicitly and explicitly. A key aim of this chapter, building on the arguments of part I, is to use the theme of social reproduction to show how the story of sociology of education is arguably one of increasing sophistication and contestation. More importantly, it is also, we suggest, a story which brings home the multiplicity of values that are at stake in education and which simultaneously reveals the difficulty of making clear and confident value judgements either about what has been done or about what ought to be done.

Each of the themes discussed in part II of the book can be seen as connecting with a different 'field of value'. The theme of inequality, which is the focus of chapter 4, also runs through the next three chapters, which, in addition, focus respectively on the value fields of knowledge, identity, and teacher autonomy. As well as reviewing some of the key insights that sociology has to offer in relation to each of these themes, these chapters allow us to advance our argument in two ways. First, in chapters 5 and 6 we show how analytical perspectives on knowledge and identity 'carry' multiple and in some cases conflicting value hierarchies such that adopting an analytic perspective, or affirming the priority of one analytic perspective over another, depends upon a preparedness to discriminate between and 'own' value judgements. Second, in chapters 6 and 7 we expressly address the relationship between sociological analysis and policymaking and argue that there is much to be gained from dialogue between sociologists and policymakers/practitioners. In particular, we contend that sociological analyses are strengthened (epistemologically and not just in terms of their practical relevance) by taking seriously the vantage point of those actors who have to decide what ought to be done.

In chapter 8 we review and summarize the main argument of the book by presenting the case for ethical reflexivity in the sociology of education. Ethical reflexivity, we suggest, is both supported by and supports a policy-oriented approach to sociology, and has the potential, therefore, to contribute to both theory and practice.

Acknowledgements

We would like to thank our colleagues in the Department of Education and Professional Studies at King's for providing such a warm and collegial working environment. Particular thanks go to Louise Archer, Meg Maguire, Anwar Tlili and Chris Winch for the conversations we have shared and for their practical support, without which the writing of this book would have been much more difficult. Our ideas have also benefited from both private and public exchanges with Martyn Hammersley, and we are very grateful to him for the constructive and stimulating spirit in which he has debated some of the core issues discussed here with us. We are grateful to participants at meetings where we presented earlier versions of some of the chapters, including the International Sociology of Education Annual Conference (chapter 4) and seminars at Roehampton University (chapter 5), the University of Sussex (chapter 6) and the University of Bergen (chapter 7). And we have had very helpful comments on individual chapters from other colleagues, among them Ingrid Helgøy, Ian Hextall, Anne Homme, Ken Jones, Pat Mahony, Heather Mendick and Sally Power. Thanks are also due to the two anonymous readers appointed by Polity for their very encouraging, thoughtful and useful feedback. In addition, we would like to thank Jonathan Skerrett and Clare Ansell, who have worked so sensitively and effectively with us on this project and made us feel glad that we were producing a book for Polity.

We are grateful to Symposium Journals and the Taylor & Francis Group (http://www.informaworld.com) for permission to use material adapted from previously published work (Gewirtz and Cribb 2003, 2006, 2008a; Cribb and Gewirtz 2007). This material has been substantially revised before inclusion here.

This volume was entirely co-written, and thus represents the coming together of different histories and influences. For that reason we are very conscious of the many other people who have contributed indirectly to a book such as this having been produced. In that regard we would especially like to acknowledge the influence of Stephen Ball, Harry Lesser, Jenny Ozga, Raymond Plant and Geoff Whitty. Of course, we are responsible for the text; but if you don't like it we would prefer it if you blamed them.

PART I

Approaching Education Sociologically

1
Understanding Education: the Role of Sociology

[P]arents are increasingly using the Internet to undertake their own independent research into the conditions with which their children have been diagnosed. No longer content to leave 'the medical side' to the experts, in some cases parents are gaining a grasp of medical discourses that goes beyond what would be typically expected of a 'lay person'. (Fisher and Fisher 2007: 521)

Many people, when they hear the word education, will automatically think of schools and schoolteachers, and indeed in much of this book we will use examples which relate to schooling. However, it is important to begin by underlining how mistaken this equation is. The quote with which we have started is from an article about parents of disabled babies who use the Internet to educate themselves about 'expert' medical diagnoses of their children's conditions. This is just one instance of a form of education that takes place outside formal settings.

In this chapter we want to use this and four other examples to explore the nature of education. Our aim is not only to illustrate the diversity of phenomena that can fall under the heading of education but also to indicate the value of sociological readings in helping us to make sense of education. At the end of the chapter we will also offer a short general account of the field of sociology of education and of some of the disputes that characterize the field. But we prefer to begin by illustrating the business of sociology of education through the examples we have chosen. In doing so, we will start to explore and unpack the ways in which education is a contested domain – that is to say, one in which there are many disputes about, for example, its purposes and its various effects on individuals and societies. Whilst education is generally taken to be a good thing, we shall see that sociological work illuminates practical contests about whether and why it is good in various ways for people who are differently located and the ways in which it is connected more widely with power and social inequality.

Education as a contested domain

Example 1: Parents of disabled babies

The example of parents of disabled babies using the Internet to learn about their children's conditions begins to illustrate both the diversity and the contestability of educational purposes and processes. For a start it reminds us that learners and learning do not always depend upon teachers, or at least not in the conventional sense. The parents referred to in the quote with which we began are using the resources of the Internet – and one another – to build their knowledge and understanding. The article from which it comes is about autodidacticism, the process of self-teaching in which these parents are cast as both learners and teachers.

This example also illuminates a particular kind of educational space – one which is less rigid and more dialogical than is typical in formal education. Whilst in more conventional educational settings the curriculum is usually divided up into discrete subjects, the 'curriculum' that is being constructed by these parents on the web is more fluid and less bounded, with the parents moving readily from conversations about parenting to ones about politics and society:

> While the Web-based communities provide rich resources of knowledge that parents share with each other, they also develop in unexpected ways . . . evolv[ing] along paths that are no longer dedicated to parenting, addressing instead political and controversial issues of the day such as . . . the current President . . . and whether social mobility within the USA is largely a myth. In other cases, parents challenge the notion of disability as deficit and learn through dialogue to develop more positive articulations of disability. (Fisher and Fisher 2007: 521–2)

We have used the term conversation to describe the kind of communication in which these parents are engaged. Yet even to talk about conversation in an educational setting is relatively unusual, as this mode of interaction can so easily be stifled by the inequalities in power that often characterize education. The fluidity and openness of the conversations that these parents are having with one another, and are learning from, are arguably made possible because there is a presumption of equality among the members of this self-learning community. Whilst such conversations are not impossible in formal educational settings, they tend to be rarer for many reasons, including the fact that in formal settings so often what we learn, how we learn and the pace at which we learn is directed by others – by the teacher, by another agent or by some combination of agents, but, crucially, not by ourselves as learners.

The relationships the parents belonging to these web-based communities have with one another are very different to the relationships they have with the professionals who are responsible for diagnosing and treating their children. In these professional–client relationships the presumption tends to be one of inequality in which the professionals generally hold the upper hand, as their socially sanctioned expertise gives them the power to name the conditions of the children and arbitrate on what the appropriate treatment should be. But, in the process of becoming more knowledgeable about their children's conditions, these parents are beginning to challenge that expertise – and hence the expert status – of the professionals. For example, Lesley is a parent of a child who has been diagnosed with autism:

> Lesley's views on her son's autism, developed through parenting and caring for her son and in dialogue with others through her many Internet contacts, resonate with a growing body of research on disability . . . Lesley's view is that the inner life of those diagnosed as autistic should be seen more in terms of neuro-diversity and less in terms of disability. While her son is 'non-verbal', she provides multiple examples of the sophisticated alternative modes of communication he has developed. His (and Lesley's) communicative 'expertise' tends to be overlooked by many of the professionals involved with her son who see legitimised knowledge as skills that are defined and taught by professionals operating within the public sphere. (Fisher and Fisher 2007: 522)

So, although Lesley has developed what the authors of this article suggest are 'valuable insights and . . . views [that] might usefully be employed to adapt and to develop services' (ibid.), these insights and views are not valued by many of the professionals with whom she has come into contact. In furnishing themselves with expertise and alternative perspectives on disability, parents like Lesley find themselves in conflict with those professionals who are normally deemed to be the authorities on the conditions of their children and the arbiters of how they should be treated. As Lesley puts it:

It's very hard for people to accept that we might actually be acquiring expertise in this area. That is not intended to threaten anybody but a lot of people experience it as professionally threatening. I think they don't want to know about the things that we've found out. (Ibid.)

What this example also illustrates, therefore, is that knowledge and power are intimately bound up together. The power of professionals – to diagnose, define a condition as a problem that needs to be treated and decide what counts as an appropriate treatment – is rooted in and sustained by their access to knowledge that is socially valued – in this case, medical knowledge acquired through several years of formal training and on-the-job experience. However, once that socially valued knowledge becomes more widely distributed – e.g. through self-educating web-based communities – and once it begins to be challenged by those who want to assert the value of a different kind of knowledge – e.g. knowledge derived from personal experience and dialogue with others in similar circumstances – traditional professional–client power relationships may be unsettled. This point is underlined by Fisher and Fisher's ascription of these parents as 'subversive autodidacts', thus highlighting the ways in which education can serve to subvert dominant knowledge and practices and not just reproduce them.

These struggles over what counts as valuable knowledge also have important emotional components. As Lesley points out, doctors can feel threatened when parents challenge their expert knowledge. Similarly, it can be very upsetting and frustrating for parents when seeing their detailed first-hand knowledge of their own children's condition being ignored, especially where there is a real risk to their children's health and wellbeing.

So through the example of these autodidact parents we have begun to indicate something of the terrain and some of the issues with which sociology of education is concerned. We have, for example, begun to indicate something of the enormity of that terrain – that sociology of education cannot be reduced to the sociology of schools and schooling (or, for that matter, the sociology of any other formal educational setting or process). Although it would be fair to say that most work in sociology of education does focus on formal settings, the sociological gaze can be cast on any setting, activity or interaction in which education takes place – homes, streets, workplaces, dance studios, sports fields, TV viewing, museum visiting, our encounters with people we meet on a daily basis, or even our encounters with those we might meet just once or twice in a lifetime.

We have also seen how particular phenomena – in this case the activities of these parents – can be understood both at the level of the individual (e.g. individual parents each with their own particular motivations, although each concerned to do their best to help their babies) and at a social level (e.g. the rise of specialist web-based communities with the potential to challenge the monopoly of knowledge and power in the hands of professional groups). The sociological gaze seeks to encompass the individual and the social level of description and explanation, and to illuminate the relationships between these two levels.

Finally, we have begun to open up some central themes in sociology of education. In broad terms sociology of education is about the relationship between education and society. It is about how formal and informal educational institutions, processes and experiences are shaped by and in turn contribute to shaping wider social relations, structures, experiences, values and identities. We have already seen that this includes an interest in struggles over what counts as valuable knowledge, an interest in the role that education and the knowledge it provides can play in reinforcing or subverting established relations of power, and an interest in the emotional dynamics and consequences of educational processes.

Example 2: Bedouin girls 'dropping out' from school

We now want to turn to our second example to introduce what has arguably been *the* central debate in sociology of education – namely inequalities in educational experiences, including how educational processes are implicated in the reproduction of broader social inequalities. The example is taken from an article about the high rates of 'dropout' of Bedouin girls from school in the Negev region of Israel:

> Dropout rates among Bedouins are the highest in Israel, especially for girls. A report by Katz (1998) indicates drop out rates of 10% in the Jewish sector, 40% in the entire Arab sector and more than 67% among the Bedouins. In Rahat, the first Bedouin city in Israel, the overall dropout rate among 17 year olds reached 40% in 2002, and several of its neighbourhoods had a 100% dropout rate for girls . . . The number of female Bedouin students increases every year, but the size of this increase decreases from one grade to the next. (Abu-Rabia-Queder 2006: 5)

'Dropout' rates are one of a range of kinds of statistics that can be used to map the distribution of educational opportunity and advantage, and in this quote such statistics are used to illustrate how completion of schooling varies dramatically both in different ethnically defined sectors of the Israeli population and according to gender, with Bedouin girls being the least advantaged in this respect. This is seen to matter because of the widespread perception that access to formal education is a good thing. And if we assume that access to schooling is a good thing because it provides access to other social goods, including cultural, economic and political ones, then statistics such as these point to fundamental injustices whose effects extend far beyond the domain of schooling itself. It is for this reason that the subject of access to schooling has been so central to sociology of education.

However, this example also raises questions about whether schooling *should* be taken for granted as a good thing. In this case, it seems that at least some Bedouin parents are concerned that schooling may have harmful consequences for their daughters, and their wider families, and may thereby also undermine traditional Bedouin values. For example:

> many parents do not send their daughters to school for fear of contact with boys from other tribes, which could damage the family honor. Many girls have to walk to a distant school or travel in mix-sex buses, placing them in a dangerous zone over which parents have no control. (Abu-Rabia-Queder 2006: 5)

This concern is reflected in the following comment from one of the fathers interviewed by Abu-Rabia-Queder:

> My daughter, Manal, had too many men asking for her hand. So we preferred to get her married instead of being seen in school by different men. You know what happens with boys and girls in school. I don't want there to be any bad rumours about her. (Ibid.: 10)

What is at stake here seems to be a potential conflict between the values of schooling and the values of the home. It is, therefore, too simplistic to say that schooling is about the distribution of uncontestable benefits when it could also be seen as a process of disrupting identities and acculturating young people away from family norms and towards state norms. The question of whether it is a good or bad thing for these Bedouin girls to go to school relates to a very difficult set of questions to which we will return later in the book (for example, in chapters 5 and 6 on knowledge and identity) – that is, questions about how we decide what is good or bad in education and overlapping questions about whose interests educational processes serve. In this case it is possible to construct Bedouin families either as obstructing the beneficent intentions of the state or as protecting their traditions against the unwarranted and misjudged paternalism of the state.

Understanding education thus necessarily depends on dealing with competing perspectives and sets of value judgements. For example, if we want to explain the differential patterns of dropout from schools, it is evident from the perspectives captured in Abu-Rabia-Queder's article that different kinds of explanation will be offered by different parties. The explanation offered by the schooling authorities is likely to centre on the 'obstacles' provided by the 'lay beliefs' of the Bedouin people – i.e. the source of 'the problem' will be seen to lie in the culture of the home. The explanation offered by Bedouin parents is likely to centre on the unresponsiveness of schooling policies to their families' needs and values – i.e. here 'the problem' will be located in the culture of the school and the schooling system. Questions about explanation are, therefore, inextricably linked both to questions about the distribution of responsibility and to the identification of possible policy solutions. That is to say, in emphasizing a certain explanation we could, at the same time, be seen as implying that certain people need to change what they are doing in certain kinds of ways. So, for example, if the problem is located in the home, then the policy solution is to get families to behave in different ways, whereas if it is located in the school system, then the policy solution is to change the schooling system. The author of the paper is in part attempting to identify a more nuanced set of explanations and policy solutions that steer a course between these two perspectives by proposing 'an alternative approach to the "modern/traditional" dichotomy, perceiving the traditional nature of Bedouin society not as an inhibitor, but as a possible vehicle to promote women by weaving the modern and traditional together' (Abu-Rabia-Queder 2006: 6).

Example 3: Social-class differences in college pathways

Our third example has some strong parallels with the previous one, in that it relates to a group of students whose educational trajectory is 'interrupted', and to the question of inequalities in educational pathways and experiences. However, it is not a study of so-called dropouts but rather one of students who successfully navigate their way through higher education (HE). HE is a sector that is both educationally and socially important. It has intrinsic educational importance because it is a key site of knowledge production and provides an opportunity for (predominantly young) people to be inducted into the cultures and practices of knowledge production. In other words, it is centrally concerned with making, using and sharing the tools that enable us to understand – and change – the world. It is socially important, not only because it distributes academic credentials which give access to other socially and economically valued goods, but also because it is a social and economic force in its own right, representing a substantial proportion of investment and employment in many localities.

For many individuals and families, being able to attend a university and obtain a degree is a key marker of educational success, and, in this sense, examining the experiences of HE students can be seen as the study of the educationally successful. Nonetheless, it is important to look more closely at this group of students to understand how inequalities persist at every stage of formal education, the form these inequalities take and the diversity of student experiences attached to them.

This is the terrain that concerns Goldrick-Rab (2006) in her paper 'Following their every move', which explores the different pathways that students take through the US HE system. The paper is an analysis of the educational histories of 4,628 students, all of whom had completed a bachelor's degree, who were (after weighting) 'representative of the approximately 1.5 million high school seniors who enrol in four-year colleges and universities each year following graduation from high school' (ibid.: 66). Goldrick-Rab's aim is to map the different patterns of student attendance in HE, to look at the factors in the students' life and educational histories that correlate with certain patterns of attendance, and thereby to suggest possible explanations for different attendance patterns. Her model looks specifically at two factors: first, the number of times students take a break in their studies; and, second, the number of times students switch between different HE institutions. Goldrick-Rab is at pains to describe these different pathways in a relatively neutral language and to 'avoid any value judgements or negative connotations' in the labels that she uses to capture the pathways (ibid.: 68). For example, she talks about 'students who enrol discontinuously' rather than 'stopouts' or 'dropouts'. One of her aims is to show that statistics on students moving between institutions, considered on their own, 'conceal' very different experiences and explanations. There are, in particular, ways in which students changing HE institutions might be read by some as evidence of a highly successful education marketplace where 'educational institutions treat students as consumers' and 'students respond in kind by attending multiple institutions to meet their specific needs' (ibid.: 62). However, another reading is that discontinuous enrolment provides evidence of the imperfections of a market-based system which can lead to disrupted educational pathways for those least well placed to work the system to their advantage.

The study makes use of a very extensive data set, including complete college transcripts and multiple interviews with all the students which together provide detailed information on age, gender, 'race', high school experiences and test scores, along with information on parental education, income and occupation (used as a measure of socio-economic status (SES)). This data set obviously allows for a considerable amount of statistical analysis. Here we will just briefly summarize Goldrick-Rab's key findings and conclusions. Her central findings are that there is a significant social class difference between those students who either remain at a single institution or move between institutions 'fluidly' and those whose studies at an institution are interrupted or who move 'discontinuously' (i.e. with a period of study interruption between institutions). As she puts it:

> students from families with fewer resources have over four times (4.18) the odds of experiencing an interrupted pathway and over four times (4.11) the odds of engaging in interrupted movement than do students from upper socioeconomic backgrounds. (Goldrick-Rab 2006: 72)

Combined with other research that shows a strong correlation between 'non-traditional' pathways and the successful completion of degree study, this analysis indicates that very different degrees of struggle lie behind the various 'success stories' of this cohort of graduates:

> These findings imply that students with greater access to financial resources are better able to take advantage of the new HE marketplace. Given the significant link between social class and interrupted schooling, it seems reasonable to conjecture that low-SES students who change schools interrupt their schooling not because they are shopping, partying, or choosing to take time off to 'find themselves', but because they have suffered academically or financially in school. Thus, while some analysts have suggested that competition among institutions will benefit disadvantaged students . . . these results indicate otherwise. (Ibid.: 73)

Indeed, Goldrick-Rab's analysis suggests that superficially similar pathways of 'non-traditional' attendance may require entirely contrasting explanations:

Some students may indeed 'shop' their way through college and thus engage in concerted and intentional moves among institutions, while others may be shuttled and pushed throughout the system by various constraints. (Ibid.: 66)

One of the reasons we have chosen this as an example is that it clearly illustrates the ways in which education can be seen as a commodity in both private and public sector markets and not just as a public good. In other words, education can in some respects be seen as an item that can be purchased, and thus in many respects as analogous to any other good that one might buy in the marketplace, whether it be food, fridges, cars or houses. However, it is perhaps best understood to be more like buying a house or stocks and shares than consumable goods, in that it represents an investment that might yield dividends in the long term or by contrast may lose its value. To talk in these terms will jar with many educators who, quite understandably, will often place much more emphasis on the intrinsic value of education to the individual or on the value of education as a public good – i.e. as something which benefits society as a whole. But it is important to understand that, for some policymakers, providers and students, the commodification of education is not something to be rejected or even reluctantly accepted but is rather something to be embraced and positively encouraged. Work such as Goldrick-Rab's – and this includes many analogous studies in sociology of education – is important because it helps us look beyond the ideological claims and counter-claims about the relative advantages and disadvantages of education markets towards a more detailed description of the consequences of the differential effects of markets on different kinds of education 'consumers'. In particular, this work problematizes the notion of students-as-choosers in market thinking and, as Goldrick-Rab suggests, brings home the difference between those students for whom choice is to a large extent real and those whose 'choices' are forced upon them. In doing so, Goldrick-Rab's research points to one – sometimes neglected – form of class stratification within the population of HE students. There are, of course, multiple forms of stratification most obviously relating to the relative social prestige attached to different kinds of HE providers and different kinds of programmes of study, for example, the prestige attached to having a law degree from an Ivy League university compared with that attached to having a degree in sports studies from a state college. Nonetheless, work like Goldrick-Rab's contributes an important set of insights towards the study of HE stratification because it brings home the extent to which the 'felt experience' of HE is itself stratified. In other words, 'doing a degree' for a middle-class student without any family responsibilities or financial constraints is simply different than it is for a student who has to juggle their studies with paid work and other commitments.

Of course the kind of sociological readings that are made in this area are likely to be ethically and politically contentious. As we have noted, the phenomena that Goldrick-Rab and others are analysing might be positively evaluated by some people as a sign of the advantages of market flexibility in HE (after all, these students all graduated). And, as in the previous example, there is scope to place the explanatory emphasis in more than one place. We can, in brief, think primarily in terms of more or less *capable* consumers or of more or less *advantaged* consumers of educational goods. Goldrick-Rab's account shows that the emphasis we favour in our readings will depend upon how far we foreground the agency of the students or the structural factors that shape students' agency. But it also shows that the ways in which we conceptualize and balance explanatory reference to agency and structure may vary from case to case. And, once again, questions of explanation here are linked into questions about the distribution of responsibility and questions about possible policy solutions.

Example 4: The role of museums in defining the origins of humankind

Our fourth example is drawn from an article by Scott (2005), who has explored museum visitors' understandings of the origins of humankind and the role that human evolution exhibitions play in reinforcing or challenging those understandings. As Scott explains, there is a tendency in some of these exhibitions to conflate 'the African' with 'the primitive' and 'the European' with 'the advanced'; and, as she also makes clear, these images and associations are not confined to museums but have a widespread cultural presence:

> One idea that museum visitors often share is the misconception that Africa is evolutionarily inferior to Europe – a product of museum iconography, lingering Victorian anthropological folklore, and globalized media that continue to stigmatize sub-Saharan Africa as prehistoric. . . . A significant number of museum visitors, whether Kenyan, British or American, still seem to associate features deemed unique to indigenous Africans with a less evolved state, culturally and biologically. The misconception of an evolutionarily inferior Africa . . . strongly suggests that historical forms of racism have not disappeared into history. (Scott 2005: 75, 82)

Like our first example, this example shows how educational processes transcend conventional schooling settings and indicates that
what gets learnt or reinforced in informal contexts can be as significant as what happens in the classroom. Scott's work highlights how
racist confusions and simplifications that are embedded in localized
exhibitions and texts are part of a wider set of racist discourses that
operate on a global scale:

> In many ways, the world's museum visitors . . . are part of a 'transna-
> tional cultural elite.' They often fundamentally share exposure to similar
> forms of mass globalized media – television, films, magazines, and the
> Internet. This becomes part of the important cultural information they
> bring with them to the natural history museum. (Scott 2005: 78)

Amongst other things, Scott's work provides a compelling example
of the ways in which the practice of science education – on the surface
one of the most value-neutral parts of the curriculum – is shaped by
ethical and political value judgements and has ethical and political
effects. There are well-known controversies about the teaching of
human evolution, with various religious groups contesting its validity, but here we can see that, even accepting the scientific validity of
evolutionary theory, important social implications can follow from
the kinds of resources and images that are used in its teaching.

However, Scott also points out that, although the '"up from
Africa" evolutionary progressive narrative is internalized by a range
of culturally and nationally diverse peoples', this narrative does not
go unchallenged, particularly by black visitors:

> Those who identify culturally with the African continent (such as
> Kenyan, African-American or Afro-British visitors) often have more
> complicated relationships to exhibition representations of Africa than
> other visitors. Black museum audiences often identified with Africa not
> only as the cradle of mankind, but as an important site of cultural herit-
> age as well. Furthermore, black visitors frequently displayed an acute
> sense of what it means to be interpolated as primitive in the museum
> and in world politics. . . . Among audiences at all the museums, black
> visitors were more likely to initiate discussions regarding the racial
> implications of exhibitions there. Occasionally these audiences sub-
> verted the conventional 'up from Africa' evolutionary progress narra-
> tive. (Scott 2005: 83)

Scott's analysis of visitors' engagement with museum exhibits
rests on a view of learning as an active process of meaning making.
On this view, the racist representations of museum exhibits are

not simply transmitted to and accepted by a quiescent population of visitors, but rather visitors bring with them a diversity of prior knowledge, beliefs and forms of interpretive expertise. In some cases this knowledge and expertise enables visitors to engage critically with and challenge the objects on display, whilst in others misconceptions and prejudices are reinforced in the interaction between the visitor and the museum objects.

Scott's discussion of the nature of the interaction between museum visitors and museum objects touches on the fundamental debate in sociology of education, introduced above, about the reproduction of social inequalities. Whilst some sociologists have tended to emphasize the role of social structures and social institutions in creating and reinforcing hierarchies, others have explored the ways in which hierarchies are reproduced through human agency. As we have already begun to see, the interaction between structure and agency is an important theme in sociology and one that recurs throughout this book. It is also the focus of the final example in this chapter.

Example 5: Girls, boys and the 'heterosexual matrix'

The setting for our final example is the primary school classroom and playground, and this example concerns the ways in which young children talk about and 'perform' gender and sexuality in their everyday school lives. It is drawn from the work of Renold (2005, 2006), one of a growing number of sociologists interested in exploring the ways in which the identities of children and young people are constructed in the mundane interactions of daily school life. Through an analysis of children's conversations about their relationships with each other, Renold exposes the ways in which heterosexuality is an invisible, taken-for-granted norm that powerfully regulates the ways in which children talk, think about and act out their relationships with one another. The taken for grantedness of heterosexuality as the norm is also apparent in government policy documents, for example, the UK government's *Sex and Relationship: education guidance* of the time. According to Renold:

> Throughout the guidance there are numerous references that unofficially promote 'heterosexuality' despite specifically stating that the guidance 'is not about the promotion of sexual orientation' (DfEE, 2000, p. 5, para. 9). . . . For example, (hetero)familial discourses (e.g. marriage and babies) are explicitly prescribed: 'children should be taught about the nature of marriage and its importance for family life and for bringing up children' (DfEE, 2000, p. 11, para 1.21). Other

(non-hetero)sexualities are not only invisible (e.g. gay, lesbian or bisex-
ual identities are never explicitly named), but, rather, they are discur-
sively constituted in negative discourses, making an appearance solely
in relation to homophobic 'bullying' or 'harassment'. (2006: 490–1)

This kind of government guidance is, Renold suggests, 'part of
a local and global culture that presumes, if not expects, gendered
performances that are the straightest of straight'. The presumption
of heterosexuality as normal is part of what Butler (1990) has called
'the heterosexual matrix' – a dominant model of talking and thinking
about gender which assumes that 'to be a "real" boy or girl would
involve desiring or growing up to desire the opposite sex' (Renold
2006: 493) and which thereby makes heterosexuality 'compulsory'
(Rich 1983) or the only 'thinkable' option. Renold's research, which
she undertook in two English primary schools, revealed the dominance of a boyfriend/girlfriend culture in which the children's conversations and practices were embedded in a range of discourses of
heterosexual romance. For example:

> Beyond girls' own emotionally charged discussions of who 'liked',
> 'loved' or 'fancied' who, girls' heterosexual practices included: kissing
> and holding hands; the setting, fixing or breaking up of relationships
> (usually by 'messengers' delivering secret love letters or dumping
> letters); sexualized playground games (such as 'blind-date'); and
> empirically testing a range of consumer products (including a com-
> puterized 'Match-Making Diary' and a mini 'Snog Log Book' from a
> popular girl's magazine). Collectively these heterosexualised practices
> were a central and increasingly compulsory component of the ways in
> which girls were 'doing girl'. (Renold 2006: 495–6)

Although not all of the girls 'bought into' the (hetero)sexualization
of contemporary girl culture, they were all 'ultimately positioned in
relation to it' (ibid.: 496). For example:

> by the end of Year 6, the only girls who did not participate or desire
> participation in their boyfriend–girlfriend culture (either as 'girlfriends'
> 'potential girlfriends' or 'go-betweens') were a group of middle-class
> high-achieving girls . . . These girls, however, were collectively and deri-
> sively known as the 'square girls' precisely because of their rejection of
> sexualized 'girlie' culture, boys as boyfriends and their preoccupation and
> investment in school work and academic achievement . . . (Ibid.: 497)

The use of the derisory tag 'square girls' and the often deep and
permanent psychic scars such tags can inflict is just one example of

the injurious nature of the heterosexual matrix or compulsory heterosexuality. As with the first example, we are reminded here of the powerful emotional currents that run through formal and informal educational processes. As Renold goes on to explain:

> although all children experienced some form of gendered and sexualized teasing . . . , it was those girls and boys who actively persisted to subvert and resist dominant and hegemonic identities that were routinely targeted. Over one-third of children were routinely positioned and positioned themselves as Other to hegemonic heterogendered scripts, with all of them reporting being systematically teased, excluded and humiliated for choosing not to invest in and project (thus directly challenge and resist) normative[1] forms of age-appropriate heterofemininity and heteromasculinity . . . (Ibid.: 499)

Another harmful effect of the heterosexual matrix is the way it operates to constrain the kinds of relationships boys and girls can have with one another at school. Because boy–girl relationships are so pervasively heterosexualised, to the extent that 'only those in committed relationships can talk to each other without fear of being teased' (Davies 1993: 127, cited in Renold 2006: 499), it is virtually impossible for the children to develop boy–girl friendships that are not sexualized:

> Aside from one self-identified tomboy (Erica . . .), no girl in the study seemed able to cultivate and maintain a boy–girl friendship free from heterosexual innuendo or outside of a dating discourse in which she/he is positioned as 'girlfriend' or 'boyfriend' for hanging out with the opposite gender. (Renold 2006: 500)

So what can Renold's account of mixed gender relationships in schools tell us about the value of sociological readings of educational processes and the kinds of insights such readings can produce? First, by placing the children's own social worlds and issues of gender and sexuality at the heart of her analysis, Renold reminds us that so much of what goes on in schools and of what is important to children in schools is unrelated to the formal curriculum and to the primary concerns of the majority of teachers. The importance of these informal school processes lies not only in the fact that they are so central to children's lives but also in the fact that they may have long-lasting, deep-seated and sometimes damaging psychic effects. This is just one example of many we could have used to illuminate the ways in which sociological work seeks to question and look beyond official accounts of what goes on in schools and of the outcomes of schooling.

Second, like our other examples, Renold's analysis indicates some of the ways in which sociological readings can help us to understand the processes by which status hierarchies are reproduced in society, in this case by examining how discourse in the form of 'a ubiquitous hegemonic heterosexual matrix' serves to coerce children to act out and construct their gender identities in particular ways.

Third, the analysis – like all the examples we have used in this chapter, and indeed much work in sociology of education – is underpinned by a normative agenda in that it (a) illuminates the complex patterns of goods and harms and hierarchies of value that are produced, circulated and negotiated through educational processes; (b) espouses values (either directly or by implication conveying a view that there is something wrong in the world that needs to be remedied); and (c) advocates that something (more or less specific) should be done. In this case, what is taken to be wrong is the privileging of heterosexuality over other kinds of sexuality, and one of the remedies for this injustice is taken to be the elimination of hierarchies of sexuality.

Finally, the analysis highlights some of the tensions that pervade a good deal of work in sociology of education around the question of 'what is to be done'. For example, Renold's analysis, in common with much work in sociology of education, as we shall see later in the book, appears to hover in the space between pessimism and optimism – the pessimism stemming from an appreciation of the durability and apparent impermeability of social structures which severely constrain the possibilities for successfully challenging established hierarchies, and the optimism arising from sensitivity to the ways in which people actively negotiate and in some cases work to side-step or erode dominant structures and hierarchies. Thus, for instance, Renold uses the example of Erica, the girl referred to in the quote above, who 'publicly celebrated her "tomboy" status' (2006: 503), to argue that assuming the identity of a tomboy 'has the potential to offer girls within an increasingly heterosexualised pre-teen girlhood an escape route from compulsory heterosexuality'. The 'ambivalent gendered and sexual positioning' represented by the tomboy identity provides grounds for optimism for those, like Renold, who are interested in subverting the heterosexual matrix, as what Renold calls 'tomboyism' seems to provide an example of how it is possible to trouble, disrupt or even begin to undo prevailing gender and sexual norms. However, this is an optimism tinged with pessimism, as Renold notes that 'the pressures of active heterosexuality' mean that, towards the end of their primary schooling, it becomes increasingly difficult for girls to hold on to the tomboy identity – and 'Erica was no exception':

in the final few months of primary school I observed Erica engaging in a series of public performances through which she declared a string of romantic attachments to boys (within and outside the school) and eventually struck up a boyfriend–girlfriend relationship with an older Year 7 secondary school boy. (Ibid.: 504)

Here Renold is interested in capturing something about Erica as an individual but also, at the same time, in capturing something more general about the nature of the social world. As we indicated with our first example, the sociological gaze seeks to understand both individual actions and social processes and, at the same time, the relationship between the individual and the social. Renold's account, like other similar studies in contemporary sociology of education, illuminates the enormous power of the social world of education not just as it is manifest in the conspicuous features of schooling structures, pedagogy or curriculum but as it is evinced in the 'taken for-granted' assumptions behind routine interactions.

Sociology of education as a contested domain

In this chapter thus far we have been looking at extracts from sociological writings on education in order to illustrate the potential for sociology to help us understand education. Now we want to change tack and begin to explore the sociology in sociology of education. What is the glue that holds together the examples that we have looked at? What is it that makes them sociology?

In brief, sociology is the study of social relations, processes, institutions and structures, whilst sociology of education is the study of these things with a particular focus on educational processes and on how educational and other social processes are mutually implicated and intertwined. Sociology encompasses a concern about economics, politics, culture and the psyche but is not confined to any one of these things. However, to say this isn't to say very much, because it leaves open the question of what the difference is between a sociological eye on these phenomena and a routine 'common-sense' eye. That is to say, why isn't anybody with an interest in society thereby a sociologist? There is no clear-cut answer to this question. Anyone, regardless of professional affiliation, can think in more or less sociological ways, but, at root, a sociological approach involves studying society in a systematic manner in order to understand better how social phenomena 'hang together' – i.e. how they connect to and interact with one another, cause or shape one another, or constitute one another.

Sociology is typically presented as a social science. But the question of whether sociology is best understood as a science is a controversial one. There are aspects of scientific methods that most sociologists would embrace – for example, a concern with systematically collecting and analysing data about social phenomena. In other words, and not surprisingly, most sociologists would want to distinguish between their accounts of the social world and the impressionistic pictures and personal opinions or prejudices that are often evident in more everyday contexts. Lying behind this distinction is an interest in 'getting things right', that is, in saying things about the social world that are valid. This interest in 'getting things right', in critically examining and providing the evidence that supports claims, and in attempting to deploy a cool and disinterested eye is what links together many social scientists with natural scientists. But the central controversy about the scientific nature of sociology comes to a head when we scrutinize this idea of 'validity' more closely and in particular if we ask whether it is possible for sociologists to achieve a 'view from nowhere' (Nagel 1986) – that is, a view that is objective in the sense of being impersonal and acultural in the way that many people regard some of the 'truths' of physics. Faced with this question, it is probable that most sociologists would be sceptical about this aspiration and would stress the inherently perspectival and interpretive nature of social science. For this reason it is sensible to see sociology as an art as well as or as much as a science.

In this respect sociology might be seen as a cousin of literature as well as a cousin of the natural sciences. Writers of literature use their imaginations to provide interpretations of social experience in illuminating and powerful ways that enable readers to understand how individual experiences arise from the complex of social relations and environments through which people move, to help readers see connections and patterns – many of which may be hidden from the point of view of the individual actor – or simply to remind readers of things they half know but keep forgetting. Sociologists, like other scholars in the social sciences, can play a similar function to this one of 'opening up', interpreting and illuminating social life, and, furthermore, they often do so by using genres that are closely analogous to those of the humanities (e.g. history or biography) or to creative writing (e.g. using detailed, and sometimes even fictionalized, portraits of people, places, periods and problems, etc.).

Sociology of education, like sociology more generally – as we indicated in the preface – is a subject full of controversy and contestation, and this contestation extends to debates about the nature of the field, its centre of gravity and the question of its boundaries. Contestation is an important part of the nature of sociology partly because sociology is very much a reflexive discipline, i.e. it is a discipline that asks questions about itself and not just about other things. We have seen that sociologists of education are, for example, interested in questions about the nature of knowledge, the relationship between knowledge and power, and the competing purposes and diverse effects of education. All of these kinds of questions can be asked just as much about sociology of education as about any other educational phenomenon. A reflexive sociologist of education will necessarily ask about the nature of knowledge in sociology of education (e.g. who decides what counts as worthwhile knowledge in sociology of education?) and about the relationship between this knowledge and various forms of social power (e.g. how can and do the accounts given and the claims made by sociologists of education exercise influence over what happens in the world?). And reflexivity will extend, more generally, to asking about the diverse and competing purposes of sociology of education and about its social effects.

Conclusion: values and purposes in sociology of education

The best way to get a feel for the contests that characterize sociology of education is to look at the rival perspectives that make it up, and in the next two chapters we will present an overview of many of these perspectives and discuss their differences in emphasis and some of the tensions between them. However, to conclude this chapter we will say a little more to introduce some of the tensions and disputes that cut across (and sometimes cut apart) sociology, including sociology of education, because these disputes are important to the central argument of this book. In fact, one of our key interests is to celebrate, participate in and hopefully make a contribution to the reflexive nature of sociology of education.

The cluster of disputes we have in mind can be approached through the tensions we have just introduced between sociology as a science and sociology as an art: in brief, how far ought we to see sociology of education as about discovery or about interpretation? The former seems to place the emphasis on the cool, detached, impersonal and, above all, accurate representation of the social world. The latter suggests the possibility of imaginative readings, of variety, and perhaps of personal involvement or partisanship of various kinds.

Both of these lists seem to point to things of importance. No doubt they can be combined to some extent but, on the other hand, there do seem to be some underlying contradictions suggested by the two lists that cannot be entirely ignored or erased. These disputes – which we might very loosely summarize as being about how 'impersonal' or 'personal' sociology can and should be – are entangled with two sets of important debates about, first, the place of 'value judgements' in sociology and, second, the purposes of sociology.

The work that we have cited in the examples, and other work in sociology of education, often reflects or revolves around values. In other words, as we noted in the preface, the work has a normative as well as a descriptive/explanatory agenda. In the first two examples we have looked at – the parents of disabled babies and the schooling of Bedouin girls – what is at stake is the question of what and whose knowledge is valued. These two examples, and the fourth one about human evolution exhibitions, also raise important questions about what values are embedded in the official knowledge of powerful institutions. In the first example, official knowledge privileges medicalized as opposed to more holistic conceptions of 'treatment' and medically defined as opposed to more socially defined conceptions of disability. In the second example, powerful institutions privilege the official school curriculum over a culturally responsive curriculum that recognizes distinctive cultural values such as family honour. The crucial importance of the embedded nature of values is evident in the fourth example, which highlights the dangers of insidious but potent racism being propagated by arguably well-intentioned science education exhibits. The third example about the disrupted pathways that some US students are forced to take through HE highlights the tensions between the values of 'choice' and equal access to education. And the fifth example highlights a concern about the 'identity damage' caused by superficially 'innocent' playground activities. The themes of equality and different kinds of educational advantage and disadvantage run through all of the examples, but the third and fifth in particular are a good illustration of the complexity of the value of equality – which is perhaps better seen as a 'field of value' rather than as 'a value' – with the third example centring on the question of the equal distribution of educational goods and the fifth on the equal recognition of diverse identities.

Indeed, it is very difficult to write about these examples meaningfully without drawing upon a set of overtly value-laden terms such as 'racism', 'identity damage', 'exclusion', 'oppression' and 'equality of opportunity'. To use these terms, and to talk about the things to which they are intended to refer, seems to be very different from what happens in physics or chemistry when we talk about 'mass', 'velocity', 'evaporation', etc. The latter seems to be a purely descriptive set of language practices, whereas the former set of terms has some strongly 'normative' content – i.e. these terms amount to – state or imply – the judgement that the things being described are somehow bad or wrong, at least in certain respects. In highlighting this distinction at the end of this opening chapter, we are partly just 'flagging it up' as an important feature of the apparent differences between social and natural science. But we are also intending to signal a longstanding debate within the social sciences about how social scientists can and should handle value judgements, which we will return to at the end of the book.

There seem to be two broad ways in which to go here, both of which are potentially problematic. On the one hand, sociologists could seek to avoid the use of such terms or somehow 'recast' them so that they are given non-normative meanings. If they take this route, it seems arguable that they will lose the ability to talk about a very important dimension of social life, or at least to include this talk in the sociological work they do. On the other hand, sociologists could embrace the use of these and similar terms and thereby embrace the idea that sociology is an inherently normative, as well as descriptive, subject. If they take this route, it seems arguable that they may have to abandon any idea that they are committed to neutral, detached or disinterested conceptions of knowledge comparable to some conceptions of natural science knowledge. As we proceed, we will keep this seeming conundrum in mind – hopeful that there is a way to solve or dissolve it.

The question of how self-consciously normative sociology should be depends upon having an answer to the question of what sociology is for, and we will conclude this chapter with a brief consideration of the purposes of sociology of education. One possible conception of the discipline is that it is a problem-solving one aimed at addressing a range of educational and social problems, such as the various problems of 'relative disadvantage' that we have just reviewed – problems about different kinds of inequality, and about the pervasiveness and effects of power, and the multiple ways in which power operates. These kinds of problems recur throughout sociology of education and will recur throughout this book. But in what, if any, sense are these problems for the sociologist?

Clearly the problems we have reviewed are not necessarily the personal problems of professional sociologists. (Of course professional sociologists may have some similar problems of their own, but they are, in general, likely to be relatively privileged members of society, in relatively well-paid posts.) Nor does the more general problem for society of the existence and effects of relative disadvantage seem to be the problem of sociologists in the sense that it is their job to 'sort it out'. Indeed, this is a job in which anyone and everyone could take an interest and to which many individuals and agencies, including voluntary and state organizations, can legitimately contribute. Rather the fundamental sense in which any of these matters are problems for sociologists is that they are phenomena which sociologists are interested in understanding and/or explaining. In short, there are social problems and there are academic problems, and these are different things. Poverty, for example, is a social problem in the sense that it is a real 'lived' problem for poor people and in the wider sense that society as a whole arguably suffers as a result of poverty. (This is arguable both on theoretical grounds and empirically – see Wilkinson 2005.) But poverty is also an analytical and explanatory problem. For sociology and other academic disciplines poverty poses problems – for example, about how to analyse the meanings and nature of poverty, how to understand the experiences and effects of poverty, and how to understand the social mechanisms that produce poverty and the reasons behind its persistence.

So we now have a working summary of the nature and purpose of sociology – it is the systematic study of social relations, processes, institutions and structures which aims at contributing to our *knowledge* of these things. Sociology may encompass the study of social problems, focusing a lot of attention, for example, on the issue of relative disadvantage, but – unlike some other fields, such as social policy – it is aimed not at practically addressing or solving these problems but rather at understanding them.

The above statement captures our idea of the difference between sociology and more obviously applied fields. But we do not wish to leave it there. Whilst accepting that sociology is principally aimed at knowledge of the social world, and whilst accepting that knowledge can be an end in itself, we also want to ask whether that is all there is to say. And whilst accepting that many others have responsibility for addressing social problems, we want to use this book to pose the question of whether sociologists can themselves make any broader contribution than this central one of 'knowledge production' (and, if so, whether or not they have any responsibility to do so). Indeed, as part of the reflexive project of sociology it is worth asking how far sociologists are – whether they like it or not – inevitably implicated in dcbates about practical and policy dilemmas. In relation to the two examples about inequalities of access discussed in this chapter, we drew attention to, and briefly illustrated, the relationships between description and explanation, on the one hand, and assumptions about the distribution of responsibility for 'problems' or the framing of potential policy solutions, on the other. We will discuss this issue more fully in chapter 8, but for now will simply note that the relationship between sociological work and policy is not simply a question of what sociologists explicitly intend. Sociological work can have policy effects – produced partly as a result of its implicit emphases – that are independent of what its authors intend.

2
Understanding Structure and Agency

In this chapter and the next we will review the sociological perspectives that have been particularly influential in sociology of education. In the space of two chapters we obviously cannot claim to present a comprehensive review; rather our approach will be to focus on the main perspectives that have helped shape the discipline and to look at specific examples of writing – from books and articles – that help show the perspectives in action. This body of work is very diverse and deals with a large range of themes and problematics which can be classified in many ways. Sociological work, for example, can be classified according to its substantive focus, its theoretical approach, and its epistemological and/or methodological orientation. In addition, as we suggested at the end of the previous chapter, these dimensions of classification can be complemented by asking about different approaches to the question of values or different conceptions of the purposes of sociology. In our review we will try to illustrate something of this multi-dimensional complexity, and in so doing we hope to tread the thin line between the acknowledgement of untidiness and the presentation of a false tidiness. We have chosen to organize the two chapters by reference to two very broad overarching themes which are at the core of sociology of education – first, structure and agency and, second, critique. Although both these themes apply to work reviewed in both chapters, this chapter foregrounds the theme of structure and agency but also introduces the idea of critique through the example of Marxism. In the next chapter, we will look at some more examples of critical approaches and thereby raise some questions about the nature of critique. Both chapters are organized around examples of what might be seen as classic work in sociology of education from the 1950s to the 1980s.

This chapter will make reference to a number of sociological theorists but it focuses on four broad approaches: structural functionalism, symbolic interactionism, Marxism, and some work in the 'new sociology of education' which cuts across these approaches. Our discussion of these approaches is largely structured around the descriptive/explanatory agenda of sociology, but we also provide some indication of the different normative perspectives that underpin or are conveyed by the work. In the next chapter the emphasis is in many respects reversed, as one of our aims will be to draw out more explicitly some of the normative work done by the sociology of education.

Structural functionalism

In its early years – the 1950s and 1960s – sociology of education was dominated by work in the structural functionalist tradition. Heavily influenced by Durkheimian ideas, the central concerns of structural functionalism are the problems of social order and its close relatives, social solidarity and social cohesion. More specifically, structural functionalists are interested in how social order, solidarity and cohesion are maintained and developed and what role the various systems and institutions of society play in all of this. In this tradition, society is understood as analogous to the human body, with the various social systems – e.g. the church, the family and the political, economic and education systems – likened to organs of the body, each fulfilling a distinct function and dependent on one another. Each of these systems is in turn understood to be made up of a number of interdependent sub-systems with their own discrete roles and functions. These sub-systems are themselves broken down into different functional components, and so on. So, for instance, the education system is comprised of different sectors, such as the schooling, further and HE sectors, and each of these operates as a sub-system. For example, the HE system is comprised of universities, bodies that regulate them, professional associations representing those who work in them, etc. Each of these institutions has its own component parts (e.g. faculties, departments) and a complex division of labour amongst the different roles needed to help the institution run smoothly (e.g. administrators, cleaners, lecturers, librarians, researchers and technicians). The structural functionalist perspective is concerned with exploring how these interacting and interdependent components of society fulfil their individual functions and how they combine to contribute to the smooth functioning of society as a whole.

Structural functionalists believe that the central explanation for why society is structured in the way it is – for example, the reason why schools, teachers, religion and families came into existence and continue to exist – is society's 'need' to create and preserve the conditions of social stability and solidarity. Structural functionalist explanations tend therefore to be teleological. In other words, the end point – social stability – is used to explain the existence of the various elements that contribute to this end point coming into being. Teleological forms of explanation are often criticized on the grounds that 'this type of explanation defies the laws of logic, for one thing cannot be the cause of another if it succeeds it in time' (Cohen 1968: 58). The structural functionalist idea of society having needs or agency independently of the people that make it up has also been a source of much criticism. Durkheim (1961: 59) conceptualized society as a 'sentient being' existing 'above and beyond' individuals, which has its own laws, akin to the laws of nature that determine what it is that individuals do. According to this view, it is society that shapes individuals and not the other way round, and it does this in part by promoting a shared set of values that Durkheim refers to as 'the collective or common conscience'.

Parsons: 'The school class as a social system'

In sociology of education, structural functionalism is reflected in many of the contributions to one of the early readers for students in the discipline. Halsey, Floud and Anderson's *Education, Economy and Society* (1961) focuses on the relationship between the structure and functioning of schools and the changing demands of a 'technological' society and the economy in an age of 'advanced industrialism'. Although not explicit in its theoretical orientation, the collection includes seminal papers by, amongst others, Talcott Parsons and Ralph H. Turner, which typify the structural functionalist perspective in sociology of education during this period. In 'The school class as a social system', originally published in 1959, Parsons explores the role of US schools both in socializing individuals into the norms and values he believes were demanded by society and in selecting them for and allocating them to their future social and economic roles. Whilst acknowledging variability in schooling practices, Parsons argues that there are nevertheless certain structural features common to elementary schools which enable them to perform two crucial functions in the maintenance of social order. First, alongside and in interaction with the family and the peer group, schools, he argues, play a crucial role in shaping children's personalities and specifically their commitments and capacities in ways that equip them for performing their future adult roles. This shaping has both cognitive and moral or social dimensions, with children developing the empirical and theoretical knowledge appropriate for their future occupational roles as well as appropriate attitudes developed through encouraging 'responsible citizenship in the school community'. For Parsons these attitudes include 'respect for the teacher, consideration and cooperativeness in relation to fellow-pupils and good "work-habits"' (Parsons 1961: 440).

Second, Parsons argues that, as children progress through the elementary school, they are increasingly differentiated from each other on the basis of a combination of their cognitive and moral achievements, or in other words 'their capacity to act in accord with [societal] values' (1961: 440). These differentiations at elementary school play an important part, in conjunction with processes of socialization in the peer-group and family, in determining a child's status and role in later life. The unequal rewards associated with different levels of achievement at school, however, represent a potential 'source of strain' on the smooth running of the school system and society more generally, because those who are disadvantaged by the system are likely to be dissatisfied and hence potentially uncooperative and troublesome. But the problem of strain is circumvented, Parsons suggests, by the existence of a common set of values, shared by the school and the family, around a commitment to the value of achievement and the principle of meritocracy. These common values, according to Parsons, perform 'a crucial integrative function for the system' (ibid.: 446).[1]

Symbolic interactionism

The tradition of structural functionalism is typically contrasted with that of symbolic interactionism.[2] The influence of symbolic interactionism in sociology of education is sometimes dated to the early 1970s but has its roots in earlier work, including that of the influential 'Chicago School' sociologist Becker, who was working in the 1950s, and originally in the social psychology of George Herbert Mead and the biographical sociology of W. I. Thomas. In practice, symbolic interactionists study the actions and perspectives of individuals and groups living and working in particular settings, paying particular attention to the systems of meaning through which they account for their experiences and make sense of the world and the ways in which the meanings that they draw upon are produced through social interaction.

The contrasts between structural functionalism and symbolic interactionism are quite striking and help to illuminate a cluster of core problematics in sociology, including the one that makes up the central theme of this chapter – the tensions between descriptive and explanatory accounts that centre on 'structure' and those that centre on 'agency'. Whereas structural functionalism is centred on the structure of society as a whole and the various ways in which society shapes the lives of individuals, the tradition of symbolic interactionism emphasizes the ways in which society is shaped through the interactions of individual agents. Hence, familiarizing oneself with work in these two rival traditions is one productive way of understanding the importance and power of structural and agentic explanatory accounts, some of the tensions between these forms of explanation, and some of the potential strengths and weaknesses of both sets of emphases. These two traditions also exhibit a range of other, overlapping, contrasts. For example, the structural functionalist tradition emphasizes the 'objective' nature of the social world, foregrounding a sense in which society operates independently of people's subjective responses and interpretations, whilst symbolic interactionism foregrounds the ways in which subjectivities not only help produce but are themselves an important part of the social world. Also, these emphases on subjectivity and interpersonal agency as contrasted with an emphasis on 'objective' social systems mean that work in the symbolic interactionist tradition often focuses upon micro-level interactions and the minutiae of people's everyday lives as opposed to macro-level work that looks at large-scale social phenomena.

Becker: 'The teacher in the authority system of the public school'

An early example of work in this tradition in sociology of education is Becker's PhD research on the role and career of the Chicago public schoolteacher, which was published in a series of articles (Becker 1952a, 1952b, 1953). 'The teacher in the authority system of the public school' (Becker 1953), as the title suggests, deals with precisely the kind of subject matter that would interest someone working in the structural functionalist tradition – the system by which authority, and hence stability, is maintained in the social institution of the school. However, Becker's approach to this subject matter is very different from that of a structural functionalist. Rather than focusing on the ways in which the actions of teachers are shaped by the system of authority that operates in the school, Becker is interested in the way that systems of authority are actively produced and maintained through the interactions of teachers and other key agents. This interest is signalled in the first sentence of the article, in which Becker defines institutions, following his 'Chicago School' colleague (and PhD supervisor) Everett Hughes (1942), as 'forms of collective action which are somewhat firmly established' (Becker 1953: 128). For Becker, the 'shared understandings' of relations of control and authority within the institution of the school that structural functionalists would argue precede and shape social action and individual beliefs are produced and reproduced by teachers' conceptions of their role and of the conditions that are necessary for them to perform that role. These conceptions shape and in turn are shaped by the interactions of teachers and other 'institutional functionaries'. Moreover, the systems of authority expressed in these shared understandings cannot be taken for granted but are subject to contestation and conflict, and hence are fragile and demand active preservation.

Becker's thesis is grounded in an analysis of sixty in-depth unstructured interviews with Chicago public schoolteachers. He uses the voices and perspectives of these teachers to explore potential and actual challenges to their authority and the strategies they use both to defend or preserve their authority when it is under threat and to assert their own definitions of situations over competing definitions. The sources of threat can be external to the institution, as in the case of parents exercising their own 'latent authority' by ignoring or rejecting the authority system established by the school, or internal, for example where a principal fails to support a teacher when the authority of the latter is challenged by a parent or pupil. Becker identifies a range of strategies teachers use to circumvent potential challenges from parents (particularly 'higher-class' ones) which could undermine their authority, subject them 'to forms of control that are, for them, illegitimate – control by outsiders' (1953: 131), and potentially destroy the authority system of the school. These strategies include teachers never admitting their mistakes, never criticizing other teachers, and using sanctions against principals who flout the conventional expectation that principals support teachers in the face of external challenges, regardless of whether such challenges are legitimate.

The contrast between Becker's analysis of the authority system of the school and Parsons's analysis of the school class as a social system is not simply one of theoretical orientation but also one of method and style – a contrast that typifies the differences between the traditions from within which they were working. Parsons's analysis represents a fairly abstract form of theorizing – what C. Wright Mills (1959) called grand theory – and the voices of the social actors being written about are entirely absent. Becker's analysis, in contrast, is rooted in actors' voices, and these are frequently quoted in the text, giving the reader a glimpse into what, from a teacher's perspective, it might have been like to work in the Chicago public school system in the late 1940s/early 1950s. However, although work in the symbolic interactionist tradition tends to focus on relatively small-scale case studies of the day-to-day lives and subjectivities of social actors, it does not necessarily eschew 'grander' theorizing beyond the case, and in this particular article Becker seeks to draw out some 'points of general relevance' for the sociological study of institutions:

> an institution like the school can be seen as a . . . self-contained system of social control. Its functionaries . . . are able to control one another; each has some power to influence the others' conduct. This creates a stable and predictable work setting . . . In contrast the activities of those who are outside the professional group are not involved in such a network of mutual understanding . . . . To the teacher . . . the parent appears as an unpredictable and uncontrollable element, as a force which endangers . . . the existing authority system over which she has some measure of control. For this reason teachers carry on an essentially secretive relationship vis-à-vis parents and the community, trying to prevent any event which will give these groups a permanent place of authority in the school situation . . . . This suggests the general proposition that the relations of institutional functionaries to one another are relations of mutual influence and control, and that outsiders are systematically prevented from exerting any authority over the institution's operations because they are not involved in this web of control and would literally be uncontrollable, and destructive of the institutional organization, as the functionaries desire it to be preserved, if they were allowed such authority. (Becker 1953: 140–1)

Becker's words here, including the reference to educational institutions as 'systems of social control' (along with the reference above to institutions as 'forms of collective action'), point to the inadequacy of any clear distinction between structure and agency. Indeed, it may be more appropriate to think of them in terms of two sides of the same coin that makes up 'the social'. This latter notion – i.e. the interpenetration of structure and agency – is one that has been recognized by many sociological theorists, although different theorists express this idea within different frameworks and using different vocabularies.

In reviewing and distinguishing approaches to sociology of education, there is an inevitable tendency to simplify and to some extent caricature the work that is ascribed to particular traditions. So it is important to emphasize that the contrasts we have drawn between structural functionalism and symbolic interactionism should not be read as implying that the major theorists we have mentioned were somehow blind to one half of the social world. In reality, the work of major theorists tends to be very rich and to encompass an appreciation of the complexity of the social world, including the interpenetration of structure and agency. Nonetheless, the contrasts are important because they illuminate the fact that different traditions of work have different theoretical centres of gravity and result in important differences in emphasis in the approach taken to the practice of sociology. It is also important to emphasize that a lot of work cuts across different traditions and defies straightforward labelling. Indeed, the various traditions that we are now going on to summarize can be seen as cutting across and reflecting elements of both functionalism and symbolic interactionism. This certainly applies to three very influential critical traditions that we will go on to consider – Marxism in this chapter and feminism and critical race theory in the next. These three traditions have a number of things in common. First, none of them are simple, one-dimensional traditions. Rather they are traditions of 'disagreement', each representing a cluster of different positions and perspectives. Second, they are all primarily concerned with the operation of power in society and the ways in which power is produced by, and produces, patterns of social inequality. Third, and closely related to this concern with power and inequality, all are explicitly ideological. That is, they are strongly associated with political projects directed at emancipatory social change. Finally, and this relates to another use of the idea of ideology, all three traditions seek to expose the ways in which phenomena that are typically presented as natural and neutral are in fact socially constructed in order to serve particular interests.

Marxism

Marxist perspectives are united in their interest in the relationship between economy and society, in particular in how the relationships between social classes that are necessary to sustain a capitalist economy are reproduced and legitimized in non-economic arenas, including schools. For example, Marxist sociologists of education are interested in the different school experiences of working- and middle-class students and the ways in which they are thereby differentially prepared for their respective roles in the workplace. At the heart of Marxist analysis is a concern with the conflict between social classes and the conflicts and the contradictions inherent in economic systems. Put simply, according to Marx, capitalist economies require the domination and exploitation of the working class by capitalists, but this system produces alienation and dissatisfaction amongst the working class which has a destabilizing effect, threatening the smooth functioning of the economy and the ability of capitalists to accumulate wealth.

It is commonplace to talk of two Marxist approaches – sometimes labelled structural and cultural Marxism – which are loosely associated with different currents in Marx's own writing. The former has resonances with functionalism and the latter with interactionism. In explaining the nature of the social world, structural Marxism gives primacy to the economy, arguing that social and cultural practices and relationships are heavily determined by the economic base of society, including both the physical and technological 'means of production' – for example, the machinery – and the 'relations of production' – i.e. patterns of ownership and employment. In contrast, cultural Marxist explanations of how capitalist social relations are reproduced give primacy to social action, and to the ways in which people actually create the unequal conditions of social life. From this perspective, whilst social structures constrain the actions of individuals, structures are also the product of individual and collective action. This emphasis on action foregrounds the importance of, and the scope for, human agency to effect social change, whilst the structural approach is more overtly deterministic – i.e. the nature and direction of social change is seen as necessarily flowing from pre-existing economic and social conditions and objective social forces. In crude terms, cultural Marxism emphasizes freedom and structural Marxism emphasizes determinism, and once again this contrast of emphasis echoes the differences between interactionism's emphasis on agency and functionalism's emphasis on structures.

In practice, structural and cultural Marxism represent a spectrum of approaches. In this section we will look at examples of work from the structural and cultural ends of the spectrum and then go on to look at an example of state-centred theory that cuts across these two tendencies. A clear example of work at the structural end of the spectrum is Bowles and Gintis's *Schooling in Capitalist America*.

Bowles and Gintis: Schooling in Capitalist America

In this classic text Bowles and Gintis (1976) develop the idea of the 'correspondence principle' as a means of characterizing and explaining the relationship between education and the economy. According to this principle, there is a 'correspondence' between the social relations of the capitalist economy and the social relations of schooling, with schools playing an essential role in producing the stratified labour force and the range of technical and cognitive skills, dispositions and forms of self-presentation and consciousness that the capitalist enterprise demands from its workers. Bowles and Gintis claim that schools for working-class children have a division of labour and structure of authority akin to the factory, and that in these schools young people are taught to be docile, obedient and compliant through the practices of rote learning and rule following. By contrast, according to Bowles and Gintis, the young people attending elite schools are prepared for their future professional and managerial occupational roles through teaching practices and forms of teacher–student relationships that train students to be autonomous, self-directed learners and instruct them in the skills of leadership. This stratified system and its stratifying effects, Bowles and Gintis argue, are legitimated through the promotion of an ideology of meritocracy which, they contend, renders economic inequality acceptable by promoting the belief that poverty is a consequence of innate personal failings. They suggest that these differentiated forms of schooling – and the ideology of meritocracy – are directly produced by shifts in the mode of production, arguing that: 'the fact that changes in the structure of production have preceded parallel changes in schooling establishes a prima facie case for the causal importance of economic structure as a major determinant of educational structure' (Bowles and Gintis 1976: 224). As a number of commentators have noted, these arguments closely mirror Parsons's structural functionalism, particularly with regard to their apparent determinism, the macro-level focus of their argument, and their neglect of both micro-level teacher–student interactions and the content of what is taught in schools (see, for example, Sarup 1978: 177–8). Also paralleling aspects of Parsons's arguments, Bowles and Gintis focus on the socializing role of the informal aspects of schooling, i.e. what is implicitly taught through the way the school is organized – what Bowles and Gintis, and others, call the 'hidden curriculum'.

However, what marks out the arguments of Bowles and Gintis as different from those of Parsons is their very different normative perspectives. Parsons seems implicitly to endorse the roles that schools play in preparing children for their future adult roles, appears to accept stratification in society and the workforce more generally as inevitable and necessary for the smooth functioning of society, and does not ask questions about whose interests this system serves, privileging instead the interests of society considered as a whole. In contrast, Bowles and Gintis challenge socio-economic stratification and the forms of education that help reproduce it and argue for alternative, Marxist-inspired, egalitarian economic, social and educational formations. For Bowles and Gintis, an 'adequate education system in a good society' should serve three purposes. These are perhaps most succinctly summarized in their reply to critics of their thesis (1988), where they restate their position that, first, such a system should promote personal development through the inculcation of appropriate knowledge and intellectual skills, as well as through developing 'those affective and interpersonal skills which allow individuals to control their own lives, and foster the self-esteem and personal dignity which lead them to demand the resources to exercise such control'. Second, it should 'act as an equalizing force', disrupting rather than reproducing privilege and disadvantage (Bowles and Gintis 1988: 235). And finally the education system should act as 'a stabilizing force . . . by training youth to accept and affirm the dominant culture'. In a capitalist society these aims are, they suggest, fundamentally incompatible because, 'in the process of performing its stabilizing function, schools consistently thwart full personal development and legitimate rather than attenuate social inequality' (ibid.: 236). For Bowles and Gintis, it follows that what is needed is the building of a broad-based socialist movement committed to 'the ultimate dismantling of the capitalist system and its replacement by a more progressive social order' (1976: 246) coupled with 'revolutionary education'. The latter involves:

> the dissident teacher . . . teaching the truth about society . . . inspiring a sense of collective power and mutual respect . . . demonstrating that alternatives superior to capitalism exist . . . fighting racist, sexist, and other ideologies of privilege [and] criticizing and providing alternatives to a culture that [quoting Woody Guthrie] 'makes you feel you're not any good . . . just born to lose'.

Although this last quote indicates that Bowles and Gintis believe that change can be effected through collective social action and the development of a dissident teachers' movement, their work has nevertheless been subjected to substantial criticism on the grounds that, in large part – because it adopts a relatively abstract, macro-level theoretical approach – it tends to depict teachers and students as passive, their actions determined by the structures and demands of corporate capital (e.g. see Sarup 1978 and Giroux 1983). This depiction of teachers and students as passive has been challenged by, amongst others, those working in the cultural Marxist tradition who, drawing on interactionist methodologies, prefer to characterize teachers and students as active creators and meaning makers, albeit operating within identifiable structural constraints.

Willis: Learning to Labour

The cultural Marxist position in sociology of education is classically represented by Paul Willis's *Learning to Labour* (1977), an in-depth ethnographic study centring on the in- and out-of-school experiences and perspectives of a group of twelve working-class, non-academic 'lads' growing up in a small industrial town in the English Midlands. Using evidence gleaned from close observation of the lads, and representing their voices extensively in his writing, Willis attempts to show how these young men created a counter-school culture characterized by opposition to authority, a rejection of conformity and a deeply entrenched sexism and racism that, Willis argues, very closely mirrored – and was influenced by – the shop-floor culture of their fathers. Willis suggests that, in constructing this counter-school culture, and in differentiating themselves from their more conformist working-class peers, whom they called the 'ear'oles', the lads were systematically preparing themselves for the future manual labour roles they aspired and looked forward to. Paradoxically, this involved valuing a stance of not thinking about the future. As Joey, one of the lads, put it:

> We wanna live for now, wanna live while we're young, want money to go out with, wanna go with women now, wanna have cars now, and uh think about five, ten, fifteen years time when it comes, but other people, say people like the ear'oles, they'm getting their exams, they'm working, having no social life, having no fun, and they're waiting for fifteen years time . . . when they've got married and things like that . . . . I'll say they'll be the civil servants, toffs, and we'll be the brickies and things like that. (Willis 1977: 98)

For Willis, these young men's beliefs about the superiority of, and their optimism about, manual work 'lead finally to an objective work situation which seems to be entrapment rather than liberation' (ibid.: 119).

Unlike Bowles and Gintis, who emphasize the ways in which capitalist economic and social structures determine the social relations of schooling and the inculcation in schools of forms of consciousness appropriate for the capitalist workplace, Willis is trying to show the role played by subjective processes – the lads' interpretations and insights – and the creative 'activities and struggles' arising from them in the production and reproduction of 'what we think of as aspects of structure' (1977: 120–1). Hence, for Willis, processes of cultural production contribute to the reproduction of capitalist social relations. However, the lads' interpretations, insights, actions and struggles, Willis contends, are not open-ended but are limited by 'the determining conditions which hold their present and future possibilities' – including the uncertain relationship between educational qualifications and economic success, the limited opportunities for upward mobility, and the essential meaninglessness of all industrial work, whether mental or manual. In other words, the young men can see – or in Willis's terms 'penetrate' – what their teachers and careers advisors fail to see, or obscure: that there are '[o]bjective grounds . . . for questioning whether it is sensible to invest the self and its energies in qualifications when both their efficacy and their object must be greatly in doubt' (ibid.: 128). Hence, for Willis, cultural practices and structural forms mutually reinforce each other.

Like Bowles and Gintis, however, Willis does not restrict himself to the tasks of description and explanation but adopts an overtly political position, attempting to formulate pedagogic alternatives for teachers committed to progressive social transformation. He recognizes that such teachers have to confront the problem of 'what to do on Monday morning', that they cannot simply sit around waiting for the revolution to happen, and that they are confronted on a day-to-day basis with the dilemma of having to respond to the immediate problems facing their students, whilst knowing that these very responses 'may help to reproduce the structures within which the problems arise' (1977: 186). Willis does not attempt to resolve this dilemma but rather delineates some pointers for helping teachers working with 'disaffected youth' to begin to think and act otherwise. For example, he encourages teachers to take seriously and critically engage with the perspectives and insights of the students, to explore how their students' insights might be extended to more systematic analyses of society, to expose and oppose oppressive ideologies and cultural practices rather than mystify or reinforce them, to acknowledge structural constraints, and to organize politically on behalf of and with students if structural change is desired. For Willis, inspired by the cultural

Marxism of Gramsci, this project represents part of a broader process of the 'politicization of culture' which, he asserts, is a precondition for, 'and an organic element of, longer-term structural change':

> The identification and understanding of the cultural level is an action to bring it closer to self-awareness and therefore to the political, to rec-ognise in the materiality of its outcomes the possibility of the cultural becoming a material force. (Ibid.: 192)

Or, as Gramsci put it, getting 'a mass of people . . . to think coher-ently . . . is not a question of introducing from scratch a scientific form of thought into everyone's individual life, but of renovating and making "critical" an already existing activity' (Gramsci 1971: 325, 330, cited in Willis 1977: 185). Willis's Gramscian-inspired conten-tion that teachers are not working on blank slates but need to start with an intimate knowledge of the cultural practices and beliefs of their students is a key feature of cultural Marxism that is not appar-ent in the more abstract prescriptions for a revolutionary pedagogy associated with the more structural approach of Bowles and Gintis.

A third strand of Marxist work that began to emerge in the late 1970s and early 1980s paid attention to an aspect of social reproduc-tion that had previously been neglected in sociology of education. As we have seen, both structural functionalist and structural Marxist approaches tend to assume that school processes are directly shaped by the 'objective demands' of capitalist economies, whilst cultural Marxist approaches draw attention to the role of students' cultural practices and subjectivities in mediating the relationship between the economy and schooling. In none of these accounts does there appear to be much recognition of the state's contribution to the work schools do in reproducing social inequalities, which, as Dale (1982) notes, is perhaps surprising given the fact that education systems are largely state funded and provided. This is a gap that state-centred socio-logists of education attempt to fill, and in doing so they draw their inspiration from neo-Marxist theories of the state and, in particular, the work of Gramsci, Poulantzes and Offe.

Whilst cultural Marxism emphasizes the relative autonomy of the cultural sphere, state-centred theory emphasizes the relative autonomy of the political sphere. Cutting across structural and cultural Marxist approaches, it seeks to illuminate the interactions between structure and agency through an analysis of state policy-making both as a response to the 'objective demands' of a capitalist economy and as a site of political struggle and class conflict 'where

hegemony must be worked for [and is hence] not a foregone conclusion' (Apple 1982: 14).

To illustrate this approach, we will use one of the most widely
cited texts on state-centred theory in education, Dale's (1982) paper
'Education and the capitalist state'.

Dale: 'Education and the capitalist state'

Like many Marxist sociologists, Dale is upfront about the normative
agenda which drives his analysis. His ultimate purpose in this paper,
he tells us, is to provide an explanation of 'patterns, policies and
processes of education in capitalist societies' that can help inform
a politics of 'resistance'. According to Dale, neither Bowles and
Gintis's macro-approach nor Willis's micro-approach can adequately
inform a politics of change, because for the former schools can only
be changed once capitalism is overthrown, whilst the latter is 'unable
to indicate the source and nature of the control over . . . schools .
. . which it would be crucial to establish before bringing about any
change in them' (Dale 1982: 129). Since it is the capitalist state as
'the immediate provider of education' which is the source of control,
'it is in the analysis of the state', Dale argues, 'that we may begin to
understand the assumptions, intentions and outcomes of various
strategies of educational change' (ibid.: 130).

For Dale, drawing on the work of Offe (and, through Offe,
Luxemburg), the state is not a crude instrument of class rule (i.e. it
is not 'a committee for managing the affairs of the whole bourgeoisie'
– Marx and Engels [1848] 2002). Rather it has a relative autonomy
that enables it to operate at a distance from the short-term, differentiated, conflicting and – as far as the overall health of capitalism
is concerned – irrational interests of individual sectors of capital.
This relative autonomy is held to be necessary for the survival of
the capitalist economy, since, left to its own devices, and without
the controlling power of the state as a 'higher authority' to keep it in
check and arbitrate between competing capitalist interests, capitalism will self-destruct. In this formulation, the role of the state is to
secure the conditions that will best protect capitalism from its own
self-destructive tendencies.

In order to secure these conditions, Dale argues, the state has to
respond to three 'core problems': '(i) the support of the capitalist
accumulation process, (ii) guaranteeing a context for its continued
expansion, [and] (iii) the legitimation of the capitalist mode of production and the state's own part in it' (1982: 133). These problems,

which are, Dale argues, 'permanently on the agenda of the state apparatus' (ibid.: 132), are the source of the state's policies, including its education policies, and mean that the policy process is inherently contradictory and unstable, because policies designed to remedy one problem generate other problems which in turn have to be remedied, generating new problems (or, more accurately, 'old' problems in new guises), and so on. The example Dale gives to illustrate the inherent contradictions that drive state education policies is the development of elitist systems of education. The capitalist accumulation process, he suggests, requires a system 'devoted to the early recognition and fostering of "ability"' (ibid.: 137). However, such a system threatens the legitimacy of both capitalism and the state, which is highly dependent on the myth of equality. Elitist education also threatens the context for capital accumulation by alienating significant sections of the population and by thereby constituting a potential source of social unrest. Hence, the shift to a less stratified system of education provision in the UK – for example, in the 1970s – can from this perspective be understood as a response to the need for the state to secure its legitimacy and guarantee a context for the continued expansion of capitalism – i.e. a context free from social unrest and disorder where children are kept 'off the streets' (ibid.: 146). Such contradictions evident in policymaking, Dale contends, reverberate throughout the system, manifesting themselves in local struggles over such issues as streaming or tracking in schools.

However, according to Dale, these core problems do not account for everything the state does. For a more comprehensive explanation of state policymaking, he argues, we need to look not only at the core problems of the state but also at how state apparatuses are organized and at the political struggles that shape policy outcomes, for example, 'struggles between the "bureaucrats" and "technocrats" within the state apparatus' (1982: 145). Of crucial importance also are the political struggles of teachers, as policy outcomes also depend on the 'nature and effectiveness of the teaching profession's resistance to them' (ibid.). Because struggle is endemic to the system, Dale, echoing Gramsci's military analogy, argues that the policy process is characterized by 'a continuing series of rarely conclusive skirmishes on shifting terrain, between shifting alliances, in an over-all context of a system attempting to carry out contradictory functions, through means that may conflict with its objectives' (ibid.: 157–8). From Dale's anti-capitalist perspective, this analysis provides grounds for optimism, for '[i]t is in the spaces and interstices created by these and other contradictions that we must look for resistance to coalesce' (ibid.: 158).

Dale's analysis thus focuses upon the structural contradictions of capitalism and thereby simultaneously highlights opportunities for agency – an agency that extends beyond the capacity to shape classroom subcultures and includes forms of political agency with the potential to obstruct and disrupt macro-structural forces.

The work of the authors we review in the next section of this chapter combines aspects of the three broad approaches we have already considered but also involves a much more fine-grained scrutiny of the interpenetration of structure and agency, introducing new theoretical lenses and categories in an attempt to make this interpenetration visible and intelligible. Compared with the Marxist writers we have considered, Bourdieu and Bernstein are less explicitly ideological in their approach to sociology, although their work has a serious critical dimension.

Some work in the 'new sociology of education': Bourdieu and Bernstein

As we have already noted, much sociology defies easy categorization, and this is the case with the work of Bourdieu and Bernstein. Drawing on a mix of Durkheimian,[3] Marxian and Weberian influences, the early writings of both of these scholars were key sources of inspiration for a 'new direction' in sociology of education that began to take root in the late 1960s and early 1970s – a direction that was to become known as the new sociology of education. Although, as Whitty (1985) has pointed out, its newness has perhaps been overstated, what marked the new sociology out as different, at least from the approaches that dominated the discipline at the time – the political arithmetic tradition[4] and particular variants of symbolic interactionism – was its concern to put the school curriculum and school pedagogies under the sociological spotlight. Those working in the political arithmetic tradition had focused on inequalities of access to formal education, but they had not sought to question the content of the education to which access was unequal. And even the interactionists, who were taking a close look at internal school processes and students' experiences of school, did not appear to pay much attention to the details of what was being taught and how. As Young observed of some of these studies, 'one can read them and hardly be aware that considerable periods of pupils' time are taken up, and presumably their consciousness is developed, by what they do in classrooms, laboratories and libraries and by the kinds of courses made available to them' (Young 1973, cited in Whitty 1985: 10–11). In contrast, the new sociology took school knowledge as its central concern, seeking to expose and examine its socially constructed nature and the social construction of other categories that had tended to be taken for granted in the 'old' sociology – categories such as educational 'success' and 'failure', 'ability' and 'intelligence' – and it sought to explain the persistence of such categories and their relationship to social class interests and activities (Young 1971: 6).

The new sociology began life in the form of an edited collection entitled *Knowledge and Control: new directions for the sociology of education* (Young 1971). This volume included empirical studies of classroom processes that drew on interactionist and phenomenological methodologies to examine how school knowledge was produced by the interactions of social actors (especially teachers and students) as well as more theoretical pieces concerned with the structural analysis of the curricular and pedagogic practices of schooling and their relationship to wider social relations of power and control.[5] Two of these theoretical pieces were contributions from Bourdieu and one was a contribution from Bernstein.

The relationship between Bourdieuan and Bernsteinian theory has been the subject of much debate (e.g. see Harker and May 1993) with which we do not want to get involved here. But we do want to draw attention to some broad similarities. Both were concerned to 'drill down' into the deep micro-structures of the social and cultural practices that mediate macro-power structures and individual consciousness. In doing so, they sought to illuminate aspects of the social world that had been obscured both by the grander, more macro-structural functionalist approaches and the more fine-grained interactionist studies that had tended to characterize sociology of education in its early years. This focus necessitated the development of a richer conceptual language than had previously been available.

Bernstein: 'On the classification and framing of educational knowledge'

The social practices that were the focus of Bernstein's microscopic lens were those implicated in 'the organization, transmission and evaluation of educational knowledge' (Bernstein 1971: 47). Over the course of his career Bernstein worked up, layer upon layer, through a steady process of conceptual elaboration and modification, a dense descriptive language that sought to encapsulate the complex internal architecture of interconnecting rules and principles and relations of control and power that organize, give shape to and are produced by these practices.

This particular paper, first published in *Knowledge and Control*, incorporated much of the groundwork for Bernstein's later explications of curricular and pedagogic practice and their social-reproductive consequences that have continued to have a major influence on the sociology of knowledge and the curriculum (e.g. see Moore et al. 2006; Morais et al. 2001; and Muller et al. 2004). The paper is centrally concerned with the relationships between three things: (i) society's 'structures of power and principles of control'; (ii) educational knowledge; and (iii) the 'forms of experience, identity and relation [that are] evoked, maintained and changed by the formal transmission of knowledge' (Bernstein 1971: 47, 67).

In simple terms, Bernstein is illuminating the pervasive nature of structures and the ways in which they penetrate into conceptions of knowledge and the fabric of individual consciousness. Bernstein detected, at the time he was writing, signs of a shift in the organization of the curriculum – a move from a curriculum structured around a collection of subject disciplines in which there was a clear separation and high degree of insulation between the subjects towards a more open, integrated arrangement, in which the separate disciplines or knowledge contents within disciplines were subordinated to an overarching idea. In the paper he develops a new conceptual language that can be used to analyse the separate components of this shift with a view to identifying its sources and social implications.

Bernstein argues that different types of curricula create different pedagogic possibilities and have different implications for educational identities, forms of consciousness and social relationships. For example, he suggests that curricula that are strongly classified – that is, organized around discrete subjects or disciplines – produce educational identities amongst both students and teachers that are 'clear-cut', 'bounded' and 'pure'. Students are socialized early into strong subject loyalties, and the strength of these loyalties mean that specialized curricula are highly resistant to change. Such a curriculum is associated with selectivity and differentiation and is sustained by 'careful screening procedures to see who belongs and does not belong' (Bernstein 1971: 56). For those (mainly middle-class) students who progress to higher levels of education, it may provide a positive educational identity, a sense of order and a commitment to schooling. For other (mainly working-class) students, it can have 'wounding' effects, and can be seen as 'meaningless' (ibid.: 59).

Bernstein uses the concept of framing to capture the degree of control that teachers and students have over pedagogy, and in particular the degree of control they have over what is taught, in what order and at what pace. So, despite the strong explanatory emphasis that Bernstein attaches to 'structures of power', his analysis allows room for varying degrees of agency at the level of teachers and students. Where there is a considerable degree of latitude for teachers and/or students to determine the content of the curriculum, its organization, sequencing and pace of learning, the framing is weak for those teachers and/or their students. Where there is little or no room for manoeuvre, the framing is strong. The degree of classification and framing (which can co-vary) has important implications for the social relations of the classroom: 'The stronger the classification and the framing, the more the educational relationship tends to be hierarchical and ritualized and the pupil seen as ignorant, with little status and few rights' (Bernstein 1971: 58).

In the paper Bernstein seeks to connect such micro-level structures and processes to more macro-level ones. He does this in two ways. First, he argues that the possibilities for social change at a macro-level are to some degree determined at the micro-level. For example, his analysis suggests that any move from a more strongly classified (i.e. what he calls a 'collection' type) curriculum to a more weakly classified (or 'integrated') one is likely to disturb established subject loyalties and organizational hierarchies, and that this may help to explain the resilience of the specialized collection code in English education. (Indeed, this argument might help to explain why A-levels have persisted in England nearly forty years after Bernstein thought he detected a shift towards a more integrated approach to the organization of school knowledge.)

Second, he suggests that changes at the macro-level create pressures for change at micro-levels. Macro-level changes include changes in the organization of the economy and, in particular, its division of labour, which create economic demands for new skills and dispositions, political demands for more egalitarian educational formations, and social-systemic demands, associated with the emergence of a more ideologically pluralistic society, for new forms of control. Bernstein's analysis at this juncture is classically Durkheimian in the sense that his explanation for curriculum change foregrounds issues of social order. More specifically, what he seems to be implying – in a way that is reminiscent of the functionalist perspective with which we began this chapter – is that society has a 'will to order'. That is, where social control – and the social solidarity on which control depends – is

threatened by social change, society has to restabilize itself by invent-
ing (or reinventing) new forms of social solidarity and new mechanisms for creating them – including new curricula, pedagogies and
modes of assessment – which in turn have the effect of shifting 'the
boundaries of consciousness' (Bernstein 1971: 67).

Bourdieu and Passeron:
Reproduction in Education, Society and Culture

Bourdieu was an incredibly prolific sociologist whose work extended
far beyond sociology of education. However, he paid particular attention to education because he believed it played such a pivotal role in
the reproduction of class privilege and social inequality, which was his
primary scholarly interest. Here we focus on just one of his texts (co-
authored with Passeron), which attempts to explicate the mechanics
of the reproduction of social inequalities and, like the Marxist texts
we have reviewed in this chapter, seeks to unmask the relations of
class domination that, the authors suggest, are obscured by the ideology of meritocracy. Bourdieu and Passeron's approach, however,
is distinctive in at least three senses: (i) in its attempt to produce a
fine-grained analysis of how inequalities are reproduced through the
interactions between the pedagogical practices of schooling and the
cultural practices of students and their families; (ii) in its Weberian-
inspired attempt to illuminate the full range of competing interests
and struggles (political, religious and cultural, as well as economic)
that combine to help produce particular educational, social and
cultural formations and the ways in which these struggles and formations 'co-produce' one another; and (iii) in its emphasis on the role of
symbolic formations in the reproduction of inequality.

Bourdieu and Passeron argue that the knowledge and culture that is
both taught in formal education institutions and valued by dominant
forces in society is essentially arbitrary 'not simply in its content, but
also in its form, since it is imposed by an arbitrary power' (Bottomore
1977). They see the imposition of such arbitrary cultural standards as
a form of symbolic violence – in other words, an instrument of domination that enables dominant groups to impose their understandings
and perspectives as legitimate and simultaneously to conceal the
inequalities of power that both enable and are reinforced by this exercise of power. So, for Bourdieu and Passeron, it is not predominantly
through coercion that class privilege is maintained but through symbolic systems of representation (e.g. language, science, art, etc.) that
help to manufacture a taken-for-granted consensus. Crucial to the

success of this consensus-producing process, they argue, are forms of pedagogic action or pedagogic work (in the family, educational institutions and society more generally) that are able to transmit cultural values in such a way as to have a lasting effect on those who are being addressed by that work. For such a lasting effect to occur, the pedagogic action must inculcate durable ways of interpreting and evaluating the world and ways of being and acting that are animated by a taken-for-granted acceptance of the naturalness of what is in fact arbitrary. Bourdieu and Passeron use the concept of 'habitus' to signify these durable 'schemes of thought, perception, appreciation and action' (1977: 40), or what they also refer to as systems of dispositions, where the term disposition is used to 'denote a manner of being, a habitual state (especially in the body), and, in particular, a predisposition, tendency, propensity or inclination' (Bourdieu, 1972: 214, cited in Bourdieu and Passeron 1977: 67–8n.). Habitus represents a form of cultural inheritance analogous to genetic inheritance, or, as Bourdieu and Passeron put it, 'it is the equivalent, in the cultural order, of genetic capital in the biological order' (ibid.: 32). One's habitus, they argue, is acquired through unconscious processes of internalization and in turn provides an unconscious driving force for our actions. Here the concept of habitus is an example of the way in which sociologists have tried to move beyond the idea of a clear distinction between structure and agency. Habitus is neither structure nor agency; it is effectively both simultaneously. It is one way of giving a name to what in our discussion of Bernstein we referred to as the pervasive nature and constitutive effects of structure at the level of consciousness and action.

In *Reproduction*, Bourdieu and Passeron suggest we cannot escape our habitus even if we think we can: 'The questions of the man who thinks he is questioning the principles of his upbringing still have their roots in his upbringing' (1977: 37). Habitus is strongly classed, and it is through our habitus that we gain a sense of our place in the world – a sense, for example, of whether educational success or a more socially valued form of educational provision (e.g. an academic as opposed to a vocational track) is something 'for the likes of us'. Hence, for Bourdieu and Passeron, educational inequalities are produced not simply – or even primarily – through the formal selection mechanisms and assessment practices of educational institutions but by the self-selective and self-exclusionary choices that are the product of our habitus:

> most of those excluded from studying at the various levels of education eliminate themselves before being examined . . . Thus, previous

performances being equal, pupils of working-class origin are more likely to 'eliminate themselves' from secondary education by declining to enter it than to eliminate themselves once they have entered, and a fortiori more likely not to enter than to be eliminated from it by the explicit sanction of examination failure. (Ibid.: 153)

In a similar vein to Willis, Bourdieu and Passeron argue that the self-exclusionary choices of working-class students are informed by a realistic appraisal of the objective probability of their succeeding in a stratified education system in which opportunities for social mobility are severely limited:

Even when it seems to be imposed by the strength of a 'vocation' or the discovery of inability, each individual act of choice by which a child excludes himself from access to a stage of education or resigns himself to relegation to a devalorized type of course takes account of the ensemble of the objective relations (which pre-existed this choice and will outlast it) between his social class and the educational system. (1977: 155)

Moreover, the very objective relations and opportunity structures that 'condition' our choices and 'dispositions towards education and towards upgrading through education' – and that hence determine our 'likelihood of entering education, adhering to its norms and succeeding in it' – simultaneously 'contribute to the actualization of objective probabilities' (ibid.: 156).

So, whilst in some respects the concepts of habitus and disposition appear to resonate with Parsons's structural functionalist position on how social order – and the legitimacy of that order – is maintained 'through the internalization of shared values, beliefs and norms' (Jenkins 1992: 81), Bourdieu and Passeron explicitly argue that the concepts provide a means of transcending the structure/agency dichotomy. As the example of working-class orientations to schooling demonstrates, habitus is presented as both the product of objective social hierarchies and relations of domination and a producer of practices which combine to reproduce social structures. Hence habitus plays a crucial mediating role in what Bourdieu and Passeron call 'a system of circular relations which unite structures and practices' (1977: 203).

Conclusion

As will become evident in the next chapter, where we review some more approaches to sociology of education, and indeed throughout the book, the relationship between structure and agency is one of the central theoretical challenges facing all sociology. The approaches we have reviewed in this chapter differ in many respects – for example, they focus on different kinds of questions and develop and use contrasting theoretical lenses – and as a result they shed different kinds of light on the structure–agency relationship. As we have said earlier in the chapter, there is a danger of producing caricatures of the positions that we have inevitably had to review in a summary fashion, but nonetheless there are discernible differences in emphasis between them. One difference relates to how structures are conceptualized. For example, structures can be seen, on the one hand, as more or less 'hard' or ontologically basic or, on the other, as 'soft' or ontologically secondary. On the former model, social structures would be seen as broadly analogous to physical structures, for example, the configuration of the planets in the solar system, which seem to provide relatively fixed and unchangeable phenomena around which human agency has to operate. The idea of a softer social structure could be understood by looking at examples such as financial currencies, which are clearly humanly produced and are open to change but nonetheless for most people most of the time provide limits for what it is possible for them to do. An even softer example would be the rules of playground chase, which give shape to and constrain the possibilities of play for the children participating and yet which might, in certain circumstances, be renegotiated and radically changed relatively easily and quickly.

Another core question that emerges from the approaches we have reviewed is the role played by the notion of agency in different accounts. In some of the accounts, agency seems to be presented as an alternative and independent explanation for social phenomena. In these cases, agency is used as if it represents a break or a gap in the structural nexus through which social phenomena are causally explained. This idea seems to be in the background, for example, when Dale writes about anti-capitalist resistance as an expression of political agency made possible by the contradictions of capital. On other occasions, agency is invoked but is at the same time effectively explained as a product of some aspects of the structural nexus. For example, in the case of both Bernstein and Bourdieu, the emphasis they place on the density and pervasiveness of structure effectively undercuts more open-ended conceptions of agency as somehow occupying space outside of structure. There is little point in analysing this tension in much more depth here because what we are pointing to is, in essence, the longstanding and highly recalcitrant philosophical problem of the possibility of free will. However, it is worth noting that some of the work we have reviewed does raise the problem of how much scope there is for agency in the social world and, indeed, of whether any unproblematized notion of agency even makes sense.

The question of the relationship between structure and agency is predominantly a question about the explanatory function of sociology, and the work that we have reviewed in this chapter shows something of the range of different ways in which sociologists have sought to explain educational and social processes by reference to different conceptions of structure and agency. However, the work we have discussed – most obviously the work which describes itself in one way or another as critical – also provides further illustration of the strongly normative dimension of sociology of education. In other words, sociology of education embodies ethical and political value judgements and in some cases the advocacy of more or less specific changes. As we have said in the preface, the descriptive/explanatory and the normative dimensions of sociology are closely interrelated because, on the one hand, sociologists only apply explanatory lenses to things that they think matter in one sense or another, and, on the other, the credible advocacy of change depends upon some understanding of the way things are, why things came to be that way, and the processes through which things might be made different. Of course, the normative dimension in sociological writings is not always entirely explicit, as in the case of the priority attached to social order by the structural functionalist perspective. We will return to this question of implicit and explicit normativity at the end of chapter 3.

Furthermore, the debates about the proper conceptualization of, and the relationships between, structure and agency are in themselves debates of substantial normative relevance. As can be seen from some of the examples we have considered, sociologists often point to the relative importance of agency as a way of indicating the capacity for people to bring about change rather than simply to be subject to the determining effects of social structure. Lying behind a great deal of work in sociology is the question of how far it is possible for things to be different from the way they are. Whilst mapping the multitude of ways in which educational and social processes produce diverse forms of inequality, sociologists frequently get caught between a sense of the inevitability of structures of oppression and inequality on the one hand and the possibilities (albeit often heavily constrained) for social transformation on the other. As we said in chapter 1 when discussing Renold's work, sociologists both individually and collectively tend to hover between optimism and pessimism. Characteristically, it is the possibilities of agency, including both the degrees and kinds of agency that are available and the potential influence of agency, which allow for more optimistic readings; and hence this sometimes seemingly technical dispute about the structure–agency relationship is simultaneously a dispute with fundamentally important political and emotional overtones.

3
Varieties of Critique

In this chapter we continue our review of influential perspectives in sociology of education. As we have already made clear, some sociologists are not interested simply in describing and explaining educational phenomena but are at the same time motivated by a normative perspective. Such sociologists often have an interest in criticizing educational phenomena and sometimes in attempting to change things. In the previous chapter we looked at this tendency through the example of Marxist sociology, which is the tradition of critique that has been most visible in the history of sociology of education. As we signalled there, there are some strong parallels between Marxism and other critical perspectives. However, there are also important differences, and in this chapter we will consider the contribution of feminist theory, critical race theory and poststructuralism to the formation of contemporary sociology of education.

The theme of the previous chapter – structure and agency – because it is so central to sociology, will continue to be visible in this chapter, although we have chosen not to foreground it so much here. Another theme which began to emerge in the previous chapter, the nature of knowledge, will become increasingly more evident in this one. In our discussion of Bernstein and Bourdieu we showed how the very idea of knowledge and the constitution of knowledge came to be problematized in the new sociology of education such that the concern became not simply the question of access to some agreed body of knowledge but also the question of how forms of knowledge embody, and act to reproduce, hierarchies and patterns of inclusion and exclusion. Similarly, in the account we offered of Marxist sociology of education we showed the importance, from a critical perspective, of disrupting and challenging dominant and supposedly neutral conceptions of knowledge which, in practice, serve to perpetuate and mask patterns of exploitation and oppression. This notion of knowledge as 'guilty' will run through the approaches we consider in this chapter.

As in the previous two chapters, our aim, in reviewing examples of work in sociology of education, is principally to illustrate and explicate a range of topics, perspectives and approaches. Although this chapter is about critique, in this part of the book we are ourselves engaged not in critique but rather in description. As will always be the case when providing descriptive accounts, there is a danger of treating all approaches and perspectives as if they are equally valid, and hence of being seen – justifiably – as insufficiently uncritical and undiscriminating. This is an important worry and one that we come back to in part II of the book. But for now we should stress that even the process of setting contrasting accounts side by side provides some measure of implicit or indirect criticism. That is to say, authors working in the traditions we look at in this chapter tend to define their own positions by contrasting them with other positions both within and outside their own traditions in sociology. In simple terms, there is a limit to how far pieces of sociological work can be complementary to one another. To some extent, what sociologists offer are *rival* accounts of the same phenomena, and to this extent they cannot all be right. Hence, a central part of the task of reading sociology, we would argue, is to be aware of the explicit and implicit contests between different pieces of work and to be prepared to try and arbitrate between them, or at least to get clear about what is at stake in these contests. These contests operate across a range of axes. For example, there are different claims about what the social world is fundamentally like, competing conceptions of what counts as valid knowledge, and competing genres of persuasion or argumentation. Related to all of these there are also what we are calling normative disagreements – i.e. competing accounts of 'what matters' in education – which produce substantially different frames of reference and emphases in sociological readings. We hope that the examples reviewed in this chapter will illuminate such contests between the different perspectives and thereby lay the groundwork for part II of the book, where we explore some of these tensions more explicitly.

Feminism

Whilst at the core of Marxist theory is the project of dismantling the natural and neutral appearance of the capitalist system and unmasking

and challenging the forms of oppression it generates, feminist sociologists have a particular interest in dismantling and challenging the
natural and neutral appearance of the sexual division of labour, the
gendered distribution of social roles and resources, and the ways in
which men oppress or dominate women. Feminist sociology is a very
diverse field containing many different perspectives which produce a
plural, and some might even say highly fractured, domain of inquiry.
There is a plethora of labels appearing under this heading, including, for example, black feminism, psychoanalytic feminism, eco-
feminism, lesbian feminism and separatist feminism. Labels of this
sort indicate both the contested nature of the field and its links with
the politics of identity, but also suggest that there are some broadly
common concerns that enable each one of these kinds of currents to
be labelled 'feminist'. Within sociology of education the dominant
feminist perspectives have been liberal feminism, a range of radical
perspectives, among them radical, Marxist, socialist, black and
lesbian feminism, and poststructuralist feminism. However, these
labels should not be taken to denote clear-cut perspectives. Rather
they should be taken as standing for a range of frequently overlapping
perspectives, each with their own distinctive descriptive, explanatory
and normative emphases. In the remainder of this section we focus
on liberal and radical/socialist feminist perspectives. Poststructuralist
feminist perspectives will be discussed later in the chapter as part of
a wider consideration of poststructuralist sociology.

In broad terms liberal feminism is characterized by its political
commitment to using existing democratic processes and structures to
equalize opportunities for women and girls. The focus is on identifying the attitudinal and structural barriers to equal access to economic
and educational opportunities, and then removing these barriers
through legislative reform and personal and professional development activities aimed at challenging gender stereotyping and sexist
attitudes. A widely cited example of work that lies broadly in the
liberal tradition but which, as we shall see, has a distinctively radical
edge to it is Byrne's *Women and Education* (1978).

Byrne: Women and Education

This book starts with:

> an impassioned call to all educated women (and men) to accept their
> own responsibility and direct duty, to walk back down the ladder which
> they have climbed, and to build in all the missing rungs to help less

fortunate girls and women . . . to the freedom of status, career, and
personal fulfilment to which only the fullest educational opportunity is
the key. (Byrne 1978: 12)

Commitment to the meritocratic ideal – the idea that everyone
regardless of sex, class or race should have an equal chance to
compete for the social and economic rewards associated with the
higher rungs of the 'ladder of opportunity' – is central to the liberal
feminist position.

It is this fundamental political commitment that shapes Byrne's
analytic approach. First, she uses statistics to demonstrate gender
inequality in the distribution of educational resources, education
and employment opportunities, and pay, pointing, for example, to
the predominance of women teachers in the lower-paid sectors of
education, to lower levels of financial investment in the education of
girls, to the under-representation of girls in secondary school science
and technology courses, and to the under-representation of women
in higher education, in science, engineering and technology-related
occupations and in top management positions, even in sectors, such
as further education, where women are well represented.

Second, she seeks to challenge the explanations of these inequalities that prevailed at the time – explanations which locate the cause
in innate differences between the sexes – arguing that the causes are
social rather than biological and identifying a combination of attitudinal and structural barriers to gender equality. Byrne draws on a
range of kinds of data to support her case, including surveys exploring the attitudes of teachers and girls, her own observations (as a local
authority administrator) of gender-differentiated curricula, textual
analysis of gender stereotyping in school textbooks, and statistical
analysis of gender imbalances in the teaching profession. She also
uses autobiographical writing to illustrate some of her arguments,
a device that is fairly typical of feminist work, reflecting its concern
with subjective experience.

Among the attitudinal barriers Byrne identifies are the myth of
women's dependency in marriage and the stereotyping of girls as
passive, physically weak, caring, technically inept, arts oriented,
and innately interested in domestic activities and of boys as active,
strong, technically minded, spatially aware and good at mathematics. She rejects the assumptions of homogeneity underpinning these
stereotypes, which leads her in turn to reject altogether the use of
gendered distinctions in schools. She is concerned both about the
effects of gendered discourses on boys and girls who do not conform

to normative conceptions of femininity or masculinity, 'who are
then labelled as deviant rather than simply untypical, whatever that
means' (1978: 51), and about the effects of gendered discourses on
girls' motivation, arguing that:

> the assumption of women's economic dependence on men in marriage
> . . . is a principal cause of girls' lower motivation to continue in long-
> term education and training, to strive for the same qualifications, to
> seek work, advancement, and independence in the same measure as
> boys. (Ibid.: 61)

The myth of women's dependency is also, Byrne argues, the reason
why teachers tend 'to accept lower ceilings of attainment and
motivation in their girl school leavers' (ibid.).

As well as looking at attitudinal barriers, Byrne points to structural
inequalities in the organization of the school curriculum and the
teaching workforce. For example, she notes the persistence of separate
curricular routes for girls and boys – which limit the opportunities of
girls (especially working-class girls) for further education and skilled
employment – despite the passage three years before the publication
of her book of the UK Sex Discrimination Act, which had rendered
such practices open to legal challenge. And she analyses patterns of
teacher employment and the gendered division of labour in schools
(with, for example, men predominating in leadership roles) as a form
of hidden curriculum which conveys messages to schoolchildren
about what are 'appropriate' roles for men and women.

For Byrne, the solutions lie in eliminating sexist organizational
and teaching practices in schools through national policies, including the introduction of a common core curriculum aimed at enabling
all students to leave school with the qualifications needed for skilled
employment. Byrne also calls for the elimination of masculinist termi-
nology in schools that makes 'girls feel they are being allowed into the
"male club" rather than entering an open mixed environment with a
new ethos' (1978: 145), compulsory training for teachers to counter-
act sex-role stereotyping, and the establishment of an independent
board to monitor stereotyping or sexism in curricular materials and
to publish guidelines on good practice. Beyond schools, she suggests
that such reforms will help contribute to '[t]he gradual restructuring
of men's and women's roles so that men take full share of domestic
burdens and women of economic responsibility' (ibid.: 76).

Radical and socialist feminists reject the reformist approach
advocated by liberal feminists such as Byrne and the ideology of

meritocracy underpinning it, arguing for far more deep-seated changes to the organization of education. Unlike liberal feminists, who seek to secure for women equal access to the top rungs of prevailing hierarchies, radical and socialist feminists seek to dissolve hierarchies. This includes, for many, dissolving the division between formal knowledge acquired within formal educational institutions and personal knowledge acquired through living, and hence also the division between teaching and learning and between expert and layperson. In the models of education preferred by radical and socialist feminists, everyone in the classroom is a teacher and a learner, with learning reconstructed as a cooperative activity. Stratification of the student population on the basis of age and ability, stratification within the teaching workforce, and the stratification of knowledge and of educational institutions are all challenged on the grounds that they are central to the hidden curriculum of formal education through which students learn that inequalities and hierarchies are normal, natural and necessary and that, for substantial proportions of the population, failure is inevitable. Within the feminist cooperative model there is no place for failure, which is viewed as a barrier to learning and unnecessary, and hence there is no place for hierarchical systems of grading which inevitably 'establish some students as clever and others as mediocre' (De Wolfe 1988: 50). On this model, 'learning is an end in itself and not a passport to a particular place in society' (Spender 1988: 48). As well as seeking to dismantle the fundamental structures of society and construct new – feminist – forms of education, radical feminist sociologists have opened up distinct areas of inquiry within education, including violence against girls and women, the sexual harassment of girls and women teachers, and the treatment of sexuality in the curriculum.

A range of radical and socialist feminist perspectives were brought together in a pivotal anthology, *Learning to Lose: sexism and education*. First published in 1980, the collection was updated in 1988 to include chapters on lesbian and black feminism, which had been neglected in the first edition, reflecting a wider tendency within the women's movement at the time to assume that the experiences of white women were those of all women.

Spender and Sarah: Learning to Lose

Learning to Lose is the collective product of a cooperative feminist study group comprised of women, many of them teachers, who were active in the women's liberation movement in the 1970s. The chapters are written in an accessible style aimed at opening up the ideas of the women's movement to feminist teachers, 'enabling them to feel part of it, thus strengthening their voices' (Mahony 1988), and giving them a language with which to articulate what is wrong with the education system and how it needs to change. As with Byrne's analysis, there is an emphasis on the personal experiences of the researchers. The choice to value personal experience is a political one, grounded in the belief that the 'objective' approach of male-dominated social science, by ignoring women's accounts of their own lived experience, enables 'the objective facts about women's existence' to be 'distorted' and 'continue unquestioned' (Brewster 1988: 5). So, for radical feminists, the sharing and analysis of personal experience, because of the structural inequalities, oppressive practices and sometimes deep emotional scars it reveals, represents a political act, a first step in 'redistributing power' (ibid.: 6).

This wide-ranging collection offers a radical critique of the education system of the 1970s, aspects of which echo some of Byrne's arguments. For example, like Byrne, many of the contributors point to the ways in which curriculum materials and teachers' expectations reproduce sex-role stereotypes, channelling girls into traditionally female subject choices, and conveying 'a subtle and pernicious message that females are inferior, [hence] do[ing] untold damage to the self evaluation of girls' (Lobban 1977: 106, cited in Spender 1988: 27). However, this is accompanied by a more deep-seated critique of the nature of the knowledge that is being taught in schools. Rather than seeking to secure for girls equal access to the same curriculum as boys, the contributors to this collection advocate a fundamental rewriting of the curriculum, arguing, on the basis of analysis of curriculum texts, that what was being taught in schools in the 1970s was men's history, men's science, men's geography, etc. – masquerading as objective, universal knowledge. Within this male curriculum, women were rendered invisible, their contributions were trivialized or they were represented in derogatory ways, or, in the case of sex education, their sexuality was not recognized (Jackson 1988). *Learning to Lose* is also marked by a more deep-seated critique of the social organization and pedagogic practices of schooling than is apparent in Byrne's work. Whilst Byrne argues for co-education as the best means of securing equal access for girls to valued knowledge and further education opportunities, many of the contributors to this collection are hostile to co-education, arguing for single-sex schools where girls are exposed to women teachers who 'are involved in exercising some authority on their own behalf and that of other females, namely their pupils', and to an alternative to patriarchal cultures, with opportunities to develop women's solidarity and 'know the strength that can come as a result of collective action' (Sarah et al. 1988: 64, 65).

The collection focuses more on description and critique, and on the construction of alternative approaches to education, than it does on explanation. However, where explanations are attempted, they tend to focus on the core concept of patriarchy and, in some cases, the working together of patriarchy and capitalism. Several of the contributions were influenced by a functionalist version of Marxist feminism which linked the oppression of women to the demands of capitalist production. In this interpretation, sexist – or patriarchal – ideologies that are reproduced in the school (e.g., those of domesticity, femininity and women's dependency, which sustain male supremacy) are shaped by the requirement that working-class girls need to be prepared to be both low-paid workers in the economy (like their male counterparts) and subordinate to men in preparation for their future roles as 'domestic workers and child bearers and rearers'. Moreover, women 'must learn to give this labour freely, based on a notion of individual love' (Payne 1988: 12). Hence, patriarchal ideology is seen to be firmly rooted in the material realities of capitalist production, and equality of opportunity is understood as 'a myth . . . created to mask the practices of the school' which enable the dominant group, consisting of white males, to 'perpetuate its own success' (Scott 1988: 98).

Contributors to *Learning to Lose* advocate an alternative, socialist feminist, form of education, involving individual and collective action. At the individual level, this means feminist teachers constantly trying to raise both their own awareness of how sexism operates and the consciousness of their students, giving teachers and students 'a sense of themselves as part of a social group with power to change society' (Sarah 1988: 179). Feminist teachers are encouraged to look for every opportunity to expose and challenge the sexist ideology of the school, to make explicit the 'hidden' sexism in the organization of the school, and to use non-sexist language and also non-sexist teaching materials, which make girls and issues of gender equality visible in the curriculum and contain positive and non-sex-stereotyped images of girls and women. A number of contributors argue that through such consciousness-raising activities sexist ideology can begin to be undermined, since '[o]pposition to, and decline of patriarchy and capitalism grow in part out of a change in consciousness' (Scott 1988: 115–16).

The feminist education advocated in this book also involves challenging the patriarchal bias in the knowledge that is taught, questioning the objectivity of that knowledge and transforming patriarchal knowledge in ways that make women visible, reflect women's lives and experiences, expose sexual divisions, inequalities and oppression, and explain how these are produced. The development of women's studies and black studies courses in universities in the 1970s represented a core part of this strategy but was fraught with tension, as feminist academics had to grapple with how to reconcile the individualism, competition and hierarchical grading systems demanded by university assessment practices with the feminist commitment to cooperation, collectivism and non-hierarchical practices.

Feminist teachers were also engaged in collective action to challenge and prevent sexual harassment in the workplace (Whitbread 1988). However, radical and socialist feminist educators believed that sexist ideologies could not be eradicated through classroom or within-school practices alone, and so they were also engaged in collective political movements outside of the school – both the women's movement and the socialist movement – in order to challenge the oppressive structures, in particular the sexist division of labour and the material dependence of women on men within capitalist patriarchal societies. As one of the editors puts it, '[i]f sexism in education is to be eliminated, the whole patriarchal social order and the ideology that legitimates it must be confronted' (Sarah 1988: 162).

However, much of the radical feminist writing of the 1970s and 1980s was produced by white women and tended to neglect the experiences of black teachers and black girls. As black feminist writers within sociology of education pointed out, black women teachers and students suffer dual oppression. As well as experiencing overt and covert sexism, they experience overt and covert racism, as documented in Evans's contribution to the second edition of *Learning to Lose*, which draws on her personal experience as a teacher in London secondary schools from the mid-1970s to the mid-1980s as well as on a wider black feminist literature. For example, Evans writes of the way in which her white colleagues disparaged black female students, typically describing them as 'those loud black girls' (the title of her chapter); black images were either absent around the school or in the curriculum or were presented in ways that portrayed black people as inferior and uncivilized; and black women workers dominated in the lowest status jobs in schools – as cleaners, cooks and support workers. For black women educated in the 1950s onwards it was arguably racism more than sexism that oppressed them:

For Black schoolgirls sexism has . . . played an insidious role in our lives. It has influenced our already limited career choices and has scarred our already tarnished self-image. But it is racism which has determined the schools we can attend and the quality of education we receive in them. Consequently this has been the most significant influence on our experience of school and society. (Bryan et al. 1985: 58, quoted in Evans 1988: 187)

The black feminist literature challenged the universalist assumptions of radical feminism, pointing to the historic and culturally specific nature of girls' experiences. For example, whilst for white feminists the family was constructed as a site of oppression, for black feminists it was more often constructed as a source of sustenance and empowerment, as a haven from the racism and sexism experienced outside the home. For Evans and other black feminists, the women's movement had 'perpetrated a type of cultural imperialism that takes the oppression of white women as its norm and develops its theory from the experience of a small minority of women in global terms' (1988: 189).

In parallel, a lesbian feminist literature emerged which described the double oppression of lesbians as a consequence both of sexism and of heterosexism and homophobia. In the final chapter of the second edition of *Learning to Lose*, Trenchard (1988) reports on an interview study of 136 young lesbians. These young women reported that lesbianism tended to be either ignored or trivialized by their teachers. They also described their experiences of homophobic abuse in schools, the failure of teachers to challenge homophobic remarks, the tendency of teachers to treat heterosexuality as the norm and lesbianism as 'other', and the emotional consequences of all this, including feelings of alienation, stress and anxiety and, in some cases, attempted suicide. However, Trenchard avoids constructing these students as victims, instead choosing to emphasize the ways in which many of them were strong and positive about their lesbianism, able to critique the way in which lesbianism is treated in schools and to develop constructive suggestions for transforming schools in ways that enable young lesbians to be educated in environments free from discrimination.

As we hope is clear from this discussion, feminism is a good example of a sociological tradition where internal disagreements are evident. And central to the differences between alternative currents in feminist analysis are normative disagreements. This is not to say that values are the only things about which feminist scholars might disagree. Feminist scholars have profound disagreements about evidential claims, for example, and about what are the most productive theoretical and argumentative resources for feminist analysis. However, bound up with these are important disagreements about values, including what count as feminist values. It is, for example, not possible to be equally and wholeheartedly committed both to the liberal feminist objective of increasing girls' and women's access to traditionally valued educational goods and to the radical feminist objective of dismantling and restructuring our notions of what is educationally important. In evaluating the rival claims made within critical traditions, therefore, we inevitably find ourselves having to focus upon and make judgements about competing value positions. This is also the case when evaluating the rival claims made *across* critical traditions. The critical race theory (CRT) tradition, to which we now turn, which is broadly located within the anti-racist movement, defines itself in part by contrast with certain feminist and Marxist currents as well as with liberal educational movements such as those centred on the idea of multiculturalism.

Critical race theory

Like Marxism and feminism, CRT has a transformative political as well as an intellectual agenda. Politically, the aim is to work towards racial justice through critical scholarship combined with forms of radical action. Intellectually, the goal is to produce forms of analysis that can both expose and explain the persistence of racism and race-based inequalities throughout society. The CRT movement grew up in the United States in the 1970s, but its influence has begun to be felt beyond US borders (e.g. see Gillborn 2005, 2008).

CRT has its roots in the US critical legal studies (CLS) tradition of the 1960s, a form of legal analysis that sought to challenge traditional liberal approaches to jurisprudence. Heavily influenced by neo-Marxist theories of ideology, the CLS approach challenged the presumed neutrality and objectivity of legal discourse and legal structures, seeking to expose them as ideological formations that served to legitimate and reinforce unjust and oppressive social structures. However, just as white feminists were criticized by black feminists for their universalizing assumptions, so critical black legal scholars challenged some of the universalizing assumptions of CLS. For example, in rejecting formal structures, such as rights, rules and bureaucracies, and embracing informal ones based on ideas of goodwill and community, CLS, these critics argued, risked reinforcing racial injustice, because informal structures are heavily susceptible to the operation of prejudice.

It was from such critiques that CRT was born. Central to CRT is the idea that racism is 'normal, not aberrant' in society (Delgado and Stefancic 2000: xvi) and that, 'because it is so enmeshed in the fabric of our social order, it appears both normal and natural to people in this culture' (Ladson-Billings 1998: 11). CRT seeks to unmask and explain racism in all its manifestations, ranging from macro-level economic and legislative structures to the multiple forms of 'micro-aggression' that shape the everyday experiences of black people. In doing so, like the feminist research discussed in the previous section, it places emphasis on the value of giving voice to 'the feelings and intangible modes of perception unique to those who have historically been socially, structurally, and intellectually marginalized' (Barnes 1990: 1864, cited in Tate 1997: 210). Hence there is an emphasis in CRT on storytelling or narrative forms of scholarship. The narrative form is understood as being analytically generative, because it provides insights grounded in experience that forms of more abstract theorizing or quantitative analysis do not make available, and politically generative, because it represents a form of communication that has the power to convince and persuade. Storytelling is also understood as playing a therapeutic role, as a means of countering the 'wounds of pain caused by racial oppression', in particular the wounds caused by the internalization of stereotypical images of themselves to which members of marginalized groups are so frequently exposed (Ladson-Billings and Tate 1995: 57).

In attempting to explain the persistence of racial justice, CRT offers a thoroughgoing critique of the liberal civil rights doctrine, with a particular focus on the principle of colour-blindness and the structures and processes of anti-discrimination law. The principle of colour-blindness, which lies at the core of US civil rights discourse, is problematized by critical race theorists, who argue that colour-blindness is, in fact, necessarily an expression of 'color-consciousness' (Crenshaw et al. 1995: xxviii) and that, moreover, underlying colour-blindness is a presumption that blackness represents a physical malady or abnormality (Williams 1997). 'When students begin to internalize this shame or sense of abnormality', according to Dixson and Rousseau (2005: 16), 'colour-blindness can become a form of microagression.' CRT scholars argue that colour-blindness can perpetuate discrimination when it is associated with a refusal to acknowledge either race-based inequalities or that race-based inequalities are a result of racism, as in the case of the mathematics teachers studied by Rousseau and Tate (2003), who either denied the existence of race-based patterns of achievement in their classrooms or, where they acknowledged them, explained them by recourse to class-based explanations rather than considering the possible role played by institutional racism.

Liberal anti-discrimination law, which emphasizes incremental change, has been criticized from a CRT perspective both for its 'painstaking' slowness (Ladson-Billings 1998: 12) and for its tendency to benefit more white than black people. Bell suggests that it is only when the interests of white and black people converge that black people benefit from civil rights laws, that '[t]his convergence is far more important for gaining relief than the degree of harm suffered by blacks or the character of proof offered to prove that harm', and that:

> even when the interest convergence results in an effective racial remedy, that remedy will be abrogated at the point that policy makers fear the remedial policy is threatening the superior societal status of whites. (Bell 2004: 69)

This, Bell suggests, was the case with school desegregation, and he identifies a range of methods that white people have used to preserve segregated school environments, and hence 'their superior social status', whilst maintaining support for the principle of desegregation. Amongst the examples he gives are:

> opposition of New York City school teachers to community control . . . the resistance of unions to plans that require that they stop excluding minority workers . . . suburban zoning and referendum practices designed to keep out low-income housing. (Bell 1979: 11–12)

In an extension of Bell's arguments, Harris (1993) uses the concept of 'whiteness as property' to explain such status-preserving strategies. Harris argues that, since the time America was first conquered by white people, whiteness has been established as a form of property that has enabled white people to 'buy' privilege, and that this continues to be the case in the US, even though segregation is no longer permitted by law:

> Even after the period of conquest and colonization of the New World and the abolition of slavery, whiteness was the predicate for attaining a host of societal privileges, in both public and private spheres. Whiteness determined whether one could vote, travel freely, attend schools, obtain work, and indeed, defined the structure of social relations along with

the entire spectrum of interactions between the individual and society. Whiteness then became status, a form of racialized privilege ratified in law. Material privileges attendant to being white inhered in the status of being white. After the dismantling of legalized race segregation, whiteness took on the character of property in the modern sense in that relative white privilege was legitimated as the status quo. (1993: 1745–6)

This idea was taken up, and introduced into sociology of education, by Ladson-Billings and Tate in their seminal article 'Toward a critical race theory of education', which uses a CRT perspective to challenge some of the key assumptions of liberal multicultural education.

Ladson-Billings and Tate: 'Toward a critical race theory of education'

Like other theorists in the CRT tradition, Ladson-Billings and Tate remind us that, if we are to fully understand how racism works, we need to listen to the voices of marginalized people:

> without authentic voices of people of color (as teachers, parents, administrators, students, and community members) it is doubtful that we can say or know anything useful about education in their communities. (1995: 58)

Their discussion is organized around three central propositions. First, they argue that, although '[r]ace continues to be a significant factor in determining inequity in the United States' and is 'endemic and deeply ingrained in American life' (1995: 48, 55), issues of race and racism have been neglected in most critical education research. Whilst not seeking to underestimate the important role that class and gender bias play in the production of educational and social inequalities, Ladson-Billings and Tate argue that:

> class- and gender-based explanations are not powerful enough to explain all of the difference (or variance) in school experience and performance. Although both class and gender can and do intersect race, as stand-alone variables they do not explain all of the educational achievement differences apparent between whites and students of color. Indeed there is some evidence to suggest that even when we hold constant for class, middle-class African American students do not achieve at the same level as their white counterparts. . . . [E]xamination of class and gender, taken alone or together, do not account for the extraordinarily high rates of school dropout, suspension, expulsion, and failure among African American and Latino males. (Ibid.: 51)

Their second proposition is that 'US society is based on property rights' (1995: 48), so that, despite the gains of the civil rights movement, race-based inequalities in access to property rights mean that 'Blacks remain disadvantaged and deprived because of their race' (Bell 1987: 239, cited in Ladson-Billings and Tate 1995). In many US states, a substantial proportion of funding for public schools comes from local taxation based on property values, and this, coupled with residential segregation, according to Ladson-Billings and Tate, effectively means that 'those with "better" property are entitled to "better schools"' (1995: 54). To illustrate this point, the authors use data from Kozol's (1991) hard-hitting exposé of the 'savage inequalities' of US schooling. Kozol found that, in 1987, average per-pupil funding in the state of New York ranged from $5,500 in the city of New York to $15,000 in the most wealthy state districts. As a consequence of these disparities, middle-class schools have greater access to the material resources that can be used to support learning, including 'science labs, computers and other state-of-the art technologies', and to 'appropriately certified and prepared teachers' (Ladson-Billings and Tate 1995: 54). These 'property differences', Ladson-Billings and Tate argue, also have ramifications for the curriculum, evident, for example, in the far greater range of subject choices available to students in mainly white middle-class school districts than are available to students in urban African-American districts.

Ladson-Billings and Tate's third proposition is that '[t]he intersection of race and property creates an analytic tool through which we can understand social (and, consequently, school) inequity' (1995: 48). This analytic tool centres on Harris's (1993) theorization of 'whiteness as property', the idea that whiteness is the 'ultimate property' that is available to white people for the purchase of advantage and which undergirds white supremacy. Ladson-Billings and Tate apply this concept to an analysis of racial injustice in education. Harris distinguishes between four 'property functions of whiteness': rights of disposition; rights to use and enjoyment; reputation and status property; and the absolute right to exclude. Ladson-Billings and Tate argue that each of these property functions is evident in education. Commenting on the first function, they point out that it is difficult at first sight to see how whiteness can be disposable or alienable. After all, if it is something that is embodied, how can it then be transferred to someone else? However, they suggest that it can be transferred when certain values, dispositions and cultural practices are constructed as 'white':

When students are rewarded only for conformity to perceived 'white norms' or sanctioned for cultural practices (e.g., dress, speech patterns, unauthorized conceptions of knowledge), white property is being rendered alienable. (Ladson-Billings and Tate 1995: 59)

The second function of whiteness, according to Harris, consists of the rights to use and enjoyment that it confers on those who own it. To illustrate how this function operates in education, Ladson-Billings and Tate turn once again to Kozol's *Savage Inequalities* and his vivid descriptions of the differences in the physical and curricular resources to which black and white students have access:

The curriculum [[which] the white school] follows 'emphasizes critical thinking, reasoning and logic.' The planetarium, for instance, is employed not simply for the study of the universe as it exists. 'Children are also designing their own galaxies,' the teacher says . . .
In my [Kozol's] notes: 'Six girls, four boys. Nine White, one Chinese. I am glad they have this class. But what about the others? Aren't there ten Black children in the school who could *enjoy* this also?' (Kozol 1991: 96, cited in Ladson-Billings and Tate 1995: 59; their emphasis)

Harris's third property function of whiteness is reputation and status:

The concept of reputation as property is regularly demonstrated in legal cases of libel and slander. Thus to damage someone's reputation is to damage some aspect of his or her personal property. In the case of race, to call a white person 'black' is to defame him or her. (Ladson-Billings and Tate 1995: 60)

Ladson-Billings and Tate show how the same idea can be applied to education. For example, schools and school programmes associated with minority communities tend to be constructed in dominant discourse as low status. So, for instance:

Despite the prestige of foreign language learning, bilingual education as practiced in the United States as a nonwhite form of second language learning has lower status. The term urban, the root of the word urbane, has come to mean black. Thus, urban schools (located in the urbane, sophisticated cities) lack the status and reputation of suburban (white) schools and when urban students move or are bused to suburban schools, these schools lose their reputation. (Ibid.)

The final property function of whiteness Harris identifies is the absolute right to exclude. Ladson-Billings and Tate argue that in education the absolute right to exclude has taken on different forms over the course of US history, starting with the total exclusion of black people from schooling, then manifested in the enshrinement of segregated schooling in law, and now seen in the phenomena of 'white flight and the growing insistence on vouchers, public funding of private schools, and schools of choice' and the various technologies of in-school segregation, including tracking and gifted and talented programmes that are currently in use (1995: 60).

In the final section of the paper, Ladson-Billings and Tate turn their attention to the main liberal response to racial injustice in education – multicultural education.[1] Although established with the laudable aim of transforming schools 'and other educational institutions so that students from diverse racial, ethnic, and other social-class groups will experience educational equality' (Banks 1993: 22), multicultural education, they argue, suffers from equivalent limitations to the ones CRT identifies in civil rights law. Namely, progress has been slow because multicultural education does not tackle the root cause of racism – white hegemony. Instead it is frequently reduced to a superficial inclusion in the curriculum of 'trivial examples and artefacts of cultures such as eating ethnic or cultural foods, singing songs or dancing' (Ladson-Billings and Tate 1995: 61). In addition, the concept of difference has been stretched in the multicultural education paradigm to include a multiplicity of kinds of difference, including those relating to divisions of language, ability, gender and sexuality as well as race and ethnicity, as if 'all difference is both analogous and equivalent' (ibid.: 62).

The problem with multicultural education, as Ladson-Billings and Tate see it, is pithily captured in their statement that it 'attempts to be everything to everyone and consequently becomes nothing for anyone, allowing the status quo to prevail'. They suggest that it is impossible to maintain 'the spirit and intent of justice for the oppressed whilst simultaneously permitting the hegemonic rule of the oppressor' and, citing Marcus Garvey, conclude that 'any program of emancipation would have to be built around the question of race first' (1995: 62).

This call for 'race first' highlights the potential tensions between the different critical traditions that we are reviewing here. That is to say, whilst it might be tempting to suggest that issues of inequality around class, gender and race are equally imperative in principle, in practice things are not always so straightforward. This applies most obviously in the realm of practical politics, where individuals sometimes have to decide which battles to fight first and how to divide their time between the competing demands of different constituencies and movements. But it can also apply in an analogous way to the framing of sociological analyses, in terms both of how research agendas are constructed and of what is written and for whom we write. There are inevitably sometimes choices to be made about what dimensions of concern to focus on, highlight or relatively foreground. (We will come back to these problems of *focus and framing* at the end of the chapter.) This indicates the scope for the existence of a set of normative differences *between* critical traditions which exist in parallel with and in addition to the normative disagreements that occur *within* critical traditions, such as those between liberal and radical feminism discussed earlier. Here, as elsewhere, we are simply underlining the fact that doing sociology seriously means taking these normative disagreements seriously. One possible reaction to rivalries between critical traditions is to focus on what sociologists sometimes call intersectionalities – that is, the inseparability of what are sometimes taken to be different facets of oppression (e.g. those based on social divisions of class, gender and race) and the constitutive and causal interpenetration of these. This stance is typically associated with poststructuralist analysis, which we will move on to next. However, it is important to see that this stance itself occupies a particular normative space which some people would reject (on the grounds that some differences need to be prioritized over others and in one way or another 'put first'), and hence it does not obviate the need to arbitrate between normative disagreements.

Poststructuralism

As our depiction of Marxism, feminism and CRT has shown, critique plays a central role in sociology. That is, as well as attempting to capture and explain the nature of the social world, it is concerned to unmask, dislodge and disrupt commonly accepted versions of what the social world is like. From the 1970s onwards there was an intellectual mass movement in the humanities and social sciences which turned this critical gaze back onto itself. In the field of sociology, for example, there was increasing scepticism, not only about dominant ideologies such as capitalism and patriarchy, but also about the claims of sociologists themselves and the possibility of knowledge in sociology. A highly contentious term with very fuzzy boundaries, poststructuralism is the label generally given to this movement. It is characterized by pervasive, highly critical and imaginative forms of scepticism about many of the taken-for-granted tenets of classical and modern sociology. Here we attempt to illuminate something of the force and sweep of poststructuralist scepticism by identifying some of the key assumptions of classical and modern sociological thought that poststructuralists reject.

Most famously, poststructuralism involves a rejection of the validity of meta-narratives, such as functionalism, Marxism, patriarchy, globalization and secularization – that is, grand overarching theoretical or conceptual frameworks that purport to capture large and central features of the world authoritatively. For the poststructuralist, such frameworks are inevitably reductionist and obscure and distort the messy and complicated nature of the social world as much as they illuminate it.

In fact, the language of 'distortion' could be seen as misleading because it suggests that there is a definite object which could be clearly represented but which is in some way being misrepresented, whereas, according to perspectives that are dominant in poststructuralism, the point about the messiness of the social world is precisely that there are no objects outside of modes of representation. Rather, objects exist only insofar as they are created by the ways we talk about them; and, moreover, there is an inevitable lack of definiteness to objects because our ways of talking are diverse, open-ended, shifting and even contradictory.

Another recurrent theme in poststructuralist writing is a warning against the widespread and uncritical reliance on the use of binary distinctions, e.g. distinctions between man and woman, young and old, able-bodied and disabled. Distinctions such as these, which often play a major role in the way we make sense of the world, are criticized for three main reasons. First, they suggest that these categories might refer to stable and fixed categories in the world, whereas the possibilities of identity are much richer and more complex and hybrid than these simple distinctions suggest. Second, each of these distinctions echoes a set of social relationships in which some identities or subject positions are dominant and others subservient, and an uncritical reliance on their use arguably serves to reinforce or reproduce these hierarchical relationships. Third, they lead to essentialism, i.e. the belief that individuals categorized as belonging to what are often labelled as different social groups (e.g. those classified on the basis of gender, race, ethnicity, dis/ability, etc.) possess an unalterable essence which determines their actions and behaviour (Burr 1995).

This rejection of essentialism, and the homogenizing assumptions which generally accompany it, strongly relates to the poststructuralist rejection of the Enlightenment conception of a singular, coherent self. This is the idea popular in religious traditions, but also in a good deal of 'common sense', that each person has a stable and definitive core, at least from birth to death, which makes them who they are. By contrast, because they reject the existence of entities outside of representations, poststructuralists conceive of the self as another product of the stories that we tell. According to this conception, the self is continually in a state of flux and is plural, hybrid, fractured and discontinuous.

Closely connected to this is the rejection of the idea of the Enlightenment conception of the rational actor that is common in much social science. For poststructuralists, it is naïve to explain or try to predict people's behaviour by using the idea that they pursue their ends on the basis of systematic and well-reasoned decision-making processes. Rather they suggest that people's motivations are more complex and opaque and are shaped by an amalgam of affective factors, including unconscious desires and non-rational preferences.

We can use a final example of poststructuralist scepticism to draw some of these points together. Poststructuralist work is often characterized as anti-universalist. This means it is sceptical about ways of talking that assume or imply that all people have certain things in common in relation to their nature, their needs and what ought to be done on their behalf. Although often associated with apparently beneficent and humanistic intentions, policies and practices undertaken on the basis of universalist assumptions are criticized by poststructuralists because of the way in which, in practice, they embody various kinds of oppression, including colonialism and ethnocentricism. Some of these ideas are taken up in Valerie Walkerdine's paper 'Sex, power and pedagogy' ([1981] 1990).

Walkerdine: 'Sex, power and pedagogy'

This short paper has played a pivotal role in sociology of education, laying some of the groundwork for the substantial body of feminist poststructuralist writing that has been produced since the mid-1980s. Walkerdine draws on Foucault's concepts of discourse and power/ knowledge to challenge the unidirectional, monolithic and static understandings of power and subjectivity she associates with some of the Marxist and radical feminist work of the 1970s. For Walkerdine, it is not always teachers who are the oppressors, wielding their power against children. She conceives of power relations as fluid, so that teachers can be oppressors of and oppressed by children at different moments. She also rejects the idea advanced in some Marxist writing that children's resistance to their teachers' authority should be read as a form of emancipatory action, arguing that resistances can have reactionary as well as progressive effects. Intertwined with Walkerdine's conception of power as complex and fluid is a conception of the subject (the poststructuralist term for the person) as equally complex and fluid. From this perspective the subject is 'produced' through a range of sometimes contradictory discourses that position individuals in a multiplicity of ways, in some cases as powerful and in some cases as powerless. So, for Walkerdine, girls and women are not unitary subjects straightforwardly shaped by material circumstances of economic dependence or physical weakness but rather 'are produced as a nexus of subjectivities, in relations of power that are constantly shifting, rendering them at one moment powerful and at another powerless' (1990: 3).

Walkerdine illustrates her arguments using observational data collected in a nursery school. The paper begins with an account and some verbatim reporting of an exchange between a nursery teacher, Miss Baxter, and two four-year-old boys, in which the boys use sexually explicit abusive language directed first at a three-year-old girl and then at Miss Baxter:

> The sequence begins when Annie takes a piece of Lego to add on to a construction she is building. Terry tries to take it away from her to use himself, and she resists. He says:
>
> *Terry*: You're a stupid cunt, Annie.
>
> The teacher tells him to stop and Sean tries to mess up another child's construction. The teacher tells him to stop. Then Sean says:
>
> *Sean*:   Get out of it Miss Baxter paxter.
> *Terry*:   Get out of it knickers Miss Baxter.
> *Sean*:   Get out of it Miss Baxter paxter.
> *Terry*:   Get out it Miss Baxter the knickers paxter knickers, bum.
> *Sean*:   Knickers, shit, bum.
> *Miss B*: Sean, that's enough, you're being silly.
> *Sean*:   Miss Baxter, knickers, show your knickers.
> *Terry*:   Miss Baxter, show your bum off.
>   (they giggle)
> *Miss B*: I think you're being very silly.
> *Terry*:   Shit Miss Baxter, shit Miss Baxter.
> *Sean*:   Miss Baxter, show your knickers your bum off.
> *Sean*:   Take all your clothes off, your bra off.
> *Terry*:   Yeah, and take your bum off, take your wee-wee off, take your clothes, your mouth off.

Sean: Take your teeth out, take your head off, take your hair off, take
            your bum off. Miss Baxter the paxter knickers taxter.
Miss B: Sean, go and find something else to do please.
            (1990: 4)

In order to explain this exchange, Walkerdine points to the existence of a variety of discursive practices through which Miss Baxter is
produced as a subject. Not all of the discourses that circulate within
the classroom produce Miss Baxter as a teacher, and the boys are
able to draw on a sexist discourse that produces Miss Baxter as a
powerless woman and themselves as powerful:

[The boys'] power is gained by refusing to be constituted as the powerless objects in her discourse and recasting her as the powerless object
of theirs. In their discourse she is constituted as 'woman as sex object',
and as that object she is rendered the powerless object of their oppression. . . . The boys' resistance takes the form of a seizure of power in
discourse such that despite their institutional positions they achieve
power in this instance. (1990: 5)

Walkerdine goes on to show how various discourses interact to
enable this particular configuration of power relation and its oppressive effects. She argues that the boys' ability to use sexist discourse
to oppress their teacher is enabled by the pedagogic discourses of
progressive education upon which Miss Baxter draws. Miss Baxter
does not challenge or condemn the sexist content of the boys' talk,
offers only a mild rebuke and does not see herself as oppressed.
Walkerdine's explanation for this stance is that Miss Baxter is using
the discourses of childhood sexuality and choice associated with
progressive education to 'read' the situation. The discourse of childhood sexuality enables Miss Baxter to construct the boys' remarks
as natural expressions of male sexuality which, if repressed, could be
psychically harmful to them. This discourse, Walkerdine suggests,
is drawn from particular variants of psychoanalytic theory which
associate 'over-regimentation' with aggression. This idea feeds into
the discourse of choice centred on the belief that children should be
free to express themselves and choose the activities they engage in so
they can develop at their own pace, learn to make rational choices,
and understand how to be responsible and autonomous agents.
Walkerdine argues that these:

discursive forces which shape the pedagogy of the classroom produce
a space which promotes the power of children and asserts the naturalness and harmlessness of their actions. They show us how the teacher is

rendered powerless to resist the power of the boys and how she fails to understand this as an example of their oppression of her: we can understand it only with the superimposition of a feminist discourse. We can understand that the individuals are not produced as unitary subjects but as a nexus of contradictory subjectivities. These contradictions are produced by the way in which the 'material' of the individual provides the potential to be the subject and object of a variety of discourses which produce that individual as sometimes powerful and sometimes powerless. There is in this no model of the unitary rational subject of progressivism who sloughs off the irrational; neither is the individual a 'real' and essential kernel of phenomenological Marxism, whose outer skins are just a series of roles which can be cast off to reveal the true and revolutionary self. (1990: 9).

Hence, according to Walkerdine, the ideal of the rational subject, which is the goal of progressive education, and the image of the unitary subject, upon which the ideal of rationality is based, are fictions 'doomed to failure from the beginning' (ibid.).

Walkerdine uses further examples of nursery school interactions to critique the feminist conception of sex-role socialization (as articulated, for example, by Byrne and in Spender and Sarah's *Learning to Lose* – see above) where girls' and women's subjectivities are understood as powerfully shaped by sex-role stereotyping and structural conditions of economic dependence. She draws on a range of exchanges in which boys and girls are engaged in imaginative play to suggest that girls are able to produce themselves as powerful through creating games that centre on domestic scenarios (e.g. playing 'mums and dads and girls') in which they are able to dominate the boys, whilst the boys try to assert their own power by trying to take the game out of the domestic setting. So although in these games the girls are casting themselves in a domestic role in ways that appear to conform to sex-role socialization theory, Walkerdine uses the example to challenge that theory, which, she suggests, incorrectly constructs girls and women as passive and dependent.

So throughout the paper Walkerdine is pointing to the fluidity of power: 'an individual's position is not uniquely determined by being "woman", "girl" or "teacher"'; and individuals do not occupy 'fixed, institutionally determined positions of power'. Rather they occupy a 'multiplicity of subjectivities' which shift from setting to setting and sometimes from moment to moment (1990: 14).

But, in addition, threaded through Walkerdine's account is the negotiation of two overlapping tensions which in many respects can be seen as a product of the combination of feminism and poststructuralism. It is readily acknowledged by many authors working in this tradition (e.g. Lather 1991) that there are tensions between the feminist and poststructuralist components in this approach to sociology of education – tensions which are of critical importance for anyone wanting to understand poststructuralist scholarship more generally.

First, feminism, although a very contested field, is basically an evaluative tradition that is ready to make judgements about what are acceptable and unacceptable features of social organization and social relations. By contrast, poststructuralism is predominantly a deconstructionist tradition fuelled by scepticism and by a concern not to generate still further forms of marginalization and misrecognition. On occasions, therefore, there will inevitably be some tension between the two forms of critique inherent in hybrid traditions, such as feminist poststructuralism, which have to hold together a critical-evaluative and a critical-deconstructionist orientation. This is, for example, evident in Walkerdine's evaluative critique of practices performed in the name of progressive education which, she suggests, whilst seeking to avoid certain forms of oppression, create other forms, notably the perpetuation of patriarchal oppression. However, this evaluative stance seems to be to some degree checked by Walkerdine's poststructuralist sensibility, which prevents her from calling for a dismantling of progressive education, presumably because she is all too conscious of the ambivalences inherent in such a call and the potentially unknown and unintended side effects of such a strategy. She writes: 'Whilst I do not find it possible to present easy answers or immediate political strategies, I think the presentation of the complexity is important' (1990: 14).

To some extent this tension overlaps with a tension in the explanatory models drawn on by feminist poststructuralists, as well as other sociologists, who often want to combine discursive and materialist modes of explanation. Whereas discursive modes of explanation highlight the socially constructed nature of social reality and point to the possibility of alternative modes of representation through which new forms of social organization and relations might be produced, materialist modes tend to foreground the sometimes recalcitrant nature of extra-discursive phenomena (e.g. economic and bodily materials) and thereby the limits of thinking and acting differently. Walkerdine treads a careful path between the two, pointing in her concluding remarks to 'certain problems of determination which do not seem to be totally resolved' by her conceptualization of power as 'produced as a constantly shifting relation' and of individuals 'as a multiplicity of subjectivities'. In particular, she notes that there are limits to the fluidity and multiplicity of the subject positions available to the girls and women she is writing about and the power relations in which they are enmeshed. These limits are framed by both 'the materiality of the female body' and the materiality of an economic system that rests on the domestic and quasi-domestic labour performed predominantly by women.[2]

Something of this careful treading between and across materialist and discursive terrains is evident in the following extract:

> Although this essay does raise problems for arguments which advocate direct and linear cause, the economic and material are clearly crucial to these examples. The confining of women to the quasi-domestic, while discursively powerful, remains a site of economic dependence. While this dependence does not directly produce a passive and dependent subject, it is not without its effects. Similarly, the girls and women do not take up any position in any discourse. Their signification as girls and women matters. It means the positions available to them exist only within certain limits. These limits are material – not in the sense they are directly caused by the materiality of the female body, but certainly by the limits within which that body can signify in current discursive practices. Nor are they directly 'caused' by the economic, but it does serve to produce women as confined to the domestic. (Walkerdine 1990: 14)

The story so far: proliferation and reflexivity

Our review, in this and the previous chapter, of work in sociology of education illustrates a story of an increasingly complex and differentiated discipline. Sociology of education has always been a field of contestation, but it seems that the degrees and dimensions of contestation have grown as the field has matured. In many respects the story we have told is one of proliferation. There is a proliferation not just of perspectives but of analytical and political vantage points within perspectives – e.g. forms of Marxism and forms of feminism. In some respects, this kind of differentiation is a response to the importance of recognizing a multiplicity of axes of social difference and division and, linked to this, a growing concern with the recognition of a range of voices and standpoints.

Another facet of proliferation is the multiplication of 'objects of study' in which sociologists of education take an interest, increasingly including such things as voice and identity. This is perhaps most conspicuous in the changing treatment of knowledge and the 'cultural turn' most famously associated with the 'new sociology of education'. This means that knowledge itself cannot be treated as an innocent educational good, albeit one that might be unequally distributed, but comes to be seen as a crucial mediator of social and educational advantage and one that has to be continually subject to the detailed critical gaze of the sociologist.

This critical interest in knowledge has also, and with good reason, produced, in many cases, a concern amongst sociologists to speak tentatively and in a way that recognizes and embraces ambiguity and ambivalence. Once one recognizes that the way one writes and talks about the social world is itself potentially part of the problem, i.e. is implicated in the ways in which social advantages and disadvantages are conferred, then some of the more confident modes of assertion that characterized earlier approaches to sociology of education become less available.

The forms of proliferation we have mentioned – namely those to do with diverse standpoints, diverse objects of study, and diverse genres and modes of assertion – are typically associated with the poststructuralist movement in sociology of education, which explicitly addresses the processes of multiplication, fracturing and contestation associated with these forms of proliferation. However, as we hope this review has shown, this complexity is not owned purely by poststructuralism but is a reflection of the evolution of the field as a whole. This complexity has demanded an increased sophistication in both the descriptive/explanatory and the critical/normative agendas of the discipline.

As we will continue to see in part II, there has been an increasing richness in the kind and range of analytical and theoretical resources deployed by sociologists to understand educational phenomena, and this has been accompanied by a growing reflexivity about the strengths, weaknesses and effects of competing theoretical frameworks. At the same time, contemporary sociologists of education have become increasingly conscious of the normative dimension, and normative effects, of what they are doing. In making this point, we want to distinguish (as we did in note 1 to the preface) between two senses of the word 'normative', both of which apply in this case. In the first sense, normative means normalizing – i.e. presenting certain things (e.g. certain identities or forms of behaviour) as 'normal' and thereby positioning those who do not share these 'normal' identities and forms of behaviour as 'other', aberrant or deficient. In the second sense, normative means embodying political and ethical value judgements – that is, judgements that certain things are ethically 'bad' or 'wrong' and ought to be different in respects that may be more or less specified.

The central argument of this book is that the increasing analytical sophistication and methodological reflexivity which characterize contemporary sociology of education have, for very good reasons, been accompanied by a growing sensitivity to normative themes (in both senses), but that the high level of self-consciousness about 'normalizing' discourses has not been matched by an equal commitment to reflexivity about ethical and political values, which, we suggest, is also critically important to the rigour of the discipline.

Conclusion

To conclude this chapter, we want to begin to indicate in a little more depth what we mean by the normative agenda (in this second sense) in sociology of education and to show the potential importance of reflexivity in relation to it. In particular, we want to ask how the normative dimension of sociology of education relates to its descriptive/explanatory dimension. As we noted at the end of chapter 1, the central role of sociology is arguably to describe, explain and help us understand various aspects of the social world – i.e. sociology is not primarily either a 'problem-solving' or a political activity but an academic activity concerned with making defensible and rigorous claims about 'the way things are'. But it is manifestly clear from the work we have looked at that many sociologists with an interest in education also see their writing as having an expressly normative dimension. That is to say, they do not wish simply to claim that 'this is the way things are' but also (a) to make more or less explicit value judgements about the phenomena they study and, in some cases, (b) to make more or less specific recommendations about changes that ought to happen.

One thing that should be clear from the work we have considered, and something which is arguably not celebrated enough, is the extent to which sociology of education – even if it is treated as purely descriptive/explanatory – illuminates values in education and social life more generally. This is one, relatively uncontentious, sense in which the descriptive/explanatory and the normative agendas do relate together – i.e. sociologists can deal with values as part of their descriptive and explanatory work. The publications we have considered in the past three chapters illustrate this very well. Sociological work often provides a detailed, vivid and analytically rich account of how education is implicated in 'goods' and 'harms' of many different kinds. And this is much more than a cataloguing of both 'who gets what' educational resource and the mechanisms that produce and reproduce multiple forms of educational advantage; as examples such as CRT show, it includes a concern with 'naming' and making visible and intelligible the ways in which value or worth of certain kinds can 'attach' or 'belong' to certain people rather than others. This process of 'naming' goods or harms, like the processes of 'giving voice' and 'telling stories' that we referred to earlier, can itself be seen as a way of helping 'others think in different ways' (Tate 1994: 264) and thus as a form of action. In this sense, all critical work in sociology of education can be seen as more than simply descriptive but as straddling the divide between the two components of normativity (in this ethical/political sense) – i.e. the divide between making value judgements and advocating action. However, even if a good case can be made for the existence of normativity in critical sociological currents, does it follow that all sociology of education is or need be normative?

Rather than supposing that there is a clear distinction in sociology of education between normative and descriptive/explanatory approaches, we suggest that it is more helpful to read all work in the field as having both descriptive and normative dimensions. Nonetheless, a distinction can usefully be made between more explicit and more implicit forms of normativity. Explicit normativity is relatively easy to identify and is, of course, characteristic of critical scholarship. In its fullest expression it consists of assertions that specific political or ethical ends should be advanced (possibly even combined with specific prescriptions concerning how they could be advanced). But it will at least consist of some more or less plain assertions that 'the way things are', in some respect or other, is unacceptable. Implicit normativity is, by definition, more difficult to identify, and such identifications are more likely to be contentious. However, it is now widely accepted that all social science is 'value laden'. And – assuming this idea is correct – what this suggests is that, whilst some sociology may strive to be detached, disinterested or even ethically and politically neutral, it is likely that value judgements of one kind or another inform, and are somehow embedded in, this work. At the very least, this means that, for readers of sociology of education, it would be a mistake to accept a simple split between normative and 'neutral' work: we always need to be alive to the normative dimension of sociological work, however much it is presented in a purely descriptive/explanatory package.

We should also note that we do not see explicit and implicit normativity as mutually exclusive categories. The idea of implicit normativity, accepting that it is a sensible one, applies to all socio-logical work. In other words, just because something is explicitly packaged as laden with certain values, there is no reason to suppose that we should not look for other values that might be 'carried by it'[3] and which are not advertised on the packaging. Someone is at least as likely to be thrown 'off the scent' of embedded values when reading work which is expressly ideological as when reading work which is expressly 'neutral'.

In the next few chapters we will provide many further examples of normativity – both implicit and explicit – and this will allow us to illustrate this idea in more depth and to develop our central argu-ment. But it is worth offering a few brief illustrations here by way of concluding these two review chapters. One way of approaching implicit normativity is to ask about the *focus and framing* of scholar-ship – that is, to ask why certain phenomena (and not others) are being investigated, why certain concepts (and not others) are used to capture these phenomena, and why certain questions (and not others) are being asked about these phenomena. And what are the effects of these choices? In this chapter, for example, we have chosen to focus upon gender and 'race' as axes of inequality and to review some writing in feminism and CRT. But we have not given any sig-nificant space to queer theory or disability theory. For that reason we could – and with some justification – be accused of neglecting crucial axes of social inequality and possibly, thereby, of reproducing some relatively blinkered conceptions of what does and does not matter. This potential problem obviously attaches to work which purports to be essentially descriptive. For example, a study which compares the attainment scores of boys and girls in mixed- and single-sex classrooms risks reinforcing, by taking for granted, the significance of certain (narrow) conceptions of educational purpose and success. Of course, we would have to read all work carefully, and consider it on a case-by-case basis, to make these readings of implicit normativity.

Another possible example of the normative function of focus and framing relates to the epistemological and methodological *style* of work. For example, as we have seen, some sociological work places a heavy emphasis on 'voice' and, more generally, on the vantage points of less powerful actors. Such work may not necessarily be presented from within a self-consciously ideological or critical standpoint but could be presented, for instance, as an example of ethnographic work concerned with 'ground-level' realities written from a broadly symbolic interactionist tradition. Nonetheless, this methodological orientation might be said to play a relatively 'democratic' or even subversive function by moving voices that may be marginalized closer to centre stage. Similarly, a style that omits reference to subjectivities altogether, perhaps focusing upon 'depersonalized' economic or institutional processes, may risk conveying messages about ontological and ethical hierarchies that exacerbate processes of marginalization. Again this is offered only as a crude generalization to illustrate the point, and any such readings would have to be made in detail, very carefully, and would always be highly contestable.

There is no clear dividing line between explicit and implicit normativity. Perhaps the best way to illustrate this is to consider the central issue of social inequality. When sociologists write about some example of inequality (in relation to a valuable social resource such as wealth or power) they are utilizing a concept that has both a descriptive and a normative sense. To say that there is an inequality of some kind between a and b can be merely to make a descriptive point – i.e. to say (i) 'a has more x or y than b'. But to assert that this state of affairs is 'a bad thing' in some sense – most typically to say (ii) 'this is unjust, or damaging, to b' – is to say something different and something more. As we have seen, some sociologists are perfectly prepared to make assertions like (ii); but in many cases – both inside and outside of critical currents of work – assertions like (ii) operate more as unspoken or hidden premises. That is to say, in many cases they are implied or assumed but not stated. Much work in sociology operates on this 'hidden premise' principle. Texts can imply things like (ii), invite us to think (ii), or even require us to assume (ii), but do so without ever stating (ii) explicitly. In principle, this leaves open the possibility of these writers saying that they are not specifically committed to asserting (ii) but are simply raising questions relevant to (i) (e.g. what are these inequalities, and how are they manifested and reproduced?) because these questions are important for anyone who happens to believe (ii). Here the degree to which the normativity is implicit is a function of the degree to which (ii) is asserted, assumed or implied.

This 'hidden premise' model of implicit normativity applies to all norms, not merely those relating to inequality. For example, a functionalist sociologist may analyse the conditions necessary for underpinning and sustaining social order or social solidarity. And they may present this work as purely descriptive/explanatory – e.g. 'p and q produce social order and social solidarity'. However, it is quite possible that they will be operating within a framework that takes for granted that social order and social solidarity are important 'goods' – i.e. on the 'hidden premise' model, they can thus be seen as more or less implicitly advocating p and q. Once again, such sociologists could opt to present their work as fundamentally neutral, but in order to do so properly they would at the same time have to spell out that they are not prioritizing certain ends (e.g. social order, solidarity) or advocating certain means (e.g. p and q), and this may well in many cases substantially reduce the practical relevance and rhetorical power of their writing.

The 'hidden premise' model sheds light on the importance of *focus and framing* referred to above. The way in which sociological work is focused and framed contains a hidden premise that specific phenomena are a matter of importance and deserve our attention. Furthermore, in practice, some kinds of phenomena (e.g. certain forms of exclusion) are likely to be framed as 'problems' or as providing grounds for pessimism and some other phenomena (e.g. forms of 'resistance') framed as potential 'solutions' or as providing grounds for optimism. Again these associations are as likely to be implied as much as stated, but the sheer fact that certain things are treated as a 'locus of concern' and others as a 'locus of promise' does strong normative work. We will return to this idea in the next chapter.

There are arguably three broad approaches to managing the normative dimension of sociology of education. The first is the approach used by many critical scholars of explicitly owning certain normative positions and the value judgements and practical implications that flow from them. The second is the approach used by those who wish to highlight the descriptive/explanatory function of sociology and to sideline the normative dimension, and who do so by insisting that, whilst the interpretation and application of their work might involve making normative assumptions, they will try to separate out the normative dimension of their writing from the more neutral and disinterested empirical work that they are conducting. The third approach is what might be seen as a poststructuralist response, but one which has gained quite broad currency within sociology of education, which entails operating with a high degree of self-conscious caution and writing in a way that recognizes competing sets of values and which embraces plural and sometimes even contradictory normative standpoints. The latter two approaches, whilst very different, have in common a considerable wariness about the making of normative judgements. In the next part of the book we hope to provide a fuller account of why this wariness is understandable and in many respects to be applauded, but, at the same time, we want to suggest that such wariness cannot be the end of the matter.

PART II

Key Themes

4

Social Reproduction

In this part of the book we wish to look in more depth at four major themes in sociology of education — social reproduction, knowledge and the curriculum, identity, and teachers' work – and we will use the opportunity to consider some more recent writings in the field as compared with the more 'classical' sources drawn upon in the previous part. Our main purpose is to take forward our argument about the increasing descriptive/explanatory sophistication of sociological work on education and the ways in which, in our view, this gives rise to the need for more attention to, and reflexivity about, normative questions. This chapter continues the argument of chapter 3 by illuminating the ways in which increasingly differentiated descriptive/ explanatory lenses draw attention to both the importance and the difficulty of making normative judgements. This chapter also illuminates the ways in which making discriminations between sociological readings depends, in part, upon the making of normative discriminations. This interdependence between the descriptive/explanatory and normative currents in the sociology of education is then explored in more depth in chapters 5 and 6, on knowledge and identity respectively. In these chapters we aim to show how rival sociological interpretations are bound up with competing value hierarchies, such that arbitrating between the former depends upon a willingness directly to address and make judgements about the latter. As this part of the book develops, the argument about normativity comes increasingly to the fore and, in some places (especially in chapter 7), this results in shifts in genre as we temporarily leave behind the concern with describing sociological work and focus in on some of the central normative arguments raised by it. In doing so, we increasingly ask questions about the evaluative and prescriptive potential of sociology, and in chapters 6 and 7 we explicitly argue that there is merit in sociologists 'putting themselves in the shoes of' policymakers and practitioners and that this has the potential to strengthen sociology.

As will have been apparent from the chapters in part I, since the inception of the discipline, social reproduction has arguably been the central theme in sociology of education. The concept of social reproduction is often associated with the Marxist tradition in sociology, in which it has relatively specific connotations relating to the persistence of social class divisions within capitalism:

> Every social process of production is, at the same time, a process of reproduction . . . Capitalist production, therefore, . . . produces not only commodities, not only surplus value, but it also produces and reproduces the capitalist relation, on the one side the capitalist, on the other the wage-labourer. (Marx [1867] 1969: 531, 532, cited in Giroux 1983)

Here, however, we are using the concept of social reproduction in a more open-ended sense to refer to all the mechanisms, processes and practices by which multiple social hierarchies, divisions and relations of wealth, power and influence are sustained and re-created over time.

Social reproduction arguably represents the central normative theme as well as the central descriptive/explanatory theme in sociology of education because, as has been made clear in the earlier chapters, sociologists of education typically have a preoccupation with questions of inequality. In a nutshell, sociology of education matters (as opposed to being a purely academic pursuit) because inequality matters. This is not to say that inequality is a straightforward value, or that there are not other fields of value that deserve to be taken seriously by sociologists and others. Indeed, the next three chapters each relate to other crucial fields of value – knowledge, identity and autonomy. It is simply to underline the fact that inequality in all of its complexity provides a fundamental axis around which much work in the discipline is organized.

In recent years ideas about social reproduction have become more sophisticated (see, for example, the discussion of CRT and feminist poststructuralism in chapter 3) as sociologists have attempted to grapple with and respond to some of the weaknesses in earlier, radical left theories of social reproduction. In this chapter we want to identify some of the key questions and problematics brought to the surface by these more recent readings of social reproduction. These problematics, we will argue, all reflect shifts in dominant conceptions of knowledge and the social world, and of the relationship between sociological knowledge and agency, and they raise important epistemological as well as normative questions about reproduction theory. Before identifying these problematics we will first outline how and why social reproduction theory has evolved in recent years and then illustrate this evolution by reviewing some examples of recent scholarship on this theme.

From grand theory to context sensitivity: the evolution of social reproduction theory

The radical left theories of social reproduction which dominated in the 1970s and 1980s (for example, those of Bowles and Gintis, Willis, and Dale reviewed in chapter 2) were marked by a tendency towards grand theorizing. The practices and processes of schooling were understood as principally serving the requirements of capitalism. These theories differed in the emphasis put on the extent to which structural forces – or alternatively the creative actions of individual agents and collectivities – were primarily responsible for determining the processes and outcomes of schooling. But the basic claim was that schooling was essentially a tool of capitalism which served ruling-class interests. Since the mid- to late 1980s there has been a move away from such grand theorizing, and the centrality given to the analysis of class as the primary axis of inequality and oppression, to more complex, differentiated and context-sensitive forms of theorizing. These more differentiated approaches (exemplified by the contributions to Spender and Sarah's *Learning to Lose*, the CRT approach and Walkerdine's analysis of power and pedagogy reviewed in the previous chapter) have sought to describe and explain local difference and complexity. In particular, in rejecting the universalism and determinism characteristic of the earlier theories, the newer approaches have sought to unpack the ways in which processes of social reproduction work differently at different times and in different spatial locations for different constituencies. These constituencies are defined in relation not only to class divisions but to a wider range of intersecting axes of social differentiation, including those pertaining to class, race, gender, sexuality and dis/ability. Such approaches have not always involved a denial of every insight of the earlier theories, but they are clearly marked by greater caution about some of the more sweeping and confident generalizations inherent in the earlier claims. As Nash puts it:

> We must do our own ethnography, study our own culture, which may
> be expected to have its own problematics, and do so while remaining in
> touch with influential theses without granting them an overbearing power
> to shape our perception of a reality that may well be different. Sociology,
> in this sense, is a bit like housework: as soon as it is done it is time to
> start over again. In fact, if the sociology of education is to be much use
> to teachers . . . this is what should be taught: the need to recognise and
> respond to cultural practices that affect scholastic success as they emerge
> and change at different times and places. (Nash 1999: 47–8)

From this perspective the relevance and validity of theories are necessarily at least partly contingent on the historically and spatially specific processes they seek to capture and explain.

This theoretical shift reflects three interrelated developments: (i)
disputes arising from within the new sociology of education; (ii) substantive socio-economic changes; and (iii) the rise of poststructuralist
perspectives. The disputes arising from within the new sociology of
education can be summarized through a consideration of Giroux's
critical readings of neo-Marxist and Bourdieuan-inspired accounts
of reproduction. In particular, Giroux draws attention to the relative
neglect of agency in reproduction theories, arguing, for example, that
theorists deploying functionalist versions of Marxism (e.g. Bowles
and Gintis 1976 and Althusser 1971):

> overemphasized the idea of domination in their analyses and . . . failed
> to provide any major insights into how teachers, students, and other
> human agents come together within specific historical and social con-
> texts in order to both make and reproduce the conditions of their exist-
> ence. (Giroux 1983: 259)

Similarly, whilst welcoming the contribution of state-centred theories
advanced by Dale and others (see chapter 2) to understandings of how
social and cultural reproduction work – through contradiction and
struggle – in the political sphere, Giroux argues that these theories say
'little about how human agency works through such conflicts at the
level of everyday life and concrete school relations' (ibid.: 282). And
whilst he sees Bourdieu's 'cultural-reproductive' model as a significant
advance on the more economistic versions of reproduction, because
it takes 'seriously the notions of history, sociology and psychology',
he argues that it too underplays 'the power of reflexive thought and
historical agency' (ibid.: 271; Bourdieu and Passeron 1977).[1]

In highlighting the specificities of historical context and agency,
Giroux's critique also underlines the need for accounts of reproduction

to be sensitive to race and gender as well as class, arguing, for example, that, in Bourdieu's work up until that time, classes are reduced to homogeneous groups, providing 'no theoretical opportunity to unravel how cultural domination and resistance are mediated through the complex interface of race, gender, and class' (1983: 271–2).[2]

Finally, Giroux identifies some analogous strengths and limitations in resistance theory. This tradition of work, exemplified by the writings of Robins and Cohen (1978), Corrigan (1979), McRobbie and McCabe (1981) and Hebdige (1979), as well as Willis (1977; see chapter 2), was praised both for its emphasis on the importance of cultural production and human agency and for its more complex readings of the curriculum – as embodying emancipatory as well as oppressive possibilities. However, these accounts were also taken to task for marginalizing issues of gender and race, for assuming that all modes of oppositional behaviour constitute resistance, for downplaying the socially regressive and oppressive aspects of some students' oppositional behaviour (in particular its racism and sexism), and for ignoring students who do not translate their critique of the dominant school ideology into 'extreme forms of rebelliousness' (Giroux 1983: 288). Here Giroux's critique also serves to illustrate the normative construction of accounts of reproduction and some of the contestability of these normative constructions. In other words, and to use the labels that we introduced in chapter 3, these accounts are based on the judgement that certain things are a 'locus of concern' (e.g. 'cultural domination') and that other things are a 'locus of promise' (e.g. 'resistance'), but the interpretation and application of terms such as cultural domination and resistance, and the judgements that lie behind them, are open to debate. In brief, labelling something as 'resistance', for example, does not stop it embodying forms of oppression.

The shift towards more complex and context-sensitive modes of analysing social reproduction processes was also a reaction to a whole set of socio-economic developments which rendered some of the earlier assumptions problematic. For example, the decline of traditional working-class employment in the manufacturing industries, and the decline in trade union power and the shop floor culture that went with it, called for new explanations for the continuation of some of the schooling practices and student responses that Willis described. Similarly, the rise in female paid employment called for new explanations of the role of schooling in the production of girls' identities. And new patterns of global migration brought to the surface a recognition of the need for more complex understandings of identity formation and the role of schooling in reproducing inequalities around axes of race and ethnicity.

The third factor influencing the shift from a grand narrative approach to more context-sensitive understandings of social reproduction was the development of poststructuralist theoretical perspectives. As we have seen, these challenged the value of all-encompassing meta-theories which try to shoehorn every social formation, process and relationship into a single explanatory framework. Heavily bound up with the rise of the new social movements, poststructuralist theories also drew attention to a whole range of axes of social division that had previously been obscured by a preoccupation with class as the social division that was seen to matter most. And, as discussed in chapter 3, there was a more intensive, detailed focus on the construction of identities and subjectivities, micro-relations of power and the role that discourse plays in their construction. Partly as a result of the influence of poststructuralist theory, it is generally no longer viewed as acceptable to read off people's identities directly from their social location. Rather there is an emphasis on the fluid and hybrid nature of identity and the possibility and reality of the formation of more complex identities – identities which transcend people's positions in social hierarchies. Similarly, there is a recognition that schooling serves a whole range of purposes and encompasses a whole range of practices, not all of which are oppressive or connected with the requirements of a capitalist economy and some of which can contribute to the promotion of social justice.

Four examples

It would be unrealistic to attempt to provide a comprehensive or exhaustive review of current thinking on social reproduction in such a short chapter. Rather, what we would like to do here is to give examples of some of the different kinds of approaches and ideas that have evolved in recent years. We will do this by focusing on four pieces of work, all based on qualitative research, which seek to explore particular aspects of social reproduction: an article on race and the discursive construction of success in British secondary schools (Archer 2008); a paper on the enactment of gender justice in Australian high schools (Keddie and Mills 2007); an article on young children's negotiations of classroom contexts in two English primary schools (Benjamin et al. 2003); and a chapter on the class strategies of metropolitan middle-class parents in France (van Zanten 2004). In different ways each of these articles builds upon the critical perspectives discussed in chapter 3. As we will see, each of them can also be read as echoing and building upon Giroux's concern that reproduction theory should incorporate an interest in context sensitivity, agency and multiple axes of inequality. We will proceed by presenting each of the four examples on their own terms and then draw out some of the core problematics that cut across them.

The impossibility of minority ethnic educational success

As we have already noted, earlier radical left accounts of social reproduction tended to focus on class inequalities to the virtual exclusion of other axes of inequality. However, there is now a substantial body of work in sociology of education that is concerned to explain the persistence of racialized and gendered patterns of inequality within and beyond the education system and their interrelationship with classed patterns of inequality. Building on earlier work in the black feminist tradition (e.g. that of Evans discussed in chapter 3), a series of studies has looked at the experiences of specific racialized populations, documenting the persistence of racist stereotyping by teachers and white students and its role in the production of racialized inequalities in experience and attainment, whilst also drawing attention to differences in the experiences of differently racialized and gendered categories of students (e.g. Mirza 1992 and 2008 on black girls and women; Mac an Ghaill 1988 and Sewell 1997 on black boys; Brah 1992 and Shain 2003 on Asian girls; Basit 1997 on Muslim girls; Archer 2003 on Muslim boys; and Gillborn and Mirza's 2000 complex mapping of inequalities of attainment across the social divisions of race, class and gender). While much of this work focuses on the production and reproduction of educational failure, there is also a growing interest in the experiences of students deemed to be educationally successful (e.g. Power et al. 2003 on the middle classes; Delamont 1989 and Walkerdine et al. 2001 on middle-class girls; Gibson 1988 on Punjabi Sikh students; Byfield 2008 on black boys; Ahmad 2001 on Muslim women; and Archer and Francis 2007 on British Chinese students). In the US, work adopting a CRT approach (e.g. Fernandez 2002; Teranishi 2002; Solorzano 2001; Duncan 2002) has paid attention to the 'counterstories' of students of colour as a 'tool for exposing, analyzing and challenging majoritarian stories of racial privilege' (Solorzano and Yosso 2002: 32).

In 'The impossibility of minority ethnic educational "success"', Archer brings together insights from the growing body of work cited above and from four of her own ethnographic studies to scrutinize and theorize the complex, differentiated and 'multiple ways in which minority ethnic pupils are Othered in relation to the dominant identity of the "ideal pupil"'. Hence, she claims:

> The article moves beyond the notion of a singular Other position, engaging with the slipperiness of power and entanglements of 'race', gender, class and sexuality . . . to explain how complexly located minority ethnic pupils are always-already positioned as other . . . such that even 'high-achieving' minority ethnic pupils may experience success as precarious. (2008: 89)

Applying a feminist poststructuralist discourse-analytic perspective to teacher and student interview data, Archer sets out the different ways in which minority ethnic students' performances of educational underachievement and success are constructed in dominant discourses. Echoing the findings of earlier studies of racialized teacher discourse, she draws on her own interview data with teachers and an ethnically diverse sample of students to show how black students continue to be 'demonized' through being constructed as 'loud', 'challenging', 'excessively' sexual, and suffering from 'unaspirational' home cultures. She vividly illustrates the potentially damaging consequences of such 'demonizing' discourses. For example, she describes one girl's experience of having been laughed at by a teacher when she expressed an interest in becoming a lawyer. Following this experience, which can be read as a form of micro-aggression, the girl changed her career aspirations, deciding to become a PA or legal secretary, and this, Archer suggests, demonstrates 'the power of even a single encounter to stifle girls' ambitions and push them into gendered and classed career pathways' (2008: 98).

But Archer goes on to show that it is not only students from racialized groups traditionally associated with 'underachievement' who are pathologized in teacher discourse. She argues that 'even those minority pupils who ostensibly perform successfully within the education system can be pathologised and Othered' (2008: 98). Using examples from her research with Francis (Archer and Francis 2007), she shows how British Chinese students – commonly associated with '"traditional" academic success' – are simultaneously 'eulogized' and 'pathologized' by their teachers:

> British Chinese pupils were overwhelmingly represented as a homogenous passive, quiet and hardworking mass . . . [They were] positioned . . . outside the discourse of the ideal learner and outside constructions

of normative masculinity and femininity . . . with an image being evoked of Chinese girls as educational automatons, who are too quiet, too passive and too repressed . . . [whilst the] boys tended to be positioned as effeminate and subordinate – and hence not 'properly' masculine (by virtue of their association with 'passivity', 'quietness' and 'hard work'). (Archer 2008: 99–100)

Teachers' explanations for girls' passivity drew on stereotypical constructions of Chinese families as 'tight' and 'close'. Archer notes the similarities between these explanations and 'popular discourses around South Asian femininities, with South Asian girls similarly positioned as victims of oppressive home relations' (ibid.: 100; Rattansi 1992; Brah 1992; and Shain 2003). Archer also notes that teachers tended wrongly to assume that their Chinese students were middle class, which, she argues, illustrates 'the normative view of "the achieving pupil" as middle-class' (2008: 100).

However, Archer shows that such discourses do not go uncontested, emphasizing the agency of the young people she studied. So, for example, whilst, for the teachers, loudness tends to be associated with an absence of engagement with schooling, and therefore constructed as a problem, some of the girls Archer interviewed 'described their loudness as a desirable and valued aspect of their performances of a "strong" agentic and "independent" Black . . . or Turkish . . . femininity' (2008: 95). Similar contestations were evident around constructions of black students as displaying 'hyper(hetero)sexual' masculinities and femininities. Whilst the students' performances of sexuality – manifested in their preoccupations with wearing branded clothing and 'looking good' – tended to be constructed as a problem by teachers, as signalling an 'anti-school' stance and hence as incompatible with success, according to Archer, for the students themselves, performances of sexuality and style were worth investing in because they helped 'to generate a sense of value and self-worth' (ibid.). Hence the students were operating with hierarchies of value that were different from those of the teachers, which makes it difficult, if not impossible, for students simultaneously to achieve high status in the eyes of their peer group and their teachers.

Archer also gives examples of students and parents challenging representations of minority ethnic families as 'unaspirational' and 'unacademic' – or alternatively, in the case of British Chinese students, as 'too hardworking' – whilst at the same time noting a perceived absence of opportunities for such challenges to be mounted. For example:

many Black and Muslim boys across the different studies talked about the 'impossibility' of success . . . due to the prevalence of racism in society and its institutions . . . However, they mostly felt denied a language and a space through which to express their concerns. Indeed, their counter-accounts were often dismissed by education professionals as merely evidence of a 'chip on the shoulder', or were even cited as evidence of the boys' 'low aspirations'. (2008: 97)

In an attempt to explain why it is that even high-achieving racialized groups tend to be pathologized in dominant educational discourses, Archer uses the conceptual device of 'a trichotomy', which distinguishes between three constructions of the pupil in dominant discourse: the 'ideal' pupil – a white, outside class/middle-class, masculinized subject position; the 'other/pathologized pupil' – an Asian, 'deserving poor', feminized subject position; and the 'demonized pupil' – a black/white working-class and 'underclass', hyper-masculine/hyper-feminine subject position. The ideal pupil is 'naturally talented', has 'initiative', exists 'outside culture' and has a 'normal' sexuality; the other/pathologized pupil is 'diligent' and 'plodding', 'conformist', 'culture bound' and 'asexual' or with an 'oppressed' or 'repressed' sexuality; and the 'demonized pupil' is 'naturally unintelligent', 'peer led', a 'victim of "bad" culture' and 'hypersexual'.

Archer suggests that these discursive distinctions enable:

the privileged identity of the ideal pupil [to be] effectively preserved via a splitting and projection of undesirable attributes onto Other groups. In this way minority ethnic success is always-already positioned as 'abnormal'/other and as potentially undesirable – it is always characterised as the 'wrong' approach to learning. Consequently, instances of minority ethnic educational achievement may be experienced as precarious, because the successful pupil subject position can never be authentically inhabited . . . Likewise, the trichotomy enables us to understand how the identity of the 'ideal pupil' can be preserved as 'male' and/or 'White' in the face of 'actual' high achievement by girls and/or particular minority ethnic pupils. This is because, despite their achievement, they are positioned as achieving it in the wrong way (e.g. via feminised 'plodding diligence' or through overly passive conformism within the classroom). Hence the trichotomy explains why the notion of 'over' achievement is only comprehensible as applied to female and/or minority ethnic Others – since 'achievement' is preserved as the rightful domain of the idealised, dominant subject position. (2008: 102)

In other words, these discourses operate as a powerful grid (in much the same way as the heterosexual matrix that we discussed in the context of Renold's work in chapter 1), determining and circum-scribing what is thinkable with regard to who can or cannot legiti-mately occupy positions of success and with regard to which forms of behaviour and attributes are or are not socially valued. In Bourdieuan terms, it is via these discourses that those conforming to notions of the 'ideal pupil' can accrue symbolic capital. But the very discourses that produce the symbolic capital of the ideal pupil also hide the fact that this capital is discursively produced, because they construct 'traditional' academic success as a consequence of 'natural or indi-vidualized personality disposition' (Skeggs 2004: 169, cited in Archer 2008: 102): '[h]ence value and worth appear to reside naturally with (and are embodied by) the powerful/privileged, whose power remains hidden' (Archer 2008: 102).

At the end of her paper, Archer turns to the question of 'how such trenchant and persistent inequalities might usefully be challenged' (2008: 103). Given that these inequalities are, she is arguing, discur-sively produced, one answer, she suggests, lies in developing strate-gies that might succeed in 'interrupting' 'the current representational regime' (ibid.). These would involve exposing practitioners, and national policymakers in particular, to opportunities to reflect on the power of discourse to produce inequalities of attainment and experi-ence with a view to 'loosen[ing] and broaden[ing] the dominant dis-courses within which minority ethnic young people find themselves positioned as learners' (ibid.).

Teaching for gender justice

In 'Teaching for gender justice', Keddie and Mills (2007) start with the question with which Archer finishes – i.e. how to interrupt 'the current representational regime' in order to achieve egalitar-ian change. The policy context for the study is what Keddie and Mills (citing Weaver-Hightower 2003) call the 'boy turn' in educa-tion policy discourses that has been evident since the mid-1990s in Australia and elsewhere (e.g. the UK, the US and Canada). The boy turn, reflected in a series of policies aimed at improving boys' per-formance in literacy and their levels of engagement with schooling, is, argue Keddie and Mills, driven 'not by issues of genuine educational in/equity, but by cultures of performativity and anti-feminism' (2007: 205). The move to a marketized system of schooling provision, they suggest, has contributed to a narrowing of definitions of what consti-tutes educational achievement and success – so that success is now defined primarily in terms of performance in standardized tests and school attendance. This, coupled with 'backlash discourses against feminist gains in education', has, Keddie and Mills argue, produced a moral panic around boys' underachievement that enables them to be constructed as the 'new disadvantaged' (ibid.: 205–6). This is despite the fact that, with regard to the narrow performance indicators that are currently being given prominence, boys have always performed worse than girls (Hayes 2003; Smith 2003; and Yates 1997, cited in Keddie and Mills 2007) and despite the fact that, beyond school, boys continue to be advantaged both culturally and economically.

The 'boy turn' initiatives that are of concern to Keddie and Mills tend to be underpinned by the principles of affirmative action and special treatment, echoing what have sometimes been called the 'girl-friendly' feminist approaches of the 1980s. Drawing on Fraser's (1997) poststructuralist critique of affirmative gender politics, Keddie and Mills suggest that 'boy-friendly' initiatives, which are designed to engage boys by recognizing their 'difference', are more likely to reinforce than disrupt gender differentiation. In particular, such initiatives risk 'reinscrib[ing] essentialised constructions of masculinity and femininity and homogenis[ing] multiplicious identities associated with, for example, sexuality, socioeconomic status, race and ethnicity' (Keddie and Mills 2007: 206). Like Fraser, Keddie and Mills argue for 'a transformative politics that challenges and seeks to proliferate alternatives to the gender differentiation of binary and hierarchical understandings of masculinity and femininity' (ibid.: 208).

Keddie and Mills illustrate their arguments using cases studies of two Queensland high school teachers, Brad and Jennifer. Both are committed to gender justice, and both seek to develop strong relationships with their students in an effort to engage them with their schoolwork, but Brad adopts an affirmative approach whilst Jennifer's approach is transformative. Brad's approach involves trying to win the respect of the boys he teaches by showing an interest in and affirming some of their stereotypically (rural) male pastimes (e.g. boxing, pig chasing, cars and bull riding), demonstrating his ability to 'cut' some of the more challenging students 'down to size' by using sarcasm, and engaging in 'macho' banter rather than challenging it. Keddie and Mills argue that, as well as risking alienating both girls and boys who are not interested in the kinds of masculinist pursuits and language that are being valorized in his classroom, Brad's approach can be 'seen as colluding with and playing into broader discourses of gender and power that promote gender differentiation and hierarchical masculinities', and hence endorsing what Brad describes as the boys' 'very, very masculine' and 'very, very chauvinistic' tendencies (2007: 212).

In contrast, Jennifer believes that if gender equality is to be realized then gender binaries need to be eroded. Hence she actively seeks to encourage a diversity of gender performances by, for example:

> allowing 'the space' in her classroom for her students to 'feel comfortable' with 'exploring and experimenting with non-traditional aspects of their gender and non-stereotypical aspects of western Anglo culture.' (Keddie and Mills 2007: 213)

She teaches her students the skills of critical analysis and feminist deconstruction to help them recognize and challenge gender stereotypes and power inequalities. She encourages discussion of counter-stereotypical issues and uses counter-stereotypical language, for instance:

> If someone comes to a class with a new hairdo . . . rather than just saying to the girls, 'oh you look beautiful' or whatever, but using the same words for the boys saying 'you look gorgeous' or 'you look beautiful' and similarly for the girls using words that I might stereotypically have applied to boys. (Ibid.: 215)

And she challenges the boys' tendency to dominate classroom time and space, insisting they show courtesy and respect for others.

Jennifer describes her own approach as 'persistent and hopeful', and indeed the same could be said of Keddie and Mills's work (and that of others active in this feminist poststructuralist tradition – e.g. Davies 1989, 1993; Lingard et al. 2002; Skelton and Francis 2005), which adopts a more optimistic reading of the possibilities for egalitarian change than was characteristic of some of the older radical left theories of social reproduction. Although Keddie and Mills believe that the current policy climate, which is 'driven by concerns about reductionist and easily quantifiable gender comparisons, tends not to be receptive to such transformative gender politics' (2007: 217), they are clearly hopeful that Jennifer's story can help to persuade others that teaching for transformative gender justice is not only desirable but also possible even within a hostile policy climate.

Pupils negotiating classroom contexts

Whilst the primary focus of our first two examples was on teachers and their discursive practices, our third example concentrates on the perspectives of students, examining the ways in which they negotiate the discursive terrain they encounter at school. Drawing on ethnographic work in two English primary schools, Benjamin et al. (2003) seek to illustrate how the young children actively produce their subjectivity by adopting, resisting or manoeuvring round the different subject positions that the discourses of the school and wider society make available to them – positions that are produced through the intersecting categories of ability, class, gender, race/ethnicity and physical appearance. Like many researchers in the area, these authors are trying to find a way of exploring (a) how agents actively create their own identities and subjectivities within conditions not of their own making, and (b) the consequences of these processes of identity construction for patterns of social in/equality.

The article is organized around a series of vignettes, a number of which concern the theme of physicality. This theme – which had been neglected in older studies of social reproduction – enables the authors to bring to the fore the central role played by discourses of the body in the reproduction of social inequalities. Benjamin et al. argue that discourses of hegemonic masculinity that privilege physical over intellectual prowess – coupled with the contemporary moral panic around boys' underachievement (see above) and the historic lack of association between working-class maleness and academic success – make the subject position 'academically successful working-class boy' unthinkable for the majority of working-class boys. Such a subject position is only thinkable for those boys who are able and prepared also to take up the unpopular subject position 'gentle, studious boy', and thereby risk becoming victims of homophobic bullying. Such a subject position, Benjamin et al. argue, is most available to boys on the extremes of the hegemonic masculinity spectrum, i.e.:

> It can be taken up by boys who are sufficiently 'resource-rich' in hegemonic masculinity for transgressions not to matter . . . It can also be taken up by boys who have little choice: those who inhabit bodies and dispositions that are so distant from the physically powerful masculine subject that they cannot recognise themselves (nor can they be recognised by others) as that particular version of the subject 'boy'.[3] (Benjamin et al. 2003: 551)

For the majority of working-class boys, however, the subject position 'triumphant sportsman' is, Benjamin et al. contend, a much more attractive one, particularly given 'the fortune, fame and power held out to them as possibilities by the football business and other gendered apparatuses of twenty-first-century capitalism' (ibid.).

Benjamin et al. suggest that, for girls, the situation is somewhat different. The sporting industry does not reach out to them in the same way. Rather, 'triumphant girl' subject positions tend to centre on the entertainment industry, with working-class girls more likely to imagine themselves 'as hetero-sexualised superstars of stage, screen, dance hall and rock venue' (Benjamin et al. 2003: 551) than sports stars. At the same time, the authors argue, it is easier for girls to position themselves as studious. Whilst carrying a lower status than music or dance prowess in the cultural economy of girlhood, the studious subject position does not, they contend, carry the same risks of peer victimization as it does for boys.

Such inequalities in access to different subject positions, Benjamin et al. argue, have potentially serious material consequences for students' capacity to participate and succeed in different kinds of activities. Boys are more likely to engage actively in physical education lessons and thereby 'access the skills, capacities and dispositions that will enable their further inclusion in physical activities of all kinds'. However, for both boys and girls 'there are costs in over-investment or under-investment in PE, with many boys neglecting the more "academic" curriculum . . . and girls learning to take up spectator-only roles, or losing interest in physical activity altogether' (Benjamin et al. 2003: 551).

By focusing on children's agency, albeit an agency that is tightly constrained by the subject positions made available by dominant discourses and powerful economic interests (e.g. the sports and entertainment industries), Benjamin et al.'s analysis (in much the same way as Renold's – see chapter 1) shows how social inequality, particularly regarding children's participation in socially valued activities, is produced by the actions of children themselves. For example, the authors describe how one particular child, Leanna, a girl with acute learning difficulties, is sometimes allowed to participate in and sometimes excluded from group activities by the other children, depending on the context. The girl's learning difficulties, they explain, 'are inscribed in her body, which moves slowly and in an unco-ordinated way'. The other children are happy to include her in some lessons, but in PE her 'difference' is viewed as an obstruction:

> The PE lesson highlights her distance from the norm, and, in the context of a PE lesson, that distance produces a difference that cannot be understood as neutral. In many other classroom contexts, most of the children are able to position themselves as tolerant of Leanna's 'difference'. Their tolerance ranges from an appreciation of the progress she is making to attempts to govern her . . . and sometimes appears as valuing diversity. But in a competitive situation, in which the need to triumph comes to dominate the imperative to position oneself as 'nice'

or 'caring', Leanna's diversity cannot be valued. In such a context, Leanna's 'diversity' – and her physical body – get in the way of other children's aspirations, and her difference gets configured as deficit. (Benjamin et al. 2003: 552)

This example illustrates the central argument of Benjamin et al.'s paper – that the production of inclusions and exclusions are not once-and-for-all events. Drawing on a Foucauldian conception of power (like Walkerdine – see chapter 3), they argue that inclusions and exclusions are continually produced 'moment-by-moment', often simultaneously, through numerous micro-cultural struggles and negotiations. Hence the reproduction of meanings and practices which exclude can co-exist with the production of newer, more egalitarian ones.

In constructing their arguments, the authors are motivated by a desire to contribute to the production of a more just society, arguing that 'a politically literate understanding of the processes of inclusion and exclusion is necessary both to highlight the continuing reproduction of educational inequality, and to produce the necessary conditions for egalitarian change' (Benjamin et al. 2003: 547).

Middle-class parents and educational policy in metropolitan contexts

Our final example focuses on the contribution to processes of social reproduction of the educational strategies and school choice-making practices of middle-class parents. Drawing on data from an interview study of 120 parents in two contrasting communes on the edge of Paris, one mainly middle class and the other more socially mixed, van Zanten shows how policies that are intensifying social inequalities in France are produced through 'a complex interaction between grass root influences [in this case the actions of middle-class parents] and national decisions' (van Zanten 2004: 168). Her analysis emphasizes both continuity and change in the nature of the local social formation she is studying. Thus, for example, whilst her comparison of the middle-class and lower-class parents in her study indicates a continuation of the broadly different expectations of schooling held by these two groups of parents, she also points to 'transformations in the dynamic relationship between class and schooling' (ibid.: 169). These include greater competition between 'traditional' managers and professionals, on the one hand, and a new generation of 'top managers', on the other, a concomitant reinforcement of divisions between these different middle-class fractions and an increase in direct middle-class parental influence on schooling.

Van Zanten is especially concerned to explore the strategies adopted by the Parisian middle-class parents she studied and their implications for schooling hierarchies and patterns of inequality of access to schooling. She found that the main criteria by which these parents discriminated between schools were pupil intake and location, where '[g]ood schools, both from an instrumental and a social point of view, are those located in [middle-class] residential areas and bad schools those located in mixed or lower class areas' (2004: 175). She argues that the parents' individual and collective strategies actively alter social structures by contributing to the production of new educational policies at a local level. For example, parents' interventions in school processes, as individuals, through discussion with staff, and through collective action in parents' associations, have resulted in the introduction of more setting by ability, the more frequent use of written and oral tests in schools, and more homework. Through such interventions and through the exercise of school choice, existing educational inequalities and exclusions are both 'maintained and reinforced'. In particular, 'middle-class parental influence is reinforcing social, ethnic and academic segregation within schools and between schools, especially between public and private schools' (ibid.: 187).

However, middle-class orientations and strategies are not presented as homogeneous. Rather van Zanten points to differences between middle-class fractions employed in the private and public sectors, and she argues that the stratification of provision in the metropolitan areas she has studied occurs because some middle-class voices are more influential than others. The most influential are managers and professionals in the private sector, groups who are particularly anxious about

> their children's professional and social futures in the new global economy . . . [who] want their children to be ahead, from an early age, in the race for credentials and to acquire a competitive character through confrontation with others with similar or higher educational capital . . . and tend to view education, more and more, as a private good. (2004: 170, 171, 187)

These voices are contrasted with those of public sector professionals who try 'to reconcile their private interests and the public good' (ibid.: 187). For example, they are more likely to have a cosmopolitan vision of modern society. Society is conceived as a mosaic of groups – social, ethnic, religious, geographical – who should be able to interact in public spaces without being bounded by their origins . . . The key word for these parents in terms of social integration in schools is tolerance towards others. (Ibid.: 173)

However, even the public sector professionals shy away from choosing socially and ethnically mixed schools beyond the elementary school phase:

> while many parents view social and ethnic mix as a positive element in primary education where it could help the child catch a glimpse of the diversity of stratified, multi-ethnic urban French society, their discourse changes significantly as children become adolescents. Here the need for a more restricted form of class socialization appears necessary to most middle-class parents . . . In their view, adolescents placed in mixed schools may suffer both from the lower academic and cultural level of their classmates, from their disruptive or violent behaviour and from their lack of manners and social capital. (Van Zanten 2004: 174)

Despite this, in relation to this latter fraction of the middle-classes, van Zanten argues that their continued adherence to the ideal of the public good means that:

> Although their position is not exempt [from] criticism, it could support new practices and policies oriented toward equality and inclusion. However, this can only happen if policy-makers are able to listen to their voices and to build on them rather than to let education restructuring develop in a – perhaps only apparently – uncontrolled way at the local level. (Ibid.: 187)

Descriptive/explanatory and normative problematics

Looking at these instances of writing, which we are treating here as examples of recent work on the theme of social reproduction, it is possible to discern both descriptive/explanatory and normative problematics that are intimately bound up with one another. In developing their analyses and explanations, these authors are all having to grapple with some similar challenges: how to deal with aspects of social change and how to hold together 'top-down' and 'bottom-up' and more agentic and more deterministic models of analysis. The work we have considered tackles these challenges head on in a way that reflects and promotes increasing epistemological reflexivity in the field. However, as we have begun to indicate, and will illustrate further in the remainder of this chapter, these descriptive/explanatory challenges are interwoven with a range of normative challenges in the discipline which have thus far received less attention and, when they are attended to, are in the main treated more implicitly. In the remainder of this chapter we will briefly review the descriptive/explanatory challenges before specifying the normative challenges in more detail.

Each piece of work recognizes the fluidity and complexity of the social world, and this includes being responsive to aspects of contemporary social change as well as to continuities. For example, the articles by both Archer and Keddie and Mills can be read as sociological responses to a new set of contemporary policy preoccupations with the measurement of attainment and with the making of generalizations about the educational performance of categories of student defined in relation to ethnicity and gender; Benjamin et al.'s analysis is concerned with the children's relationship to the (new) 'gendered apparatuses of 21st century consumer capitalism'; and van Zanten's piece is about how the actions of the middle-class parents she studied are both informed by social change in the form of the new class dynamics of a globalized capitalism and contribute to educational restructuring at a local level. In addition, van Zanten argues that, '[a]t a more symbolic level, they are also contributing to a radical transformation of the image and the role of public and private schools'.

Hence, these writers are striking a balance between the recognition of change and fluidity in the social world and the recognition of the patterns of reproduction they are seeking to illuminate. Their doing so is important because the danger is that the very language of social reproduction could mean that insufficient attention is focused on the nature and extent of change. For example, if social relations and social inequalities are presented in the language of social reproduction theory as maintained, reinforced, or even exacerbated, this can prevent us from asking what is different about the intensity and nature of inequalities in different places and at different times. Arguably, to talk about 'social reproduction' is in itself to invoke a meta-narrative which, amongst other things, privileges (one kind of) continuity over change. Attempts to deploy such a meta-narrative, and at the same time to move beyond the perspective of grand theory, will thus inevitably create tensions and raise problems.

In some respects all we are doing in making this point is echoing Nash's argument (referred to earlier in the chapter) that sociology is like housework that has to be done over and over again as circumstances change and new descriptions and theorizations are needed.

The examples we have discussed in this chapter all point to ways in which social change constantly produces new hierarchies, which may be interwoven with longstanding hierarchies of social class but are not necessarily reducible to or captured by the 'old' language of class. Whilst some of these hierarchies – for example, around race and gender – can be seen as reflecting greater sensitivity and discernment on the part of sociologists about dimensions of hierarchy that are equally longstanding, social change means that new forms and manifestations of these dimensions of hierarchy are brought into existence. Van Zanten's analysis, for example, is clearly couched in the language of class, but what we are seeing here is a refinement of class categories. In particular, a distinction is drawn between different fractions within the middle classes, who are competing not just for better school places for their children but for what counts as a better place. Archer's work points to the way in which new policy discourses which privilege performance in tests and competition between schools produce new and increasingly subtle forms of racism. At a superficial level, new hierarchies of attainment are created, often reflecting racialized and gendered categories. However, an analysis of teachers' discourses shows that lying alongside these hierarchies of attainment is a hierarchy of valued identities in which students are constructed as more or less ideal *independently* of their performance at school. Keddie and Mills and Benjamin et al. also point to the malleability of hierarchies, in their case showing how, at a local level, hierarchies of inclusion and exclusion or valued forms of femininity and masculinity are constantly constructed and deconstructed. All of these examples, therefore, illustrate that the hierarchies associated with schooling are by no means fixed but are dynamic, fought over and in flux. Hence, what these analyses are pointing to is the need to be wary about any assumption that there is just one monolithic process of social reproduction. Rather, they suggest it may be better to conceive of social reproduction as something that is itself reworked and reshaped by social change.

In various ways, and using a range of conceptual tools, these pieces of work are also attempting to hold together local 'bottom-up' explanations and grander 'top-down' accounts of social reproduction. Thus Archer, Keddie and Mills, and Benjamin et al. all seek to explore the micro-cultural negotiations that occur within specific school settings, but they do so using the analytical language of a discourse-theoretical framework. The forms taken by the micro-cultural negotiations are specific to the particular settings they are analysing and demand 'bottom-up' forms of explanation that are contingent on local factors. However, the 'top-down' use of a discourse-theoretical framework points to a language of description and explanation that has a more universal applicability. That is, whilst the substance of the micro-negotiations will be different in different settings, and the content of the available discourses might vary according to spatial location and historical moment, the working assumption of this kind of analysis is that the reproduction of social relations will always be realized via the interplay of individual choice-making and the subject positions made available by wider discourses. Although the theoretical resources deployed by van Zanten are different, she too is attempting to hold on to notions of local specificity alongside grander, more universally applicable theoretical schema. For van Zanten, the actions of the Parisian parents from different middle-class fractions are interpreted using a combination of Bourdieuan social reproduction theory and political-economic theories about changing forms of governance, globalization and the restructuring of capitalist economies. Thus contemporary writing on social reproduction wants to hold on to explanations of the formation of social relations and identities which take account of both local and more overarching forms of explanation.

Finally, each of these authors is aware of the tension between more agentic and more deterministic forms of explanation and, at the same time, trying to work with and, as far as possible, manage these tensions. On the one hand, all of them emphasize the importance of agency. So, for example, Archer writes about the 'strong' and 'agentic' performances of femininity enacted by some of the young women she studied and their refusal to be positioned wholly by the official discourses of the school. Keddie and Mills use the example of one teacher to show how gender binaries can be contested and potentially eroded. Benjamin et al. wish to 'foreground children's active role in making sense of social conditions that are not of their own choice'; they are keen to point out that, although the children's actions are 'contingent on . . . a web of intersecting indices of "difference"', they are 'not determined by' them. Van Zanten wants to 'analyze the policy process as a complex interaction between grass roots influences and national decisions'. Thus her analysis emphasizes the scope for agency to make a difference at both local and national levels.

On the other hand, however, whilst this work plays up the importance of agency, it also illuminates the extent to which agency is heavily constrained, at least at the more macro-levels. Thus, for example, in van Zanten's work, at the relatively micro-level of local school market structures, parents are presented as able to organize themselves collectively to make a difference. Yet labour market structures are represented as apparently more objective 'givens' which, by implication, are less amenable to the effects of political agency. Similarly, in Keddie and Mills and Benjamin et al.'s analyses of classroom settings, the children and teachers are presented as making choices about which discourses they accept, reject or move around, but the discourses are represented as constructed elsewhere. It may be that they can be reworked at a local level, but these local reworkings still appear to leave the discourses essentially intact at a more macro-level, to be accepted, rejected or manoeuvred around by other people. Archer's analysis emphasizes constraint even at the micro-level. The students she interviewed exhibited agency in the sense that they challenged dominant, pathologizing representations of themselves as 'too loud' or 'unaspirational' or 'too hardworking'. However, according to Archer, there are limits to the effectiveness of their agency in transforming teacher discourses which construct a 'successful pupil subject position' that these students can never 'authentically inhabit'.

This emphasis on agency raises fundamentally important issues for sociologists about explanation. To talk about agency is by definition to suggest that there are limits to deterministic forms of explanation. That is, unless we construct agency as essentially illusory and the illusion of agency as merely a product of some or other social force, then we are accepting that one part of the explanation for what goes on in the social world is people's choices. So, as we discussed in chapter 2, the agency/structure distinction needs to be qualified by an elaboration of how agency and structure work together at different levels. Partly this involves explications of the various conceptions of 'structure', which we are taking here to refer to the relatively 'stable', 'solid' or 'recalcitrant' constellations found in the social world (including, for example, discourses), against and around which the possibilities of agency are delineated. But it also needs to include a consideration of what the limits of agency and the 'permeability' and 'malleability' of structures are at various levels.

The descriptive/explanatory challenges with which these authors are grappling are closely linked into a range of normative concerns and challenges. All the work that we have reviewed on social reproduction has a more or less explicit normative content. For example, normative elements are evident in the authors' reflections on the potential use of their analyses. Thus van Zanten refers to the possibility of the orientations of public sector professionals being used to support egalitarian and inclusive educational practices and policies. Benjamin et al. suggest that a deeper understanding of the mechanics of inclusion and exclusion of the kind their analysis offers can contribute to the construction of arguments for egalitarian change. And Archer and Keddie and Mills expressly call for their analyses of systems of representation to be actively deployed in an attempt to transform discourses and thereby transform patterns of inclusion/exclusion.

However, it is not merely the potential use of sociological analyses that carries a normative load; the analyses themselves are constituted by value-laden readings. That is, as we noted in our discussion of Giroux's work, in presenting certain aspects of social production and reproduction as a 'locus of concern' (e.g. hyper-masculinist discourses) and others as a 'locus of promise' (e.g. deconstruction of gender binaries), these accounts of reproduction are fundamentally constituted by normative as well as explanatory discriminations.

In short, contemporary writings on social reproduction point to a range of forms of hierarchy, various aspects of social change and different possibilities for the exercise of agency, and discussion of each of these issues raises value questions about which of these forms of hierarchy, aspects of change and possibilities for the exercise of agency we value and how we decide which we value. Hence, understanding the increasing sophistication of social reproduction is very important to the central argument of this book. As we have said, we are treating social reproduction as a core, if not the core, theme in sociology of education, and the increasing complexity of social reproduction theory reflects the main developments in the field that we discussed as forms of proliferation at the end of the last chapter. This complexity relates both to an increased attention to multiple axes of inequality and to a recognition of the importance of context dependency and the heterogeneous nature, fluidity and instability of the social world and subject positions. It seems to us that this shift towards greater analytic complexity has brought about recognition of the inherent normative complexity of this shift and yet has simultaneously made it more challenging for sociologists to address the normative dimension of judgements about social reproduction explicitly. That is to say, the analytical sophistication that we have reviewed and the lessons that have been learnt from it provide obstacles to explicitly addressing normative judgements, in the sense either of making clear evaluative judgements about social phenomena or of making specific practical and policy judgements about what might be done (given the complexity, tensions within and instability of social reproduction processes and the importance of responsiveness to specific contexts, processes and standpoints). The result for contemporary sociology of education is, therefore, an understandable tendency to portray normative complexity indirectly but to shy away from deliberating about or making normative judgements.

Whilst recognizing the substantial difficulties facing those who wish to make either evaluative judgements or policy recommendations against a background of these complex models of social reproduction, we would want to argue that some degree of explicit engagement with these normative questions is important. It seems to us that this follows, for example, from the insight that social inequalities are not all of one kind. Whilst van Zanten's work seems to relate largely to questions about equality of access to schooling and the opportunities that schooling provides, the other examples all feature an interest in the importance of equal recognition of diverse cultural identities and the various ways in which educational processes support or inhibit recognition and misrecognition. It seems to us that when sociologists, or for that matter any other people, start to take an interest in, and work across, these different conceptions of equality, the question of the relationships between and the relative importance of different conceptions arises. That is to say, we are, to some degree, forced to ask what kinds of equality we should be focusing on and how far it is possible to address, either theoretically or practically, each form of equality with equal priority. This theme is considered in greater depth in chapter 6 as part of a discussion of what is known as the redistribution–recognition dilemma.

The underlying and more general point here is the one that we introduced in the preface. In order to decide which phenomena to focus on and to attempt to describe and explain, we have to decide what matters, and deciding what matters means being prepared to deliberate about what matters and why it matters.

Conclusion

In this chapter we have drawn attention to important shifts in how social reproduction has been theorized in recent years. These new theorizations have sought to overcome some of the limitations of the earlier radical left theories, in particular, by taking seriously the 'context specificity' of social reproduction; the complex interactions between various axes of social division; the fluid and hybrid nature of identity formation; the aspects of schooling that can be read as falling outside of dominant processes of reproduction – for example, because they are unconnected with them or interrupt them; non-deterministic modes of explanation; and the dynamic nature of social relations and formations.

The evolution of the theories that we have described in this chapter can be seen as involving a number of linked moves in the articulation of the normative issues relating to social reproduction, aspects of which remain 'uncompleted'. The first move is one from a reading of schooling-related processes and practices as necessarily oppressive to a reading in which some practices can be seen as potentially emancipatory – i.e. processes and practices can be seen as fulfilling or cutting across the requirements of capitalism. According to such models of social reproduction, processes and practices are appraised along a single dimension, being seen as either 'unjust' or 'egalitarian' or somewhere between these poles. The second move is one from seeing inequality solely along this single dimension, related to class hierarchy, to a recognition of the multiple dimensions of potential inequality or equality. Given this move, it becomes possible to classify the same processes and practices as combining elements of equality and inequality, depending upon which conceptions and facets of equality or social justice are brought to bear in the analysis (Cribb and Gewirtz 2003). The final move, one that is arguably implicit in the readings we have considered, but which needs to be made more explicit, is a move from 'values as given' to 'values as contested'. In many respects, the remainder of the book is our attempt to spell out this move in more detail.

In conclusion, we would like to underline two of the challenges that arise from the account we have presented here. Both of these challenges arise directly from the recognition of multiple hierarchies, context specificity and social fluidity in more recent readings of social reproduction, and fundamentally from the shift from 'context-independent' to more 'situated' conceptions of knowledge and the social world. First, there is the epistemological challenge of steering a viable course between a use of the concept of social reproduction which is so general and unspecified that it lacks any effective explanatory power and a use of social reproduction which is so context specific that it cannot explain the persistence of fundamental social inequalities across different settings. Second, there is the ethical challenge of recognizing and self-consciously addressing and appraising the range of value hierarchies deployed (explicitly or implicitly) in readings of reproduction. The direction in which theories of social reproduction have evolved highlights not only the need for more complex models of explanation which can hold the general and the particular together, but also the importance of a positive and sufficiently differentiated theory of social and educational value. What we are saying here is that the close attention paid to the complex processes of reproduction that are apparent in much of the contemporary sociological literature needs to be matched by more deliberate and detailed attempts to theorize about the normative dimension of social reproduction. The work that we have looked at shows how sociology helps to specify and capture the various 'goods' and 'harms' that are embodied in, and transacted through, educational processes. In addition, we are arguing, sociologists need to be ready to ask, and be prepared to contribute towards answering, questions about what is meant by equality, why it matters, and what the possibilities for its realization are.

5
Knowledge and the Curriculum

In this chapter and the next we will consider some curriculum-related questions in sociology of education. Here we look at theories of knowledge and their implications for the curriculum, whilst in chapter 6 we consider questions about curricula, particularly multicultural curricula, as part of our discussion on the theme of identity. As we saw in chapters 2 and 3, knowledge is one of the central threads running through sociological work on education, and one of our aims in this chapter is simply to reflect this fact and to set out some of the insights offered by sociological work on knowledge and the curriculum. However, we are equally interested in questions about the possibility and the nature of knowledge in the field of sociology of education itself. Indeed, our principal purpose is to develop our argument about the central importance of the normative construction of sociological work and to elucidate what we see as the close relationship between questions about knowledge and questions about values. At the end of the previous chapter we began to rehearse some of the many 'value hierarchies' inherent in accounts of social reproduction. This chapter – along with the rest of the book – continues to address and illustrate this topic of implicit normativity, in this instance by considering some of the value hierarchies embedded in accounts of knowledge.

But in this chapter we hope to move beyond the illustration of implicit normativity and to specify in much more direct terms why we are suggesting that an understanding of normativity has important implications for sociology of education. We will proceed by exploring what is involved in developing readings of the curriculum that (a) are sensitive to the complexity of processes of knowledge production and knowledge effects and (b) enable a holistic understanding of how it ought to be constructed – an understanding that takes into account political, social and cognitive 'interests' and the tensions between them. Through this exploration we want to trouble the assumption, which sometimes seems to operate within parts of sociology of education, that the most desirable kind of world is a world without hierarchy.

The main body of the chapter is in two sections. In the first section we review some of the ways in which the relationship between politics[1] and the curriculum has been understood in sociology of education by looking at three perspectives on curriculum theory – critical theory, poststructuralism and social realism. In the second section we explore how these might be brought together in ways that can inform thinking about curriculum design. In doing so, we will draw out some of the complementarities and tensions between the different perspectives, thus highlighting the ways in which different approaches to sociology of the curriculum give rise to rival versions of what matters with respect to curricular practice, and hence indicating – in relatively concrete terms – the kinds of normative discriminations that are at stake in advocating a particular sociological perspective on the curriculum.

Perspectives on politics and the curriculum

Obviously it would be too ambitious to try to present here a comprehensive picture of all the different sociological approaches to the curriculum. Rather what we will do is indicate three broad perspectives which represent useful and important currents of thinking. It is important to underline, however, that these perspectives are not exhaustive, and we are aware that they leave some important gaps, notably Bernstein's substantial contribution to sociology of the curriculum, which followed on from his work on classification and framing that we discussed in chapter 2. In addition, as we go on to illustrate later in the chapter, in practice, much work tends to cross the boundaries of the different perspectives.

Critical theory

This approach is represented in some of the classic texts already reviewed in chapters 2 and 3, which include Bowles and Gintis's *Schooling in Capitalist America*, Willis's *Learning to Labour*, Bourdieu and Passeron's *Reproduction in Education, Society and Culture*,

Spender and Sarah's *Learning to Lose* and Ladson-Billings and Tate's 'Toward a critical race theory of education'. From these perspectives the curriculum is seen both to reflect and to contribute to the reproduction of the ideology of dominant groups in society. In doing so, it is seen to work in the interests of these dominant groups and serves to reinforce prevailing power relationships and inequalities of various kinds.

There are, as is well documented, more and less deterministic accounts of this relationship. As we saw in chapter 2, Bowles and Gintis, for example, argue that there is a direct relationship – or 'correspondence' – between the requirements of capital accumulation and the curriculum – so that, for example, middle-class children destined for professional and managerial occupations are taught a curriculum that emphasizes choice, flexibility and independent learning, whereas those destined for semi- or unskilled occupations are taught rote learning, punctuality and obedience. Others have been more concerned to stress (a) that capital accumulation is not the only kind of interest that shapes the school curriculum and that the state needs to negotiate and grapple with competing demands, including, for example, those of social control and legitimation (e.g. Dale 1982); and (b) the role that the 'concrete practices' of schools, educators and students can play in 'mediating' the social, economic and political tensions and contradictions that characterize capitalist – and patriarchal/white supremacist – societies (e.g. Keddie and Mills 2007; Ladson-Billings 1999).

The work of critical theorists of the curriculum is heavily influenced by Gramsci's analysis of ideology, which illuminates the ways in which social control can be achieved without 'dominant groups having to resort to overt mechanisms of domination' (Apple 2004: 2). According to this analysis, dominant or hegemonic ideologies act 'to saturate our very consciousness, so that the educational, economic and social world we see and interact with, and the commonsense interpretations we put on it becomes the world *tout court*, the only world' (ibid.: 2). From this perspective, schools are believed to play a crucial role, not only in 'differentially distributing specific kinds of knowledge', and thereby 'allocating people to positions "required" by the economic sector of society', but also in distributing

the kinds of normative and dispositional elements required to make this inequality seem natural. They teach a hidden curriculum that seems uniquely suited to maintain the ideological hegemony of the most powerful classes in society. (Ibid.: 41)

This stance – and the 'problem-making' approach embedded in it – is well captured in the following quote from Apple, a leading critical theorist of the curriculum:

> the study of educational knowledge is a study in ideology, the investigation of what is considered legitimate knowledge . . . by specific social groups and classes, in specific institutions, at specific historical moments. It is . . . a critically oriented form of investigation, in that it chooses to focus on how this knowledge is distributed in schools [and] may contribute to a cognitive and dispositional development that strengthens and reinforces existing (and often problematic) institutional arrangements in society . . . [T]he overt and covert knowledge found within school settings, and the principles of selection, organisation and evaluation of knowledge, are valued governed selections from a much larger universe of possible knowledge and selection principles. Hence they must not be accepted as given, but must be made problematic . . . so that the social and economic ideologies and the institutionally patterned meanings which stand behind them can be scrutinized. The latent meaning and the configuration that lies behind the commonsense acceptability of a position may be its most important attributes. (2004: 43)

So here school knowledge is taken to be an ideological production which contributes to the reproduction of inequalities in society (around the social axes of class, race and gender) whilst simultaneously concealing its own role in processes of social reproduction by masquerading as neutral and universal.

Poststructuralism

As with critical theory, there are a range of perspectives on the curriculum that can be 'labelled' poststructuralist, and we will not attempt here to give a full and nuanced account of the different and competing strands of thought that fall within the poststructuralist umbrella. Instead we are going to offer a broad-brush account, which is inevitably going to oversimplify a far more complex theoretical terrain.

Like critical theorists, poststructuralists see the curriculum as a social construction. Indeed, there is no sharp dividing line between what we are here labelling as critical theory and poststructuralist perspectives. This distinction involves a degree of abstraction away from the more hybrid work of actual scholars and academic practices – but it roughly corresponds to what we previously identified as the distinction between critical-evaluative and critical-deconstructionist strands in sociological critique (see chapter 3). Critical theorists – in this sense – do not reject the possibility of objective knowledge and believe there are fundamental truths about the world that critical theory is able to represent and that are hidden from view in the capitalist or patriarchal or white curriculum, whereas poststructuralist accounts deny the possibility of producing any knowledge that is universally true. In other words, for the poststructuralist curriculum scholar (in the ideal-type sense we are using here) everything is ultimately a social construction. There is not a single reality – or truth – outside the construction of knowledge – only multiple realities, multiple truths that are produced through discourse and which reflect the different standpoints and interests from which the knowledge is constructed. (Once again it may be worth noting that some analogous positions are evident with the broad families of feminism and critical race theory.) Therefore, rather than trying to expose the curriculum as representing partial or distorted truths that render capitalist, patriarchal or white sense into commonsense – as in critical theory – poststructuralist curriculum theory focuses primarily on 'the processes, procedures and apparatuses wherein truth, knowledge and belief are produced' (Fraser 1989: 19). Or, as Humm (1991: 2) puts it, 'the whole point is not to construct a theory of knowledge but to put forward a series of methods for examining the production of knowledges'. In addition, poststructuralist curriculum scholars are interested in the constitutive effects of curriculum knowledge, the way in which the curriculum regulates and positions both teachers and students, and the way in which it produces particular kinds of 'pedagogic gaze' and is thereby imbued with power. The Foucauldian concept of power-knowledge is central here:

> The power implicit in particular discursive practices exerts inclusionary and exclusionary forces. The subject is 'subjected' to the gaze of a particular knowledge discourse through which the subject's ability is measured or categorized . . . Within such practices and discourses pupils are constructed as powerful (able) or not (less able). (Atkinson 1998: 31)

From the poststructuralist perspective, power does not emanate from a single source which produces the shape of the curriculum. Rather the curriculum is produced within a complex web of power, where power exists in multiple sites and is shifting and subject to continuous negotiation.

This is one example of the poststructuralist rejection of the use of the kinds of totalizing narratives poststructuralists believe to be characteristic of critical theory. Whilst critical-theoretical accounts of the curriculum tend to be organized around what their poststructuralist critics refer to as monolithic concepts, e.g. 'class', 'the state' or 'patriarchy', the emphasis of poststructuralism, in contrast, is on deconstruction, on continuously striving to 'trouble' or 'disturb' the categories deployed in texts:

> The goal is to keep things in process, to disrupt, to keep the system in play, to set up procedures to continuously demystify the realities we create, to fight the tendency for our categories to congeal . . . Deconstruction foregrounds the lack of innocence in any discourse by looking at the textual staging of knowledge, the constitutive affects of our uses of language. (Lather 1991: 13)

As we have already noted, the poststructuralist umbrella encompasses a range of approaches, and these differ from each other in a number of respects – including the extent to which they foreground the ability of agents to actively negotiate and rework the dominant discourses of the curriculum. However, both critical and feminist variants of poststructuralist curriculum theory – the former represented in the work of Aronowitz and Giroux (1991) and McLaren (1995) and the latter in the work of hooks (1994), Lather (1991), Middleton (1993) and Miller (1990) – emphasize the possibilities of agency based on the Foucauldian idea that power can be productive, that it can create possibilities as well as constraints. Such 'agentic' versions of poststructuralist theory attempt to understand 'people's multiple and simultaneous positionings in complex, changing and often contradictory patterns of power-relations' with a view to finding 'ways of resisting the encroachments and confinements of oppressive institutional structures and political ideologies' (Middleton 1995: 90, 98). These positionings and power relations relate to overlapping and cross-cutting divisions of class, race, gender, sexuality and region – including divisions 'between races or cultures within countries, between the northern or Anglo-American European nations and those of the southern "Third world", between indigenous populations and those descended from former colonists' (ibid.: 90).

From this feminist poststructuralist perspective, the curriculum is a product of the standpoints and the life histories of those who construct it. For example, in her critical exploration of the teaching of feminist theory in HE, Middleton notes that:

> Our feminist educational theory texts are like polyvocal scores. Woven through our theoretical deliberations, our struggles with feminist and sociological theories in education . . . are reflections on the everyday

practicalities of our experience – as teachers and workers; as research-ers; as participants in institutional reorganisation, wider political upheaval during times of economic crisis and administrative restruc-turing; as women whose maternal and civic responsibilities come into conflict with the demands of our professional and political lives . . .

The references we choose for our students to read are those works which *we* consider to be the most interesting and important. They are signposts in *our* intellectual journeys, significances from our academic biographies. The reading lists we compile contain the submerged nar-ratives of the academic life histories which brought them into being. And although it is important that we tell our students about our favour-ite writings, make visible to them our own feminist and educational heroes, we should not expect that these lives and works will necessarily be those that light up our students' worlds . . . They need spaces to develop theories which tap their own native imagery . . . which are indigenous or organic to their own . . . cultural, historical . . . material, and geographical situations. (1995: 99, 94–5)

Hence, as is reflected in this quote, feminist poststructuralist approaches challenge the authority of the teacher and call for greater humility on the part of teachers, who should not assume that the knowledge they want to teach is the knowledge their students want or need to learn.

Social realism

This perspective, adumbrated by Moore, Muller, Young, Maton and Nash, and drawing substantially on work from the philosophy and sociology of science – e.g. Gellner (1974, 1992), Schmaus (1994) and Ward (1996) – rejects what it sees as the reductionist and rela-tivist arguments of critical theory and poststructuralist approaches, in which, in the case of critical theory, the curriculum is reduced to the interests of dominant groups in society and, in the case of poststructuralism, to the standpoints of its progenitors.

Here we will illustrate this perspective by drawing mainly on Moore and Young's (2001) arguments for a reconceptualization of theories of knowledge and the curriculum in sociology of education. Whilst Moore and Young accept that knowledge is bound up with social and political interests, they reject the idea that it is '"always" and "only" identical with [political or social] "interest"':

If this is accepted, there are only interests and no good grounds for preferring one interest to another. It is a form of 'criticism in the head'

> or 'in the armchair' – a kind of academic radicalism of no consequence
> to anyone else . . . If all knowledge is from a standpoint and there are
> no standpoint-independent criteria for making judgements, appeals in
> terms of 'social justice' or the 'common good' become no more than
> other standpoints. Similarly, peer reviews for preserving objectivity
> and standards become no more than a form of professional hegemony.
> [Our] view . . . is that the objectivity of peer review has a social basis in
> the codes, traditions and debates of different intellectual fields that give
> it a degree of autonomy beyond the personal and professional interests
> of any particular group of academic peers. (2001: 453)

Thus Moore and Young argue that, in reducing knowledge to social
and political interests, critical theory and poststructuralist scholars are,
wrongly, denying the possibility of objective knowledge. Objectivity is
a controversial concept that causes disquiet for all of the reasons that
have been explored in the summaries of the critical theory and poststructuralist perspectives outline above. But here Moore and Young
are using it to point to the ambition that knowledge producers have
to make claims that have a currency outside the particular historical
and cultural standpoints from which they are made. In other words,
'some knowledge is objective in ways that transcend the immediate
conditions of its production' (2001: 454). It is this idea of objectivity
that underpins the traditions of peer review and, more generally, what
Moore and Young refer to as 'the social networks, institutions and
codes of practice built up by knowledge producers over time' (ibid.:
456). These things can be seen as attempts to insulate the evaluation
of knowledge claims, as far as possible, from their entanglement with
social and political interests. To give a more concrete sense of what
might qualify as objective knowledge in this sense, we could say, for
example, that the typical human being has one heart and two lungs,
and not two hearts and one lung, or that the Second World War took
place in the twentieth century.

Thus Moore and Young are arguing that critical theory and poststructuralist perspectives, in denying the possibility of objectivity, dis-
place norms or values other than those relating to social and political
interests which play a role in shaping the curriculum. These include
what Schmaus (1994) calls cognitive norms and values. These norms
and values also represent a kind of interest, but these are interests that
are 'internal' to knowledge as opposed to the 'external' interests associated with social and political power. Cognitive values represent the
aims of knowledge – for example, in the case of sociology of education, these goals might be expressed in terms of a desire to illuminate
the social construction, processes and effects of specific educational

discourses, relationships and formations – whereas cognitive norms represent the means to achieve these ends – for example, the use of Marxist or Foucauldian theory, or specific empirical approaches. Whilst the selection and application of such goals and norms may reflect the particular biographies, values and standpoints and professional and political interests of sociologists, they cannot, as Schmaus asserts, always be reduced to these non-cognitive values and interests (1994: 263, cited in Moore and Young 2001: 455), or, as Moore and Young put it:

> This in no way denies that the production and transmission of knowledge is always entangled with a complex set of contending social interests and power relations. However . . . the persistence and in some ways extension of structured inequalities always has to be seen in interaction with the social configurations of knowledge production itself . . . It is only when the cognitive interests involved in the production and transmission of knowledge are given the importance they warrant that a social theory of knowledge can avoid an all too often facile reductionism. (2001: 456)

Moore and Young argue that what is therefore needed is a 'social realist theory' of the curriculum which seeks to explore, first, the role of 'external' interests and power relations in the construction of knowledge (both in research and the curriculum); and, second, 'how the forms of social organisation that arise from "cognitive" interests may themselves shape the organisation of society itself' (ibid.: 436).

There are strong parallels between Moore and Young's argument and Nash's attempt to reconcile what he calls the 'arbitrary' and 'necessary' elements of education. Nash wants to accept the main tenets of social reproduction theory, as delineated by Bernstein and Bourdieu, whilst attempting to 'undo' some of its effects and grip on sociology of education. He accepts 'that knowledge is socially constructed . . . and that school knowledge has the symbolic power to maintain relations of social domination' (2004: 605), but he argues that:

> what may have to be undone is the assumption that the school curriculum is, necessarily and inevitably, adequately characterised as an expression of the cultural arbitrary. This is not to dispute the generally acknowledged claim that the school is engaged in forms of symbolic violence, that it has a reproductive effect and so on; but it is to assert the realist case that accurate knowledge of the world can be obtained and should constitute a non-arbitrary element of the school curriculum. (Ibid.: 606)

Implications for curriculum evaluation and design: juggling hierarchies

In this section of the chapter we want to consider the implications of these debates about the relationship between knowledge and interests for curriculum design in order to illustrate some of the practical consequences of different sociological approaches to the curriculum and thereby highlight some of the tensions and incompatibilities between them. Our starting point here is that all of the perspectives we have discussed are important and that, to have a holistic appreciation, not only of how the curriculum is constructed and what its effects are but also of how it might be reconstructed, it is necessary to draw upon and combine insights from all three. More specifically, we think it is important to ask the following three questions of any curriculum:

1 (arising from the critical-theory perspective) in what ways does the curriculum reproduce social and political inequalities?
2 (arising from the poststructuralist perspective) in what ways does the curriculum marginalize and exclude particular individuals and constituencies and/or fail to recognize individual and group identities and hence reproduce 'recognitional inequalities'?
3 (arising from the social realist perspective) in what ways is the curriculum comprised of knowledge that is rigorous and worthwhile both intrinsically and instrumentally?

The first two questions seem to us to be relatively self-explanatory, as they represent the 'meat and potatoes' of conventional sociological writing on the curriculum. The third, however, needs some explanation. It reflects the insight illuminated by the social realist perspective that knowledge can be evaluated by criteria other than those relating to its social and political origins and effects, a fact which, as we have noted, is a commonplace assumption of the peer-review process, but which is easily obscured by an exclusive focus on the – admittedly pervasive – linkages between knowledge and social reproduction. Obviously, the ideas of rigour and worthwhileness are open to debate, and conceptions of both ideas will vary according to the particular social networks and knowledge communities from which they emanate. However, the point that the social realists are making, and the one which we wish to endorse, is that, for knowledge to have the potential to be experienced by students as fulfilling and also to enable them to act in and on the social and physical worlds in ways that change the world for the better, it matters not only that that knowledge is not oppressive but also that it is rigorous and capable of withstanding as much criticism as possible.

Our working assumption that all three perspectives need to be taken seriously may jar with those who want to highlight some of the fundamental contrasts between them. For example, the social realist perspective positions the other two as having relativist tendencies – tendencies that are positively celebrated in poststructuralist work. However, we should not necessarily uncritically accept this way of constructing these two perspectives. Or at least it is important to distinguish between the arguably productive 'relativizing tendencies' in critical and poststructuralist theories and any charge of outright relativism. This latter characterization is much more difficult to sustain. In practice, both perspectives embody precisely the kinds of claims to objective knowledge that social realists regard as necessary. For example, Marxists are arguing not that processes of capital accumulation are social constructions that exist only from within a revolutionary vantage point, but rather that they represent an objective reality that exists whether or not people are aware of it. And when poststructuralists maintain that truths only exist within particular discourses, they do not assert this as merely one truth within one discourse, but rather proceed as if this stance represents the way things are. Similarly, the claim that some forms of knowledge are exclusionary is itself a knowledge claim that poststructuralists quite rightly want us to take as making a claim on truth rather than simply to read as a discourse that positions people in particular ways. In short, we take it that all three perspectives themselves embody knowledge – and, furthermore, they embody knowledge which, we suggest, is relevant to curriculum design, evaluation and development.

Sociology of the curriculum, because of the relativizing currents within it, is sometimes taken to involve the dissolution or deconstruction of knowledge hierarchies. However, in subjecting what they see as arbitrary hierarchies to critique, in effect, sociologists assert their own rival hierarchies which are rarely explicitly acknowledged. Each of the perspectives we have reviewed has embedded within it a hierarchy of what knowledge is valuable, and these hierarchies are often made visible when the writer moves from critique to prescription.

We will now look at three examples which relate to the principal concerns of the three perspectives expressed in the questions articulated above. In doing so, our intention is both to show the practical importance of each of these questions for curriculum design and to help give a concrete sense of some of the normative tensions between the rival sociological perspectives on the curriculum that need to be confronted if we want to take the insights each perspective offers seriously. The examples also show that, in practice, the perspectives overlap, with the first two cutting across the critical theory/poststructuralist divide and the third foregrounding a social realist perspective but also reflecting some of the concerns of the other two perspectives.

'Feminist praxis and the gaze in the early childhood curriculum'

The first example is MacNaughton's critique of the role of developmental psychology in shaping the early years curriculum in her article 'Feminist praxis and the gaze in the early childhood curriculum' (1997). This draws on earlier feminist critiques of developmental psychology (what MacNaughton calls 'modernist developmentalism'), critiques of the kind advanced by Walkerdine ([1981] 1990) (see chapter 3), and the Foucauldian-inspired concept of the 'pedagogic gaze'. MacNaughton argues that developmentalism, and the curricular/pedagogic practices of 'free play' associated with it, 'can support patriarchal gender relations by skewing the teacher's gaze'. Like Walkerdine, she argues that progressive, child-centred pedagogies, in their efforts 'to facilitate the development of the "natural" child' (1997: 318), help to promote and reinforce patriarchal relations of power both between children and their teachers and amongst the children themselves.

The argument is illustrated using the case of an early years teacher, Nellie, who comes to see, through her work with MacNaughton, that she had previously 'privileged the developmentalist gaze' (1997: 322). Nellie was part of a group of early years teachers who were involved in challenging traditional sex-role stereotyping in the childhood centres where they worked and who came together with MacNaughton to reflect on the process. Like others in the group, Nellie had an approach to teaching that was based on ideas drawn from developmental psychology. The approach involved teachers observing the children's development, assessing their strengths and weaknesses and planning activities based on these. Nellie decided to analyse her observations in order to see whether gender was influencing the children's choices of play activities, but when she did this she found no evidence of a gender influence. Her initial conclusion was that gender did not feature in the children's play choices. However, colleagues in the group encouraged Nellie to focus more particularly on gender in the course of her subsequent observational work. When she did this, with the help of MacNaughton's feminist interpretations of videotaped recordings of the children's play, she began to see that gender did indeed play a substantial role in the children's interactions, with, for example, boys occupying more space than girls and using a range of strategies, including chasing and name calling, to retain their dominance of space. As a consequence of this realization, Nellie transformed her approach to observation, no longer focusing on the children's developmental progress, but instead 'using power as a new observational "criterion"' (ibid.: 320). And, in turn, as a consequence of this approach to observing the children, she developed a scepticism towards the idea of 'free play', began to develop strategies to intervene in the children's play in order to challenge the boys' sexist behaviour, and developed a commitment to providing a 'counter-sexist curriculum' (ibid.: 323).

MacNaughton uses Nellie's story to argue that developmentalism, because it entails a focus on the individual child, prevents teachers from seeing the 'fundamentally constitutive' (1997: 321) role of gender in children's learning. It was as a consequence of Nellie's use of a 'developmental gaze', MacNaughton argues, that:

> She silenced gender differences in children's play choices, cloaked the construction of gendered power relations between children, and thus enabled them to continue. . . . As a result boys were able to exercise power over girls . . . and patriarchal gender relations were maintained. (Ibid.: 322)

MacNaughton identifies two reasons for this silencing of gender in the developmental approach. First, developmental approaches focus on the individual child rather than on relationships between children; and, second, as Walkerdine argued, the emphasis on allowing children to express themselves freely so as not to repress their natural development discourages teachers from intervening in their play. MacNaughton concludes that what is needed is a 'shift away from a developmental gaze and towards a feminist gaze [which] privileg[es] a search for gendered power dynamics and . . . sexism in relationships between children' (ibid.).

So here MacNaughton is deploying, and through her own work also constructing, a hierarchy of valuable knowledge. According to this hierarchy – expressed here in its most stark and simplified form – the theory which should underpin early years practice, and which should be included in the curriculum for the professional education of early years practitioners, should foreground a feminist understanding of gender relations and power, and it should favour and prioritize this feminist understanding over and above the theory inherent in 'modernist' developmental psychology.

Student scientist identities within curriculum discourse

The second example is Hughes's (2001) exploration of 'the availability of student scientist identities within curriculum discourse', in which she advocates 'an anti-essentialist approach to gender-inclusive science'. Hughes's research is a response to the contemporary policy concern about women's under-representation in the physical sciences. Whilst early feminist work in this area in the 1970s and early 1980s had focused on girls' choices and attitudes, from the mid-1980s onwards feminist researchers shifted their gaze to the nature of science teaching and the science that was being taught in schools. Such work looked at the role of the white masculinist culture of science in the reproduction of gendered and raced hierarchies within the science classroom. This included studies of what Hughes (2001: 277) describes as 'the sexist, aggressive or discriminatory practices of teachers and male students that make science a hostile environment for many female students' (e.g. Butler Kahle et al. 1993; Whyte 1985; Kelly 1987), but it also included feminist critiques of the 'objectivist' approach to science that has – at least up until relatively recently – tended to be dominant in the practice of science education. These feminist critics joined forces with progressive science educators who were asserting that the science curriculum needed to be transformed in order to counter problems of alienation from science learning and enhance the effectiveness of science teaching. These progressive educators were arguing for science to be made more relevant to students' lives by emphasizing its socially constructed and contested nature and its human and social relevance. They were also pressing for the adoption of constructivist approaches to learning that called for more open-ended investigative work and collaborative approaches rather than a simple transmission of science 'facts'. These ideas were attractive to feminists as well (e.g. Harding 1986, 1991; Seymour 1995; Hildebrand 1996; and Vlaeminke et al. 1997), who argued that:

> while an objectivist curriculum supports a masculine identity and favours boys, a symbolically more feminine, contextual, cooperative and student-centred curriculum is compatible with femininity and encourages girls. (Hughes 2001: 278)

More recently such essentialist feminist positions – which equate certain models of science with masculinity and others with femininity – have been criticized by feminist poststructuralists, both for affirming and reinforcing gender binaries and gender hierarchies and for

ignoring issues of race/ethnicity and class. This critique was the starting point for Hughes's research.

Through semi-structured interviews with, and observations of, staff
and students in one secondary school and one post-sixteen college,
Hughes examines the nature and range of subject positions that are
made available by different kinds of science curriculum. Her research
draws on a feminist poststructuralist view of subjectivity as 'complex,
shifting and constantly being constituted and reconstituted through a
range of discursive practices' (2001: 278). In this paper Hughes uses
extracts from interviews with pairs of students to explore the ways in
which they employ and combine discourses of science, gender and
ethnicity to construct different (pro- and anti-) science identities. Her
analysis shows that some students construct science subjectivities
that 'conform to, rather than disrupt, dominant discourses of gender
segregation in science' (ibid.: 283), with some boys aligning themselves with the objectivist physical sciences and some girls constructing a more humanist biological sciences identity. However, others are
able to construct identities that are based on a rejection of dominant
discourses of curriculum science. Take 'Janice', for instance:

> Janice, who describes herself as Black British, studied chemistry,
> biology and mathematics. She gave her reasons for choosing these sub-
> jects as instrumental; she wished to train as a forensic pathologist. But
> she was considered to be far from an acquiescent model science student
> by one of her teachers, who described her as unpunctual and inattentive
> . . . [T]he scientist subjectivity based on conformity and high perform-
> ance in science is not readily available to Janice; she cannot take up
> conformist, white, middle-class, female subject positions . . . and her
> achievement is not recognised as outstanding. However, reconfigura-
> tion of dominant discourses of science generates a new scientist sub-
> jectivity that is consistent with her subjectivities of gender, academic
> status and ethnicity. (Ibid.: 284–5)

This new scientist subjectivity draws on a constructivist science
discourse expressed in Janice's enthusiasm for experiments going
wrong. As she herself puts it:

> like we're doin' an experiment . . . and they said that . . . when it's
> placed in a ethanol solution your heart rate was supposed to go down
> cos alcohol's a depressant but my one speeded up and that was inter-
> esting cos like in the results you could say why you thought it did that
> that's what I prefer if my results are slightly inaccurate and slightly
> wrong at the end you've got more to say . . . rather than saying oh I
> predict this and it came true so I'm clever type thing. I'd rather . . . do

that so you can say where it's room for improvement and what went wrong and why. (Ibid.: 285)

Hence, Hughes argues, Janice's rejection of the 'clever' science student identity and her taking up of a new, strong identity that draws on discourses of originality and self-reliance shows that 'there are assured scientist subjectivities available for some female students that depend on possible interactions between ethnicity, marginality, educational background/achievement as well as gender' (2001: 288). This lends support to Hughes's rejection of essentialist perspectives that construct particular kinds of science as either girl- or boy-friendly, and she concludes that:

> While rigid and objectivist science is only compatible with a narrow range of student gender and ethnic identities, socially relevant and more constructivist science can generate a wide range of scientist subjectivities, increase the possibilities for science identities and thus open the way towards a more inclusive curriculum. (Ibid.: 288)

So we can see that, as with that of MacNaughton, Hughes's work has at its heart key discriminations about what should qualify as more or less appropriate and more or less ideal forms of knowledge for the curriculum, in this case the secondary school science curriculum, and inherent in her account is the construction of valued hierarchies of knowledge. To express this, again in the simplest of terms, socially relevant and constructivist science is being constructed as superior (in terms of its capacity for inclusivity) to the more abstract, impersonal, 'cold' science that Hughes refers to as 'objectivist' science.

Scientific realism and the school curriculum

The final example is taken from Nash's case for applying a realist perspective in sociology of the curriculum. As we have already noted, Nash is interested in drawing a distinction between what is arbitrary and what is necessary in the school curriculum and argues that 'the necessary elements of education, including respect for reality, knowledge, and truth, should be an integral part of the school curriculum' (2004: 605).

Nash illustrates his arguments using the example of the mathematics and science curricula in New Zealand. In New Zealand there are two mathematics courses in the upper years of secondary education – 'mathematics with calculus', a traditional academic course, and 'alternative mathematics', a course that plays up the practical relevance of mathematics – for example, its relevance to filling in tax forms. Mathematics with calculus is examined; alternative mathematics is not and is also 'stigmatized with an inferior status' (Nash 2004: 608). Nash indicates that the reasons for the stigmatization are not necessarily well understood and are easily misconstrued and reduced to the fact that mathematics with calculus is credentialized and therefore has a higher 'exchange value' (ibid.). In addition, the hierarchy indicated by the stigmatization, Nash points out, is a reflection of a well-known privileging of the theoretical over the practical, the pure over the applied, and so on. But Nash wants to suggest that there are more fundamental reasons why one form of mathematics should arguably be treated as preferable to another, reasons which are hidden by the priority that is often attached to credentials. According to Nash,

> schools may fail in their educational task – not because they give too little emphasis to credentials, but because they give too much . . . : it might actually be the case that mathematics in the strict sense provides knowledge about the real structures of the physical universe and in that sense is, for the most practical of reasons, the intellectual birthright of all . . . The reason, after all, why 'Mathematics with Calculus' is valued more highly than 'Alternative Mathematics' is precisely because it is more useful to any one of the myriad technologies that sustain industrial civilization. Students may need to gain a well-grounded personal sense, moreover, that mathematical and scientific knowledge is valuable, that it is applicable in the most direct sense to fields other than the strictly vocational. An informed participation in many areas of organized life, as a citizen and as a member of different communities, can only be enhanced by a scientific education. (Ibid.: 609, 619)

In this way, Nash presents a case, built on his conception of the importance of 'necessary knowledge', for widening participation in the learning of more demanding mathematical and scientific knowledge.

The hierarchy that Nash is defending here reflects a prioritization of rigour and the intrinsic and instrumental worthwhileness of scientific knowledge over a more inclusive and subjectivist conception of what counts as scientific knowledge. However, it is worth noting at this point that even Nash does not advocate that it is sufficient to teach more demanding and discipline-specific knowledge on its own; rather he suggests that this be accompanied by introducing students to the vocational and social relevance of science more generally:

> Bringing together the sciences in terms of their value, giving some attention to their history, and demonstrating to students the critical value of

such knowledge would provide a contextualization of great benefit. Through video-production, debates, scientific clubs, magazines and other activities . . . students might gain a fuller appreciation of the value of their scientific education. It may be important that teachers and others who work in schools should give students an elaborated sense of the career opportunities open to them as people who have mastered a body of scientific knowledge. (2004: 618–19)

So whilst Nash's argument is superficially very different to that of Hughes, like the latter it also represents concerns about inclusivity, equality and social relevance. Indeed, in this section we have looked at the work of MacNaughton, Hughes and Nash to underline the complementary and in many respects overlapping nature of the concerns of theorists operating from different perspectives, as well as to highlight some fundamental tensions to which we will now turn.

Knowledge contests

These examples point to two competing axes of knowledge hierarchy – one relating to equality and one relating to cognitive interests. Each of these axes is internally complex and will be subject to contestation. For example, knowledge can produce different kinds of inequalities, including distributional and recognitional inequalities. And also there are contests about what counts as the most rigorous and defensible forms of knowledge, as attested by such myriad paradigm disputes as those rehearsed earlier in the chapter. Of course, these contests about what counts as rigour and defensibility are entangled with social and political interests, but a point that we have been keen to highlight in this chapter is that concerns about rigour and defensibility are not always and everywhere the same as political contests, and that it is a mistake always to elide them. Thus, although the two axes interact, each has a degree of autonomy from the other, and many of the contests around sociology of knowledge arise because of the relative emphasis given to these two axes, with the critical (evaluative and deconstructionist) traditions tending to emphasize the political construction of knowledge and the social realist perspective the relative independence of knowledge from politics.

To illustrate this point and some of the tensions within and between the axes, we will go back to the case of the science curriculum discussed in the articles cited above by Hughes and Nash. Although, as we have noted, there are overlaps between the conclusions of these two authors, there is a clear difference in emphasis between them. Hughes's emphasis on student identity and on inclusion leads her to privilege a more constructivist approach to the science curriculum. Nash's emphasis on the rigour and cognitive power of 'official science' leads him to argue for the wider dissemination of high-status knowledge, both for the benefit of society as a whole and for social justice reasons (in that it would contribute to the redistribution of cultural capital and the economic and social benefits that arise from it).

How far it would be possible to get Hughes and Nash, or people with similar outlooks, to agree about the science curriculum is a question that is impossible to answer without sitting down and talking to them, but it is possible here to flag up some likely points of tension. The most conspicuous tension arises where we cross the line between what might be seen as weak forms of constructivism towards stronger versions, which Nash describes as anti-realist and characterizes as follows:

> If students are to act as scientists, the argument goes, then the theories they construct as a result of their observations and experiments should be taken . . . seriously as their science: in principle, their scientific theories of specific gravity or momentum, for example, are as meaningful, considered as systems of discourse, as those of other scientists. If students are to act as scientists then their activities should be guided only in the most general methodological sense by the teacher, who should certainly not impose his or her own theories . . .
> This discourse is grievously in error. It is wrong in suggesting, if not actually stating, that one theory is as good as another; wrong in thinking that school children can, in fact, re-discover Galilean science . . . and wrong about the appropriate role of the science teacher. (2004: 620)

We do not think that Hughes's vision of constructivist science is the one that is caricatured here, but it enables us to point out in a nutshell how curriculum design has to strike a balance between enabling and validating student engagement with scientific reasoning processes, on the one hand, and indiscriminately validating any and all models or claims about the nature of the world, on the other. So what we are trying to highlight here is that there are tensions between different approaches to promoting the cognitive interests of scientific knowledge and scientific reasoning.

However, the example can also be used to illustrate tensions between cognitive and equality interests and tensions within the equality axis. Even within a weak constructivist approach, educators have to find a way of drawing a line between supporting students'

perspectives and identities and challenging students' identities where
these seem to be based on and reinforce misconceptions about reality
– for example, that homosexuality is unnatural, or that women are
less intelligent than men, or that there is such a thing as biological
race. Any experienced teacher will be conscious of the difficulty
involved in walking this fine line.

There may also be conflicts between the kinds of scientific knowledge that will advance recognitional justice and those that will advance
distributional justice. Arguably, whilst constructivist science may be
more inclusive and affirming of students' identities, it may be less
successful (and this seems to us to be an empirical question) in equalizing the distribution of HE and employment opportunities, as long as
access to high-status HE and employment positions demands knowledge of official science. We will return to the sort of dilemmas posed by
this conflict and discuss them at greater length in the next chapter.

Conclusion

In this chapter we have sought to trouble the common assumption
that sociology of education exists largely to deconstruct or demolish
hierarchy. In particular, we have endeavoured to highlight the ways in
which competing perspectives in sociology each carry their own hierarchy, and thus that each perspective has implications for what kinds
of knowledge are valuable and should have relative prominence in the
curriculum. The job for a curriculum developer, therefore, is not to try
and iron out hierarchy but rather to be reflexive about both the inevitability of hierarchy and the need to juggle together different knowledge
hierarchies, each of which has a claim that deserves respect. More
generally, we hope to have expanded and strengthened our central
argument about the growing need for political and ethical reflexivity
in sociology of education. To conclude, we will summarize the main
elements of this argument as they have featured in this chapter.

Through the examples we have considered, we have highlighted
not only the fact that different analyses and critiques of knowledge
each rest upon value hierarchies but also that different analyses rest
upon different and – crucially – sometimes incompatible value hierarchies. Those who are committed to the relative independence of
'cognitive interests' (i.e. to the view that the validity and usefulness
of knowledge claims can be assessed in respects that transcend the
social and political interests served by knowledge claims) have to
balance 'intrinsic' and 'extrinsic' forms of evaluation. That is to say,

they have to balance a concern with defending rigour and validity (within specific disciplinary traditions) with a concern with the patterns of inclusion and exclusion generated by conceptions of knowledge. However, even those who are sceptical about any distinction between 'intrinsic' and 'extrinsic' perspectives on knowledge cannot avoid having to make analogous choices. This is because their critical analyses are inevitably framed by judgements about which forms of inclusion/exclusion matter, and matter the most. Above all, sociologists cannot easily retreat into a relativist position with regards to their readings of knowledge and the curriculum. This is because, in making claims about the nature of knowledge, sociologists themselves are either relying upon some conception of knowledge as reliable (i.e. relying upon the belief that what they have to say is somehow warranted) or are encouraging the idea that there is no reason to take what they are saying seriously.

We are persuaded that, to the extent that there are relativizing tendencies in sociology of education, these tendencies can play a useful heuristic and critical function as part of broader evaluative or deconstructionist projects. In particular, these tendencies remind us that social phenomena may be experienced and valued differently by people who are differently socially located, and this reminds us not to take for granted the assumptions built into official knowledge or dominant discourses more generally. But, as we have just argued, there are important limits to how far these tendencies can be taken seriously. This is a consequence of the relatively familiar logical point that unbridled relativism is self-defeating, which has practical implications for the sociological project of critique. In short, the unqualified acceptance of relativism dissolves the very possibility of critique.

This means that, in arbitrating between rival analyses of knowledge and the curriculum, we are committed to making political or ethical judgements as well as empirical ones. Indeed, determining the relative credibility and power of sociological critiques of the curriculum requires us to do empirical and normative work at the same time. For example, returning to the case of science education we have discussed, if someone wants to make choices between different conceptions of school science, they will need to be able both to describe and to explain the various effects of specific conceptions (e.g. in relation to the construction of possible subject identities or the distribution of cultural capital). They will also (and partly aided by this descriptive and explanatory work) need to be able to make judgements about which of these effects matter, and to what degree, and how to weigh these against the cognitive interests embodied in science. Therefore, if we are committed to defending the validity of our assertions in this area then, we would claim, we are committed to think not only about the defensibility of our descriptive/explanatory judgements but also about the defensibility of our political/ethical judgements. At the very least, as we will go on to argue in the remaining chapters of this book, a commitment to rigour in sociological research would require a degree of critical self-consciousness about the normative standpoints embedded in our work. The alternative is that the very rich set of approaches and the sceptical attitudes that sociologists have brought to questions about knowledge would run out of steam just as they reached the door of sociology of education itself.

6

Identity

In this and the next chapter we want to look more closely at a theme we opened up in the previous chapter – that is, the relationship between the sociology of education and educational practices. Throughout the book we have talked about and illustrated the normative agenda of the sociology of education. This normative agenda consists essentially of two components: first, the value judgements and value hierarchies that are more or less explicitly embodied or entangled in the writings of sociologists; and, second, the direct or indirect advocacy of recommendations for policy and practice. These two components, although overlapping, are distinct because it is possible to identify strongly with specific value commitments whilst remaining open-minded about what should be done to realize them in practice. In the remainder of the book we are particularly interested in focusing on the second component and, more specifically, in asking about the extent to which it is possible to have a sociology *for* education as well as a sociology *of* education.

It is notable that explicit recommendations about what ought to be done, where they exist in sociological texts (including in the examples we have looked at in earlier chapters), often occur towards the end of publications and are typically relatively brief. There are, we would suggest, at least three possible reasons for this. First, as with those writers who eschew making recommendations altogether, there may be some judgement that policy advocacy is not really the business of sociologists. We think this is a very important and respectable position (or set of positions) and will come back to it in chapter 8. Second, there may sometimes be a feeling that policy recommendations can be made relatively quickly and easily. This might be the case, for example, when sociologists are analysing the misconceptions upon which certain policy initiatives are based and are, therefore, inclined to believe that, were these misconceptions to be rectified, sounder policies would automatically follow. Third, the opposite may be the case – that is, sociologists may be conscious of the many difficulties inherent in formulating policies and so may be reluctant to spend much time grappling with the level of difficulty and detail that is needed, especially when they are already grappling with the theoretical and empirical complexities of sociological analysis. As will become clear from what follows, we are strongly sympathetic to this third line of reasoning. However, both this and the first position seem to represent important ambivalences – i.e. sociologists affirming that policy work is not really their business but doing a little bit anyway (the first position) or affirming that, although complicated, it is worth doing but then doing it very superficially (the third position).

In this chapter and the next we hope to begin to explore some of the factors that underpin these kinds of ambivalence. In doing so, we will be asking questions about the problems and possibilities of doing 'policy-oriented' sociology of education. Specifically, we are interested in demonstrating the contribution that can be made to sociology by taking seriously the vantage points of policy actors and practitioners. Rather than ask these questions in purely abstract terms, we will be focusing on two important fields of value in which sociologists of education take a particular interest – identity in this chapter and teacher autonomy in the next.

We will begin by giving a short account of the nature of identity using illustrations from work in the sociology of education. We will then turn our attention to what has and can be done in education to recognize and respond to diverse student identities by focusing upon the multicultural education movement. This movement is not just a practical or political one, but it is also effectively an academic movement within the sociology of education. That is to say, it relates to a family of perspectives and traditions articulated and advanced both within the sociology of education and within practical classroom contexts. We will summarize and consider the response that multicultural education makes to the question of identity and some of the principles and values underlying multiculturalism. There are many different definitions of multiculturalism, but here we are using the term in its broadest sense, to include anti-racist and critical multicultural approaches, as well as more narrow conceptions. Finally, we will identify and discuss some of the challenges that arise from the multicultural response that those committed to taking identity seriously need to confront, highlighting in particular the tension between a politics of recognition and a politics of redistribution, and, in doing so, we will begin to draw out the implications for the sociology of education of taking the vantage points of actors seriously.

What is identity?

In simple terms, a person's identity can be understood as the answers to the questions: who do I think I am and who do I want to be? Despite the fact that these appear to be very simple questions, intense and often complex, convoluted and theoretically obscure academic debates have raged around the concept of identity. We do not have the space here to provide an extensive review of these debates (but, for an expert and accessible entry point, see Hall 1996). Instead, what we would like to do is to identify the salient features of identity that have been emphasized in recent work in the sociology of education. Rather than reviewing competing conceptions of identity, which is the model we have adopted in earlier sections of the book, here we are going to work with a broadly poststructuralist conception, a conception which seems to us broadly correct and which we will accept, at least for the purposes of this chapter. We are adopting this approach here so as to enable a consideration of the following questions: (a) once we accept certain sociological readings of a particular phenomenon, what implications does that have for what educationalists ought to do? and, in turn, (b) what implications does that have for how we do sociology of education?

To begin with, it is important to distinguish, as Castells does, between roles and identities. Our identity is not what we are or what we want to become but who we think we are and who we want to become:

> Roles (for example, to be a worker, a mother, a neighbor, a socialist militant, a union member, a basketball player, a churchgoer, and a smoker, at the same time) are defined by norms structured by the institutions and organizations of society . . . Identities are sources of meaning for the actors themselves, and by themselves, constructed through a process of individuation. . . . [Roles] become identities only when and if social actors internalize them, and construct meaning around this internalization. (Castells 2004: 6–7)

Previous work we have reviewed in this book (e.g. that of Renold in chapter 1, Archer and Benjamin et al. in chapter 4 and Hughes in chapter 5) illuminates the ways in which the elements that make up

our identity accounts are drawn from those discursive representations that are available to us, including discourses that position us in
particular ways, for example as 'tomboy', 'girlie girl', 'clever science
student', 'gentle, studious boy', etc. However, this does not mean
that we must uncritically adopt the subject positions that are made
available to us by dominant discourses.[1] This point is well illustrated
by Shain's (2003) ethnographic study of the schooling and identity
of Asian girls.

Shain's study draws on close observation and in-depth interviews
with forty-four working-class girls of Pakistani, Bangladeshi and
Indian heritage growing up in the North of England. She shows how
in a variety of different ways and to different extents the British Asian
girls she studied reworked, manoeuvred around or refused the dominant discourse of Asian femininity which constructed them as passive
recipients of oppressive cultural practices. As Shain explains:

> Asian girls [in dominant UK discourse] are characterised as caught
> between the two worlds of home, where they are restricted, and school,
> where they experience freedom. Public discussions in the aftermath of
> inner-city disturbances of 2001[2] and the events of September 11, 2001
> have further reinforced characterisations of the poorest Asian com-
> munities, the Pakistani and Bangladeshi Muslims as isolationist and
> refusing to integrate. These communities have been accused of holding
> onto backward and barbarous practices that prevent girls from partak-
> ing in mainstream activities and encourage boys to take up dangerous
> and fanatical positions. (Shain 2003: 125)

Shain uses the stories of the girls she studied to show that:

> Asian girls, rather than being the passive recipients of fixed cultures,
> are actively engaged in producing new cultural identities by drawing on
> residual elements of their home cultures and reinterpreting them in the
> local cultural spaces they inhabit. These reinterpretations are shaped
> and influenced by a variety of factors including gender relations within
> their communities as well as in the mainstream, their class locations
> and their locality. (Ibid.: 129)

For example, some of the girls – categorized by Shain as the 'gang
girls'– drew on counter-hegemonic discourses to contest the subject
positions that dominant discourses created for them and to challenge
the racism that they identified as the main source of their oppression:

> The gang girls challenged dominant stereotypes of Asian girls as passive,
> timid and quiet, by becoming involved in a number of rule-breaking

activities, including fighting to defend themselves from racist attack. Their prioritisation of racism as a source of oppression in school led to the formation of an all-Asian female subculture, from which white students and teachers and Asian students who appeared to ally with whites in the school, were excluded. (Ibid.: 126)

These girls were happy to be both verbally and physically combative. As one girl told Shain, '[t]his boy called me a "Paki" but I got him back. I called him white "B". If someone calls me I call them back. If they want to have a fight, I'll have a fight.' These girls also actively chose to wear traditional clothing and speak their home languages at school, even though it 'marked them out for racist name-calling'. According to Shain, this gave 'the girls a sense of power over the students and teachers they identified as routinely subjecting them to abuse' (ibid.: 60, 65). This example thus also illustrates the ways in which processes of identity construction are necessarily bound up with relations of power.

Poststructuralist accounts emphasize the ways in which, in large part, individuals actively choose and negotiate their identities but also the ways in which these choices are limited by the discourses that are available to them. For some, these choices are far more limited than for others because processes of identity construction take place within networks of power and differential access to economic, social and cultural resources (Bauman 2004: 38). This point is illustrated by Archer's analysis of young people's investments in and enactments of popular branded style that we referred to in chapter 4. Archer argues that, for the working-class young people she studied, wearing popular brands (e.g. Nike trainers and 'hoodies') is one of the relatively few means available to them of asserting their worth or value within a social system that frequently constructs them as 'not valued', whereas for middle-class young people these styles represent just one of many ways of generating 'identity capital'. In the case of working-class students, popular branded style tends to be interpreted by teachers as anti-education and can therefore work to reproduce the educational and social disadvantage they experience. In contrast, in the case of middle-class students, wearing popular brands merely represents one of many ways of 'consuming and performing different cultural styles' and therefore functions as a marker of agency and individuality and reproduces their valued position in the school system (Archer et al. 2007: 233).

The processes of identity construction we are talking about here are not neutral or innocent ones but involve us in strategically positioning ourselves in relation to others. For example, we may choose to position ourselves in relation to hierarchies as relatively powerful or powerless, and incorporate what we believe to be our powerfulness or powerlessness as an important part of our identity.

Moreover, as we have already seen in the example of Shain's 'gang girls', processes of identification necessarily involve the construction of boundaries and exclusions. In defining who we think we are, we are inevitably separating ourselves off from what and who we are not – a process Butler refers to as 'disidentification', which she explains in the following – psychoanalytic – terms:

> Identifications . . . can ward off certain desires or act as vehicles for desire; in order to facilitate certain desires it may be necessary to ward off others; identification is the site at which this ambivalent prohibition and production of desire occurs. (Butler 1993: 100)

For example, Walkerdine et al., in their psychosocial analysis of what Reay (2005) has called the 'psychic landscape of social class', have written about how some of the working-class girls and parents they studied used discourses of respectability to differentiate themselves from others:

> their . . . talk on social class generally and their own class location in particular was infused with a desire to distance themselves from the painful position of being 'one of them'. 'They' were the 'scruffs', the rough working class, the 'underclass, the poor the homeless or the hopeless'. (Walkerdine et al. 2001: 40).

And Mac an Ghaill (2000: 94) has described how the dominant heterosexual males in his school-based ethnography of the cultural production of masculinities disparaged their male peers who focused on their schoolwork, 'redefining them as gay and "poncy"'. 'Disidentification with them', Mac an Ghaill suggests, 'enabled the heterosexual males to establish their own identities.' Disidentification could work the other way round as well, as is reflected in the comment of one of Mac an Ghaill's gay respondents:

> Teachers, especially male teachers, assume your being gay is a problem but there are a lot of plusses. In fact, I think that one of the main reasons that male straights hate us is because they really know that emotionally we are more worked out than them. We can talk about and express our feelings, our emotions in a positive way. They can only express negative feelings like hatred, anger and dominance. Who would like to be like them? (Mac an Ghaill 1994: 167)

As is now widely asserted in contemporary sociological texts, identities are neither fixed nor one-dimensional. Rather they are fluid, contingent, plural and hybrid. That is to say, in actively constructing our identities, we draw on a range of representations, and the way that we combine these representations is different in different contexts and at different times. The contingent nature of identity construction is illustrated in the following quotation from a Haitian student who participated in Waters's study of the ethnic and racial identity of second-generation black migrants in New York:

> When I'm at school and I sit with my friends and, sometimes I'm ashamed to say this, but my accent changes. I learn all the words. I switch. Well, when I'm with my friends, my black friends, I say I'm black, black American. When I'm with my Haitian-American friends, I say I'm Haitian. Well, my being black, I guess that puts me when I'm with black Americans, it makes people think that I'm lower class. . . . Then, if I'm talking like this [regular voice] with my friends at school, they call me white. (Waters 1994: 807)

The hybrid nature of identity means that new identities are frequently created through the combination of different discursive elements, as in the example of Meera Syal's novels about daughters of Indian migrants growing up in the UK or Chaim Potok's novels about children of Eastern European Jewish migrants growing up in New York. Such discursive mixing is vividly portrayed in Harris's analysis of the 'everyday' 'new ethnicities' of thirty young people of mainly South Asian descent growing up in West London. Amaljeet, for instance, who was born in Britain, has a Sikh mother and Muslim father who were both born in India:

> Music plays a major part in Amaljeet's life. He is a leading member of a traditional Punjabi dhol drumming band, and often performs in school on important occasions, when pupils from different ethnic groups contribute essentialised presentations of their traditional cultures. However, when asked if his band ever wear the associated traditional dress from the Punjab, he is emphatic that for them this denotes the practices of an older generation. His band in fact wear Ralph Lauren designer clothes and black Kicker shoes . . . Nevertheless, three of the seven members of the band wear Sikh turbans, although Amaljeet himself does not do so, nor does he display other visible signs of his Sikh affiliation. His band have designed a logo based on a Yves St Laurent motif. . . . Apart from Bhangra music he likes reggae, swing beat, soul and jungle but not hip hop. He is especially fond of reggae music and mentions Bob Marley, Freddie McGregor and Jah Shaka as particular favourites. . . .

Amaljeet's speech includes local elements of London English pronun-
ciation . . . and Caribbean and London pronunciations together with
London English grammar . . . and traces of lexical items directly linked
with Indian forms of English. (Harris 2006: 46–7)

As Harris goes on to point out,

Amaljeet's account of his own ethnic and cultural formation demonstrates how fluid and open these categories can be once an enabling
discursive framework allowing such accounts to be constructed and
carefully listened to is offered. His account in its unpredictability, complexity and subtlety gives a strong sense of what the empirical realisa-
tion of the . . . 'cultures of hybridity' theoretical formulation might look
like and feel like. (Ibid.: 48)

As some of these examples also show, identities can have a collective aspect to them. The answer to the question 'who do I think I am?'
may often point to some group with whom we think we are identified
and/or by whom we think we are excluded. During the 1970s the
notion of collective identity acquired a particular salience because of
the rise of new social movements around social categories, including those relating to race, gender, sexuality and disability. Collective
identities may also revolve around a religious or ethnic affiliation, a
political or territorial one, or a combination of these (Castells 2004),
as in the case of some of the 'Palestinian Arab Israeli' young people
that Pinson studied. As one of them put it:

I think that I'm first of all Muslim. I don't mind about being Arab and
what language I speak. I'm first of all Muslim and Arab and also from
Palestine and also Israeli [. . .] But here in Israel they see us as Arab
and the Arab world they see us as Jews and they don't call us Arab-
Israelis. We are between this and that, Arab-Israelis [. . .]. ('Hackima',
cited in Pinson 2008: 209)

Because identities are about the way we think and the people
we want to be, they incorporate a set of beliefs, values and commitments, and in some cases a corresponding set of attitudes and
dispositions. As we have seen, this might include political, religious
and moral beliefs as well as more materialist kinds of commitments,
for example, to certain patterns of consumption or lifestyles and
aesthetic preferences, as in the case of Amaljeet in Harris's study or
the young people that Archer researched, all of whom constructed
their identities partly around popular fashion brands. In some cases,

these young people's investments in 'fashionable or desirable identities' are directly linked to a rejection, or at least a deprioritization, of education. As one of the girls in Archer's study commented:

> I don't see . . . [university] as a path for me . . . I like to have new Nike trainers and Nike tops and a new chain every month so I don't think the [student] grant would suit me. ('Jordan', cited in Archer et al. 2007: 233)

However, the complex and constructed nature of identity means that we cannot read off from people's roles or surface features, such as the ones we have just mentioned, how people identify themselves or what they think or believe. Simply because a teenage girl spends a lot of time applying make-up and ensuring she has the latest designer accessories, it does not follow that this forms an important part of her identity or that she has the stereotypical values and beliefs that some might associate with these practices (e.g. materialistic or superficial). Or, just because someone is a woman or a mother or a teacher, it does not mean that these characteristics form a key part of their identity. It is important to underline this feature, as identity is an area where it is notoriously easy to slide into reductionist and essentialist assumptions.

The final aspect of identity to which we want to draw attention in this account is our capacity to be reflexive about our identities. A number of commentators have argued that this feature of identity is characteristic of late or postmodernity – an era characterized by rapid change, substantial global movements of people, the growth of instant communication and virtual relationships, hyper-consumerism, and so on. All of these things change our relationships with other people and ourselves and require continual reassessment of who we are and who we want to be. As Giddens puts it:

> One of the distinctive features of modernity is an increasing interconnection between the two extremes of extensionality and intentionality: globalising influences on the one hand and personal dispositions on the other . . . The more tradition loses its hold, and the more daily life is reconstituted in terms of the dialectical interplay of the local and the global, the more individuals are forced to negotiate lifestyle choices among a diversity of options . . . Reflexively organized life-planning . . . becomes a central feature of the structuring of self-identity. (Giddens 1991: 1, 5, cited in Castells 2004: 11).

Even if such accounts are exaggerated, and even though they may underplay inequalities in the distribution of opportunities for reflexivity or for realizing reflexively made choices (Adams 2006), it nonetheless seems broadly true to claim that reflexivity has become an important feature of the world in which we live.

Having, albeit briefly, reviewed what we take to be some of the main contemporary sociological insights into identity, we now shift our emphasis by focusing predominantly on how sociologists and practical actors working in the field of multicultural education have approached the question of what is and can be done to work effectively and sensitively with the complex field of identity, given these insights.

Multicultural education as a response to the question of identity

Multicultural approaches are based on a critique of more traditional ethnocentric and patriarchal forms of education which, for example, assume and perpetuate the myth that the values associated with dominant groups are shared by everyone else, and which thereby marginalize and fail to respect the identities associated with subordinate groups. The approaches are underpinned by a commitment to valuing and affirming the diverse identities of learners and therefore to eroding inequalities in the respect that is afforded to people who are deemed to belong to different cultural groups. Translated into practice, these approaches can penetrate more or less deeply into the structures and cultures of schooling. Shallower forms of multiculturalism of the kind critiqued by critical race theorists such as Ladson-Billings and Tate (1995) (see chapter 3) or Jay (2003), amongst others, might involve the incorporation of relatively superficial elements of the cultural heritage of learners in ways that are symbolic, or even tokenistic (what Harris, quoted above, calls 'essentialised presentations of . . . traditional cultures'). In the UK this has been referred to as the three S's approach (with the three S's standing for saris, samosas and steel bands) (Troyna and Carrington 1990). More far-reaching forms of multiculturalism involve rethinking components of what Bernstein called the three message systems of education – curriculum, pedagogy and assessment – so as to ensure that they do not operate in unnecessarily exclusionary ways. There seem to be three broad strategies that have been adopted here, either separately or in combination – what we might call the three R's: representation, relevance and responsive pedagogies.

A concern for representation entails ensuring that any people represented visually or textually in the curriculum are culturally diverse.

This includes a concern with avoiding particularly pernicious use of imagery such as that illuminated by Scott (2005) in her study of human origins museum exhibits, which sometimes identify the primitive with 'African' and the advanced with 'white Anglo-Saxon' (see chapter 1). But, at a deeper level, representation can also include making visible the historical and contemporary contribution of different cultural groups to the construction of knowledge. A concern for relevance involves using examples in teaching which reflect learners' everyday lives and existing enthusiasms, such as linking the teaching of sound to the technologies of urban music-making. More generally, this entails broadening conceptions of the curriculum – for example, expanding the notion of science education to include the social and cultural dimensions of the subject, which might engage students' interest more successfully than an exclusive emphasis on the science content (as advocated by feminist and progressive science educators – see discussion of Hughes's (2001) work in chapter 5). So, for instance, the teaching of the nature of DNA can be accompanied by teaching about the discovery of DNA, including interpersonal and institutional rivalries, contrasting ways of doing science, and some of the social and political debates that contemporary genetics has generated. The incorporation of such elements helps to dissolve perceived boundaries between science and everyday life. Responsive pedagogies provide a bridge between the everyday language that learners bring with them and the language of the subject discipline. This involves teachers starting from and engaging with the everyday language, culture and practices of the learners and using these as the medium to support learning and induct students into the languages and practices of the official curriculum.

Multicultural education can also take on relatively naïve and relatively sophisticated forms. The problem of naïvety arises when we assume that strategies of relevance, representation and responsive pedagogies enable us to affirm diverse identities in unproblematic ways that do not take into account the many complications surrounding identity that we have just reviewed. In particular, there are two kinds of risk that arise from this kind of apparently straightforward affirmation of diverse identities – stereotyping and relativism. Stereotyping is often linked to an essentialist position and occurs when we attempt to read off people's identities from superficial features or partial knowledge of individuals, such as their names or physical appearance, or when we assume that people will only want to learn about 'their own' culture – as in the case of a young black South Londoner in Les Back's (1996) study, who is quoted as saying that he would like to be reading Shakespeare but in his youth centre's library he can only find books about Rastafarianism (cited in Barry 2001: 235). The risk of cultural relativism is the risk of assuming that all identities deserve equal affirmation. For not all identities are equally worth respecting and, indeed, some may be seen as harmful. For example, learners may operate with identities based on beliefs and dispositions that are damaging or demeaning to others, such as racism or sexism, and which construct unjustifiable exclusions. Or they may operate with identities that could be seen as self-limiting – for example, identities that are based on an anti-school stance.

Those operating towards the more sophisticated end of the spectrum are concerned to overcome some of these risks. More sophisticated approaches start from an anti-essentialist position. They aim to resist making assumptions about people's identities, and rather seek to engage actively and continuously with the identity projects of learners by talking with and listening to them. Underlying this position are the beliefs that (a) if we are interested in affirming people's actual identities – i.e. who *they* think they are – rather than in relating to them through our own categorizations and generalizations, then we have to treat them as individuals, not categories, and this involves being ready to listen to and learn from them; and (b) the discerning of people's actual identities is not something that can be done on a one-off basis because, as we have discussed, identities are not fixed but are fluid and hybrid, and evolve and are negotiated over time.

In addition, more sophisticated versions of multiculturalism do not seek to affirm all the identities of learners equally. Rather they acknowledge that some identities may be harmful and need to be challenged – for instance, as we have just noted, identities which embody racist or sexist commitments. For example, 'critical multiculturalism' (May 1999; Kincheloe and Steinberg 1997), arguably the most sophisticated version of multiculturalism, aims continually to challenge and reshape people's identities, beliefs, values and commitments and to provide a space in which learners are enabled – through the three message systems of schooling – continually to question their assumptions, including their assumptions about who they are and what does and could matter to them. As Connolly puts it:

> The challenge is more than simply fostering a learning environment that is non-discriminatory, free from stereotypes and which is multicultural . . . , it is also about conceiving of appropriate means of engaging . . . children more critically in the ways they are encouraged to think about and experience identity, difference and diversity. (Connolly 2003: 180)

This involves the educator capitalizing on and fostering the capacity of learners to be reflexive about their identities. Part of this task is to encourage learners to differentiate between the values of different identities – i.e. to encourage what Fraser calls a 'more differentiated politics of difference' (Fraser 1997: 204). In plain terms, this means differentiating between aspects of identity that could be harmful, those that ought to be encouraged, and those which are neither particularly harmful nor beneficial but which can just be enjoyed as manifestations of difference. This kind of approach is reflected in Sewell's advocacy of teaching young men to critique the values of anti-school identities that revolve around consumerism, materialism and gangster rap (Sewell 1997; Sewell and Majors 2001).

Finally, more sophisticated versions of multiculturalism arise from an acknowledgement that there is more to education than simply respecting people's identities, and that an exclusive focus on identity can serve as a distraction from economic and political inequality and the politics of redistribution – and may even exacerbate these forms of inequality. From the critical multicultural perspective, what is needed is for educators to facilitate the understanding and skills needed to challenge existing inequalities, including those that operate around axes of class, race and gender. According to Kincheloe and Steinberg, this:

> necessitates the attempt on the part of teachers and other cultural workers to take back power from those educational, political and economic groups who have for far too long been able to shape school policy and curriculum in ways that harm students from low status groups. In a critical multicultural school, students and their family members would study both how power shapes their lives and what they can do to resist its oppressive presence. (1997: 28)

However, combining a respect for students' identities with a concern to promote greater social and political equality is a major dilemma for educators committed to social justice – and it is one that we will return to below.

Dilemmas

Whilst our summary of the more sophisticated versions of multiculturalism shows how these might overcome the limitations of more naïve versions, it also points to some of the tensions and dilemmas that might arise from trying to put multiculturalism into practice.

In what follows we will deliberately consider some of these tensions from the perspective of policymakers and practitioners – that is, we will ask about the difficulties of 'translating' forms of critique (in critical multiculturalism) into action. We do so not simply because we think that this is an important and interesting practical and political agenda but also because we believe this question of translation has important implications for the conduct of sociology itself.

There are many tensions and dilemmas that we could consider here, but due to space constraints we will focus on what we see as three key interlocking dilemmas: engaging with the full complexity of learners' identities vs. categorizing them; recognizing identities vs. problematizing and disrupting them; and living with vs. challenging hierarchy.

Engaging with the full complexity of learners' identities vs. categorizing them

In the preceding section we talked about the risks of stereotyping – that is, where we make assumptions about people's identities on the basis of superficial facts about them – and we suggested that this needs to be avoided through closer attention to the complexities of people's actual identities. In practice, however, is such a stance either possible or altogether desirable? One reason such a stance may be practically impossible arises from the complexities of identity rehearsed above. That is, given that identity is hybrid, plural and fluid, there is a fundamental problem for educators in determining the nature of an individual learner's identity, and the investment of time and energy needed to try to understand the identity of any individual learner should not be underestimated.

In addition, there are circumstances in which it makes some sense to rely on broad generalizations. For example, someone who was asked to prepare a lecture on psychology might reasonably ask whether the average age of the audience was going to be fifteen, forty-five or seventy-five. Lying behind this question would be certain generalizations about the interests and frames of reference of people of different ages. In making these generalizations, the teacher will no doubt fail to please everyone. For instance, in choosing to use a scene from Big Brother (the reality TV show) when teaching the fifteen-year-olds about group dynamics but not when teaching the 75-year-olds, they may in fact disappoint a number of participants. However, this does not undermine the value of using statistical generalizations when trying to be sensitive to the needs of particular audiences. There are countless ways in which generalizations about age, gender, and cultural and religious identities might be made by educators who are being conscientious and interested in being both effective and equitable in the way they plan and deliver their classes. The difficulty is that making cautious generalizations about your audience and stereotyping them often amounts to the same thing. We can only strive, therefore, to limit the amount of stereotyping we do, as, if we want to develop forms of education which are relevant and responsive to learners, we cannot avoid it altogether.

Generalizing about identity is, therefore, sometimes useful, and it might also be argued that it is sometimes politically necessary as a means of challenging oppressive practices. This is, however, a very contentious claim, and it is worth exploring an example to illustrate the point. Let us look at the case of students categorized as disabled. The drive towards the affirmation of rights and resources for disabled students has in large part emerged from the demands of the disability movement, and it is in this respect one expression of the importance and strategic role of mobilization and solidarity around collective identities. However, the affirmation of rights and the allocation of special resources necessarily involve processes of labelling and identification that can be experienced as demeaning or exclusionary and that inevitably fail to reflect the complexity of people's actual identities. Hence, such processes can constantly produce frustrations and frictions in the life worlds of the people they are supposed to benefit. The response of some commentators has been to call for the rejection of the 'nomenclature of disability' in favour of more inclusive forms of educational practice which avoid the reductionist and essentializing assumptions, and processes of social marginalization and personal devaluation, that can be associated with processes of categorization and in which:

> Students are not seen as disabled, defective or disordered. Rather all students are seen as different, complex and whole. All students are recognized as reflecting a diversity of cultural, social, racial, physical and intellectual identities. (Christensen 1996: 77)

Nevertheless, although this call is laudable, it does not really address the dilemmas at stake. Notably, it is unclear how rejecting the 'nomenclature of disability' will overcome the inequalities of resource allocation that disadvantage those students who are currently categorized as disabled, and indeed there would seem to be a prima facie argument for suggesting that some form of labelling may be necessary to tackle these kinds of inequalities.

Recognizing identities vs. problematizing and disrupting them

In formulating policies and practices, it is also important to be aware of the ways in which the pedagogies that are supported or discouraged by these policies and practices impact on the identities of students. There are compelling reasons for developing pedagogic approaches that both recognize and challenge identities. Recognition is important for both intrinsic and pedagogical reasons. Recognizing a person's identity is to see them and treat them in the way they want to be seen and treated. It is what is entailed in treating everyone with equal respect. In addition, to fail to recognize people's identities can be damaging to their self-esteem and sense of dignity. Recognition also makes good pedagogic sense as it increases the chance of learners feeling engaged, involved and interested.

However, as we have argued above, all aspects of identity may not be equally deserving of respect, and an important goal of education is to encourage people continually to question the beliefs, values and commitments that make up their identities. There are two broad sets of reasons to challenge aspects of individuals' identities. The first we have summarized above, namely that some aspects of identity can be seen as harmful to individuals because they are either needlessly self-limiting or harmful to others. The second reason is that certain identities can be harmful at a wider level because they reinforce structures of oppression. For example, it could be argued that identities that revolve around a sense of marginalization can paradoxically contribute to the production of the very marginalization that is of concern. This would be a contentious thing to claim and could be interpreted as a 'blame-the-victim' stance. However, it is arguably important to draw attention to the opposite danger – that is, the danger of educators colluding with learners' acceptance of structures of oppression rather than helping them find strategies to resist such structures individually and collectively.

These are some of the reasons why educators need to move beyond the mere recognition of identities. Indeed, as we have argued, education cannot simply focus on the recognition of identities because it is centrally concerned with the construction of identities. People's identities evolve over time and at any one point in time contain elements that are backward looking and forward looking. To borrow Williams's (1981) formulation, we might say that any individual's identity is composed of dominant, residual and emergent strands. Educators, therefore, need to make choices about which strands of learners' identities to focus on and work with, and making these choices is part of their responsibility for the co-construction of identity with learners. Hence, working with identity necessarily involves a series of balancing acts in which educators have to attach weight both to who learners think they are (i.e. to their dominant and residual identities) and to who they might become (i.e. their emergent identities). This entails problematizing and disrupting identities as well as recognizing them. The dilemma here is how to problematize and disrupt identities without damaging learners' self-esteem and dignity, which is in some measure dependent upon recognition.

Living with vs. challenging hierarchy

As we have seen, multicultural education aims to disrupt existing hierarchies of value so that the perspectives of dominant groups are not valued more highly than those of subordinate groups. However, the business of disrupting hierarchies generates dilemmas.

Here we wish briefly to revisit some of the arguments we developed in chapter 5 about the limits of critique. As we stated there, it is easy for someone writing from a critical perspective to imply that all hierarchies are bad. However, anyone not adopting an extreme relativist position needs to accept that some hierarchies are both inevitable and defensible. In accepting, for example, that some people are better than others at football, music or physics, we are subscribing to a hierarchy of standards. And if we are interested in promoting high quality football, music or physics then we are committed to working with and seeing the value of some kinds of hierarchy. Similarly, if we think it matters that people working in particular occupations – for example, plumbers, doctors or teachers – have the necessary skills, then we have to subscribe to a hierarchy of standards in which not everyone will make the grade. However, often closely linked to this kind of standards hierarchy is another and much more contentious hierarchy – a hierarchy in which individuals are valued or accorded worth in proportion to standards achieved. Whilst most educators would subscribe to hierarchies of standards, many would want to resist their elision with hierarchies of esteem. This example illustrates why it is important for educators to be reflexive about hierarchy. There are two issues we have in mind here. First, educators need to find ways of working with hierarchies they feel are valuable whilst not reinforcing those that they believe should be challenged. Second, they need to decide how far they should accommodate themselves to existing hierarchies even where these are of a kind that they believe should be challenged.

The first issue arises when two kinds of hierarchy are closely allied – one that is deemed to be benign and one that is deemed malign – as set out above. In practical terms this arises, for example, in trying to give feedback to someone in a way that indicates the deficiencies in their work without suggesting that they are somehow themselves deficient. Anyone who has ever taught will recognize that this is one of the dilemmas at the heart of education. Educators constantly have to make choices between privileging a concern for the development of a learner's knowledge and understanding and privileging a concern for their feelings.

The second issue can be approached by asking how an educator committed to changing the world can support learners who are living in the world as it is. We will give two examples to illustrate this dilemma. Many teachers may want to resist the hierarchies inherent in formalized systems of assessment. They may regard them as essentially measuring the wrong things, as giving a misleading picture of the full range of capabilities of students, and as not reflecting the things that learners value about themselves. If they were in charge of the education system, they would abolish them and put in place more formative and holistic models of assessment. Nonetheless, they are not in charge of the education system and need to decide how best to prepare their students. In effect, they have to choose between, on the one hand, compromising their educational philosophy in order to ensure the students get the credentials they need to progress on to further and higher education or to valued occupations and, on the other, potentially disadvantaging the students by refusing to be reined in by the demands of the examination. However, there are different degrees of compromise between these two poles that are possible, and teachers have to decide where to place their centre of gravity. Indeed, this was precisely the dilemma that faced feminist academics setting up women's studies courses in the 1970s, who, as we noted in our review of Spender and Sarah's *Learning to Lose* in chapter 2, had somehow to reconcile the hierarchical grading systems and individualism demanded by university assessment practices with the feminist commitment to cooperation, collectivism and non-hierarchical practices.

Things do not necessarily get easier even for those who are 'in charge of the education system'. A minister of education, for instance, could also be personally sympathetic to more formative and holistic models of assessment, but he or she does not operate in a vacuum. Until employers and other powerful lobbies and stakeholders in society are also convinced of the superiority of such assessment models, any reforms in this direction are unlikely to gain legitimacy and therefore be successfully implemented. Under these circumstances, the minister would effectively be in the same situation as the classroom teacher, in having to compromise between his or her own conception of what is in students' best interests, and what in practical terms is deemed by powerful interests in society to be in students' best interests.

Exactly the same considerations apply to our second example. Just as educators may want to resist the hierarchies inherent in formalized systems of assessment, so they may also want to resist the hierarchies inherent in narrow notions of curricular content. Instead, they may wish to push towards more open-ended and contested notions of what counts as knowledge (e.g. science teachers who try to pay attention to the cultural and historical contexts of the science they teach, English teachers who teach about soaps as well as Shakespeare, or music teachers who teach about rap and R 'n' B as well as Mozart). However, as with the examination example, teachers face pressures and constraints emanating from both formal assessment processes and the more informal sets of expectations that surround education which privilege a narrower conception of the official canon. In effect, policymakers and practitioners sometimes have to choose between adhering to their ideals and conforming to dominant approaches which may, however wrongly, be of significantly more instrumental value (in terms of cultural and economic capital) to students.

Identity, equality and policy

Cutting across, and in some ways underpinning, these three dilemmas is arguably a more fundamental dilemma, one that we have already touched upon in the previous two chapters, which Fraser (1997) calls the redistribution–recognition dilemma (RRD). In essence this refers to the tension between two different kinds of equality. The first kind relates to the distribution of opportunities and material resources and the second to the equal recognition of people's identities. Before concluding, we want to reflect back on the three dilemmas we have rehearsed above, try to illustrate their relevance to the RRD, and underline the central significance of the RRD for education policy and practice in a multicultural society. Then in our conclusion we will go on to discuss the potential implications of all of this for the practice of sociology.

In relation to our first dilemma, the tension between affirmative strategies designed to combat the disablism that leads to an unequal distribution of valued social and economic goods and, on the other hand, the tendency of such strategies to contribute to labelling practices that can stigmatize students categorized as disabled is a clear example of the RRD. In relation to our second dilemma – i.e. how far to recognize or problematize identities – we have argued that some identities have harmful consequences in that they have the potential to reinforce wider structures of oppression. One example of this is the anti-school identities we mentioned earlier. Placing emphasis on recognizing and valuing anti-school identities could reinforce processes of marginalization from school and the differentiated patterns of attainment and economic wellbeing consequent upon such marginalization. A comparable example, discussed by Barry, relates to how language is taught in schools. Although it is important for schools to recognize and value non-standard variants of the dominant language if they are to treat all students with respect, there are limits to how far it is responsible for schools to place equal value on standard and non-standard variants. As Barry has argued: 'There is no escaping the conclusion that, if they are not to short change their pupils, the schools should try to ensure that by the time they leave they are equipped with a command of the standard form of the language' (2001: 324).

The third dilemma concerns the tension between living with and challenging hierarchy. Whilst accepting that teachers and students might usefully contest and disrupt many of the hierarchies that are embedded in educational processes, we have argued that there are limits to the desirability of challenging hierarchies for both instrumental and intrinsic reasons. Looking at the question purely instrumentally, education provides forms of cultural capital that create life chances for students. This means that a teacher concerned with distributive justice has some obligation to ensure that all their students gain the knowledge that is valued by dominant groups in society and which provides access to socially valued opportunities, positions and goods. But in many instances this knowledge and the goods associated with it are not merely of instrumental value but also have intrinsic value, in that they can enable people to live richer, more fulfilling lives and to participate in a broader range of social and cultural activities.

For both instrumental and intrinsic reasons, therefore, we would argue that there are limits to how far teachers should compromise on transmitting and inducting children into official knowledges for the sake of showing respect for the 'street knowledge' that children bring to school. However, as we have made clear, we see this not as an either/or choice, but rather as a question of operating with both official and unofficial knowledges at the same time. In practice, this means teachers are continuously engaged in working with students to make complex discriminations, assuming neither that unofficial knowledge is less worthy than the contents of the formal curriculum nor that these things are necessarily of equal value. Part of the job of the educator is to give learners the resources to make such discriminations on a case-by-case basis, informed by an in-depth understanding of a broad range of examples. This, of course, gives scope for students to construct evaluative hierarchies that are different from those of their teachers. The crucial point that we are repeating here is that some hierarchies are not only inevitable but in some key respects desirable.

These considerations thus highlight the impossibility of achieving wholesale educational equality in every respect. This impossibility arises from the fact that there are different dimensions of equality, and it is this insight that is expressed in Fraser's phrase the RRD. As Fraser argues, in many cases the remedies for distributive inequality are incompatible with those for recognitional inequality. In addition, eliding the two kinds of inequality can be harmful. Specifically, turning too quickly to a presumed misrecognition of minority cultures as an explanation for social or educational inequalities (such as differences in academic attainment) risks both (a) reinforcing pathological readings and (b) obscuring real economic injustices that may be responsible for the inequalities. Likewise, strategies such as affirmative action, which rest upon the use of cultural labels to seek to rectify inequalities of access to high-status goods, can serve to disguise underlying structural inequalities by superficially 'changing the color of inequality' (Gitlin 1995, cited in Barry 2001: 326) rather than dismantling the structures themselves. In both cases, the 'cultural group' is being used as a proxy for need, thereby distorting perceptions both of the 'cultural group' and of the basis of need.

One policy consequence of our argument is the need to rule out two extremes. First, it is untenable to ask educators to ignore the identities of learners and to strive to teach in an identity-blind way. Educators will inevitably operate with constructions of learners' identities whether or not these are soundly based. However, at the other extreme it does not make sense for education to be defined around an unqualified affirmation of learners' identities. This is not only because of the practical difficulties of so doing but also because of the harms that such a stance might produce.

Practical actors, therefore, need to be reflexive about such conflicts inherent in working with diverse student identities and to be aware that policies which tackle certain forms of inequality or misrecognition

may lead to other forms. The role for policymakers and practitioners here, as elsewhere, is neither to evade the dilemmas surrounding
identity by conceiving of their work in technicist terms nor to operate
with a simple template or vision of what is for the best, but rather
to make explicit the range of competing value sets that are relevant
to evaluating policy effects and to try and self-consciously and self-
critically steer the least worst course through the dilemmas we have
rehearsed in this chapter. This will necessarily involve grappling with
the many moral and political dilemmas entailed in taking seriously
both the value of identity and the value of other educational and
political goals which can sometimes conflict with valuing identity.

Conclusion

In this chapter we have set out some of the complexities associated
with the nature of identity and some of the complexities related to
practical educational responses to questions of identity. But what
does all this mean for the sociology of education?

Perhaps the first thing we should stress is the sense in which sociologists and practical actors (at least in the ideal-typical sense in which
these two roles can be defined and distinguished) are differently positioned. The principal task of the former is to make sense of the social
world and of the latter to make choices about what has to be done
and to enact those choices. For this reason, the dilemmas we have
rehearsed, and many other analogous dilemmas, are unavoidable for
policymakers and practitioners but are to some extent optional for
sociologists. One possibility would be just to accept a relatively clear
division of labour of this sort. However, we would want to argue that
there is a great deal to be gained by sociologists and practical actors
working more closely together. We hope this chapter has begun to
illustrate some of the lessons that might be derived from these kinds
of dialogue. Although sociological analysis, considered on its own,
does not answer policy dilemmas, practical actors can learn from sociology about how complex a terrain identity is and the range of forms
of 'identity damage' that are possible, including the damage that can
be caused by superficial or generic policy responses. We would also
want to argue that sociologists have something important to learn
by taking the standpoint of practical actors seriously. Our central
argument here is analogous to the one that we made in the previous chapter about knowledge. Whether writing about knowledge or
identity (or other things), sociologists are inevitably caught up in the

process of making normative discriminations of various kinds which both frame and pervade their work. In the production of this work, sociologists stand to gain at least two important things from attention to practice. First, and as is widely recognized, contexts of practice provide a level of depth and detail that specify and qualify sociological generalizations and thereby enrich them. Second, and we suggest this might be less widely understood, the 'hard choices' that practical actors have to face are foreshadowed in the textual choices that sociologists make. That is to say, neither practical actors nor sociologists can 'have it all'. For example, just as practical actors cannot necessarily fully enact strategies of both recognition and redistribution because they may have to manage incompatibilities between these facets of equality, so sociologists cannot assert or imply the absolute importance of either of these values without qualification or without undermining the coherence and practical relevance of their work. We have used the redistribution–recognition dilemma in this chapter to highlight this point, both because it is a substantively important and pervasive dilemma in the field of education and because it is a relatively straightforward example of value incompatibilities, and thus one that helps to make visible the kinds of tensions that exist everywhere but are very often hidden from view.

7

Teachers' Work

Since the 1980s the sociological study of education policy, sometimes called 'policy sociology' (Ozga 1987), has become an important sub-discipline. One of the reasons for this is the veritable explosion in the late twentieth and early twenty-first centuries in the practices of education policy development and implementation, with wave after wave of 'innovations' and 'reforms'. These policy developments are not simply about shaping the broad aims and structures of education systems but are in many cases designed to reshape the detail of educational practices at the micro-level. Rather than attempting to provide a survey of the whole of the sub-discipline, we have chosen to organize this chapter around the broad theme of changes to teachers' work and, in particular, teacher autonomy. This is a theme that is central to much recent policy sociology and is one that enables us to continue the theme introduced in chapter 6, namely the problems and possibilities of doing policy-oriented sociology of education.

The chapter is in three sections. In the first section we will review changes in the policy context of teaching and their consequences for teachers' work and autonomy, and we will consider an extended empirical case study that illustrates these things. Whilst in many respects the changed policy context of teaching represents a global phenomenon, it is important to acknowledge differences in the ways in which the new policy climate 'plays out' in different national settings, and we conclude the first section of the chapter with a discussion of some examples that illustrate this point. In the second section we will shift our attention away from the empirical dimension of sociological work on this theme and focus more closely on its conceptual and normative dimensions – in short, what are the different ideas 'bundled together' in the linked concepts of autonomy and control, and why do the policy changes and consequences discussed in the first part of the chapter matter? Having reviewed some of the empirical, conceptual and normative complexities raised in this area of policy sociology, we hope – in the final section of the chapter – to develop further our argument about the importance of, and challenges involved in, sociologists taking seriously the normative dimension of policy analysis. Whereas in the previous chapter our focus was on the implications for sociology of taking seriously the question of what ought to be done by policymakers, here we concentrate on the implications for sociology of taking the evaluation of existing policies seriously (which of course is closely bound up with questions about what ought to be done).

Education policy and the reconstruction of teachers' work

Since the 1980s, two apparently contradictory tendencies have increasingly come to dominate official policymaking in education in many countries around the world. On the one hand, there has been a growing emphasis on the role of quasi-markets in the provision of publicly funded education, centred on the discourses and practices of choice, competition and devolved decision-making. These discourses position parents and students as consumers of education, and schools, colleges and universities as relatively autonomous small businesses competing with each other for student custom – and either improving or going out of business as a consequence of their subjection to the rigours of the market. In some national settings this marketizing tendency has also included an enlarged role for the private sector in the provision of publicly funded education (e.g. see Molnar 1996, 2005; and Ball 2007).

But, on the other hand, there has, at the same time, been an increased emphasis on more direct forms of central state regulation of educational institutions and the teachers who work in them. This second tendency is manifested in the construction of new systems of accountability, inspection and performance monitoring, all of which are designed to 'steer' the actions and decisions of institutions and teachers towards targets and goals established by the state. Both marketizing and centralizing tendencies draw on languages and practices borrowed from business that relate, for example, to ideas of cost-containment, efficiency and productivity. And both tendencies have been accompanied – and to some extent sustained – by the growing influence of a range of user and social movements around welfare and education policies and practices and the rise of a culture of consumerism, which, Clarke and Newman suggest, have fed into a scepticism about 'the proposition that "professionals know best"', rendering 'both the situational and wider social authority enjoyed by professionals (even public service professionals) . . . more fragile or contingent' (Clarke and Newman 2009: 44).

A range of detailed studies conducted in different national settings have sought to map the complex and uneven transformations in teachers' identities, roles and working lives that these changes have generated, as well as their implications for conceptions of – and the possibilities for – the effective professional practice of teachers. Many of these studies point to an erosion of the scope for teachers to influence education policy and practice. They suggest that, whilst teachers had previously enjoyed relative freedom to decide on the content, methods and goals of their teaching (what Dale (1981) called a 'licensed autonomy' that, according to Ozga (1988), reached its 'zenith' in the 1960s), from the 1980s onwards their autonomy has been increasingly regulated (see, for example, Ball 1994, 2003; Mahony and Hextall 1998; Robertson 2000; Smyth et al. 2000; Gewirtz 2002). Governments have used a range of mechanisms to achieve this increased regulation, among them highly prescriptive initiatives such as the national literacy and numeracy strategies in England and mandated instructional routines in the US, which have positioned teachers as recipe-following operatives (Winch and Foreman-Peck 2005: 2) – or, as Smyth et al. have put it:

> Teachers are increasingly expected to follow directives and become compliant operatives in the headlong rush to encase schools within the ideology, practices and values of the business sector – never mind that they have histories, aspirations and professional cultures that make them decidedly different to car plants, breweries or fast-food outlets. (2000: 1)

However, it is not just via prescriptive directives – or 'input controls' – that teachers' work is being regulated. Teachers' work has also been subject to 'output controls', or what Ball (2003) calls a 'new regulative ensemble', consisting of distinct 'technologies' of 'performativity'. These are modes of state regulation that require institutions and/or their employees to render their achievements into forms amenable to public display. These displays of performance are then used by the state to draw comparisons and make judgements on the basis of which institutions and/or individuals can be rewarded or punished. Such performative technologies include individual teacher appraisals, school self-evaluations, league tables of institutional performance,

and inspections. Although these technologies are designed to scrutinize, evaluate and measure what teachers do in order to enhance
the quality of their work, as Ball and others have argued, they are
frequently experienced by teachers as having the opposite effect – of
corroding the quality both of their work and of their working lives.
Ball deploys the voices of teachers to convey something of what he
calls the 'terrors of performativity':

> What happened to my creativity? What happened to my professional
> integrity? What happened to the fun in teaching and learning? What
> happened?
> I find myself thinking that the only way I can save my sanity, my health
> and my relationship with my future husband is to leave the profession. I
> don't know what else I could do, having wanted to teach all my life, but I
> feel I am being forced out, forced to choose between a life and teaching.
> I was a primary school teacher for 22 years but left in 1996 because
> I was not prepared to sacrifice the children for the glory of politicians
> and their business plans for education.
> It's as though children are mere nuts and bolts on some distant pro-
> duction line, and it angers me to see them treated so clinically in their
> most sensitive and formative years.
> (quotes from four UK teachers, cited in Ball 2003: 216)

Ball argues that the new 'regulative ensemble' requires 'new identities, new forms of interaction and new values':

> What it means to teach and what it means to be a teacher (a researcher,
> an academic) are subtly but decisively changed in the process of
> reform. . . . New roles and subjectivities are produced as teachers are
> re-worked as producers/providers, educational entrepreneurs and man-
> agers and are subject to regular appraisal and review and performance
> comparisons. . . . The new vocabulary of performance renders old ways
> of thinking and relating dated or redundant or even obstructive. . . .
> Furthermore, new ethical systems are introduced within the new regu-
> lative ensemble, based upon institutional self-interest, pragmatics and
> performative worth. (Ibid.: 218)

An important refrain running through recent sociological analyses
of changes in teachers' work, and evident in the voices of the individuals cited by Ball, has been the impact of change on teachers' emotions
and other aspects of their wellbeing. There are seen to be substantial personal costs of the combination of prescriptive, performative
and 'fast' policies (where multiple policy initiatives are tumbled out
simultaneously in quick succession with limited time for debate).

This refrain applies to studies of teaching in higher education as well as those of schools. For example, Sikes's review of the literature on changes in academic work points to turbulence (Becher and Trowler 2001: 1), 'fragmentation . . . conflict, contestation, intensification, stress, pressure, work overload, and widespread unhappiness' (Sikes 2006: 559). She cites Beck and Young's (2005:184) depiction of higher education as characterized by 'alienation and anomie . . . crisis and loss', a site where '[c]herished identities and commitments have been undermined[, which] for some . . . has been experienced as an assault on their professionalism'.

Chicago as a case study of changing teachers' work

Using the city of Chicago as a paradigmatic case, Lipman (2009) provides a detailed illustration of Ball's arguments about the impact of recent reform on teachers' work. Using the term 'neo-liberal' as shorthand for the ideological underpinnings of the policy tendencies summarized above, Lipman argues that neo-liberal reforms and associated performative technologies are 'undermin[ing] teaching as an ethical, socially just, professional practice' and creating greater inequality and disempowerment of teachers. In the late 1990s a new regime of centralized accountability was established in Chicago, based on a system of standardized testing for students and penalties for schools identified as failing. Such schools were put on 'probation' and subject to direct oversight by the school district authorities. In 2004 this was followed by a second reform that sought to close between sixty and seventy public schools and establish over a hundred new 'schools of choice', two-thirds of which would be 'charter' or 'contract' schools – schools that are publicly funded but governed and run by private sector operators. As a consequence, in 2008, one-sixth of Chicago's schools were privately run.

Lipman conducted interviews in four elementary schools. Two of these schools – Grover and Westview – served public housing projects and had an almost exclusively African American and low-income student body, below-average test scores and high teacher turnover. A third school – Brewer – served a Mexican immigrant community and had a core of staff committed to bilingualism/biculturalism, an interest in inquiry-based teaching, and above average test scores. A fourth school – Farley – served a mixed-income community and had high test scores and a nucleus of parents in professional employment. Lipman found that the reforms were experienced very differently by teachers in the four schools. In the lower performing schools, Grover and Westview, 'teachers were increasingly monitored and the schools increasingly monitored and the schools increasingly dominated by practices and discourses of test preparation' (2009: 71). In these schools:

> Over time, practices and discourses of test preparation, including regular test practice, routinized and formulaic instruction, emphasis on discrete (tested) skills, substitution of test-prep materials for regular texts, and differential attention to students close to passing the tests pervaded the pedagogic culture. (Ibid.)

In the other schools 'there were fewer accountability pressures', although teachers were nevertheless 'fearful' about possible future encroachments on their autonomy to define what and how to teach. Teachers' responses were to some extent shaped by how experienced they were:

> While some inexperienced teachers at some schools found support in the routinized and semi-scripted curricula and instructional practices encouraged by district officials and external 'partners', more experienced and self-confident teachers found the routines simplistic and professionally demeaning. (Ibid.)

In all of the schools there was a narrowing of the curriculum in response to the new climate of high-stakes testing and an associated 'de-professionalization of teachers' knowledge':

> Brewer and Grover dropped conceptual, inquiry-based mathematics in favor of procedures to quickly solve problems on standardized tests. Accountability pressures channeled Westview teachers' holistic commitment to their students into raising test scores and began to chip away at Farley teachers' sense of professional efficacy as they debated and partly revised their rich literacy curriculum to meet the state's routinized writing template and emphasis on discrete skills. At Brewer, under the pressure of high stakes tests in English, Latino/a teachers with a deep commitment to bilingualism and biliteracy began to de-emphasize instruction in Spanish, and accountability derailed the school-wide inquiry process. At Westview, teachers were compelled to put away literature texts and projects and focus on test preparation using booklets furnished by the test maker. (Ibid.: 71–2)

Lipman also describes the development in the Chicago school system of a culture of 'naming and shaming' associated with the increased performative emphasis on measurement and comparison:

> The separation of 'good' and 'bad' schools that is accomplished through testing, sorting, and ordering processes of standardized tests, distribution of stanine scores, retention of students and determination of probation lists, constructs categories of functionality and disfunctionality, normalcy and deviance that label students, neighborhoods and teachers. 'Deficiency' is made visible, individual, easily measured, highly stigmatized and punishable. Test scores are published in the newspaper, and teachers described the public shaming that accompanied the derision directed at teachers in schools on probation. One said, 'people don't want to shake your hand when they find out you teach at [Grover]' . . . In two of the schools, test scores were posted on teachers' doors, and they were publicly rewarded or castigated accordingly. (2009: 72–3)

The threat of sanctions also acted to stifle debate, particularly around the politically controversial issues of culture and race. For example:

> At Farley, African American parents initiated an inquiry into the disproportionate disciplining and lower achievement of African American and male students. However, concerns by administrators and some teachers that any public controversy would draw attention from the district strengthened tendencies to depoliticize these issues, ultimately deflecting responsibility onto the students. The result was a plan to remediate individual students rather than examine school-wide practices and ideologies. (Ibid.: 73)

Lipman found that teacher autonomy was most constrained in the schools serving predominantly black and low-income communities, as these schools 'were the ones on probation and thus least in charge of their own destiny'. In contrast, those schools serving better-off neighbourhoods were more likely to be rewarded through being designated as 'Autonomous Management Performance Schools' (AMPS) – a designation that carried with it relative freedom from district control:

> Although there are exceptions, AMPS reproduced sedimented race and class advantages and privileged status. For example, in March 2007, Chicago Public Schools announced 18 additional AMPS schools, bringing the total to 108 out of 165 schools. Although the school district is 92 per cent students of colour and 85 per cent low-income, of the 18 new AMPS schools, eight are almost or more than 50 per cent white, all but three are less than 63 per cent low income and seven less than 25 per cent low income, and 11 are selective enrolment schools. (2009: 73–4)

Like Ball, Lipman concludes there has been an 'ethical retooling' (Ball 2003) of the public sector, changing what it means to be a 'good' teacher. In the new 'regulative ensemble', being a good teacher means achieving good test scores rather than, for example, developing curricula that valorize children's home languages and cultures or that seek to develop culturally relevant pedagogies, a rich culture of literacy and the skills of critique. At the same time, Lipman argues, paradoxically, the market opens up spaces that can be used by projects geared towards the promotion of social justice which stand in opposition to neo-liberal corporate rationality and offer examples of alternative educational ideals. For example, although charter schools have their roots in neo-liberal ideology and were introduced as a means of marketizing and privatizing the public school system, 'some educators and communities of colour are taking advantage of the greater flexibility offered by charter schools to develop culturally relevant, community-centred education, in the tradition of Black Independent Schools'. So, although the charter school policy has created a cadre of teachers who are non-unionized, not always certified, insecure and often forced to work long hours in poor conditions,

> because charter schools have greater autonomy from state regulations and local district guidelines, the educational vision, flexibility, and professional authority offered by some charter schools can be appealing even if it means lower pay, less security, or a greater time commitment. (Lipman 2009: 76)

Hence, paradoxically, as the scope for creativity and 'ethical professional' practice in Chicago's public schools is narrowed, so working in the charter school sector becomes more attractive for 'dedicated, socially committed teachers'. Lipman gives the example of one charter high school which serves a low-income African American community that has been very successful both in conventional terms, as measured by graduation and college matriculation, and in terms of a progressive curriculum which 'begins with identity and difference in historical context ("Origins") moves on to "Revolution and Resistance" in the US and globally, US foreign policy (including an examination of "white man's burden" and "imperialism"), and ends with local government and political action' (2009: 77). The teachers working in these schools are caught between their ethical commitment to public education (and distributive justice), on the one hand, and their commitment to the principles of critical multiculturalism (and recognitional justice), on the other (see chapter 6):

They know charter schools are part of the neo-liberal restructuring of public education which undermines the public interest and produces educational inequities. They feel complicit in this process yet guard the freedom to engage in teaching that they believe in, teaching that nurtures critical consciousness, cultural identity and political agency and a context that provides ideological support and collaboration of like-minded colleagues. As one teacher put it, 'I know charter schools are bad for public education, but I could never teach like this in a CPS (Chicago Public) school'. (Ibid.)

By looking across several schools in one locality which are ostensibly subject to the same regulative ensemble, Lipman is able to point to some general effects of that ensemble – in this case, a narrowing of the curriculum, increasing class- and race-based inequalities, and decreasing opportunities for teachers to pursue social justice goals in their teaching. But her analysis, like others of this type, also highlights differences in the responses of teachers – differences that relate, for example, to the social class and racialized composition of the schools in which they are working, to the positioning of the schools in the local education market, and to how experienced the teachers are.

Analogous complexities are evident when the nation-state is taken as the unit of analysis, and it is to the national level that we now want to turn. In doing so, we will for the moment be ignoring the more finely textured local differences of the kind illuminated by Lipman's analysis in order to allow us to focus on some of the different kinds of complexities revealed by cross-national comparison.

Acknowledging national diversity

Although it is undoubtedly the case that the recent 'tectonic shift' (Robertson 2008) in education policy discourse – with its apparently contradictory components of regulation and standardization, on the one hand, and devolution, diversity and individualism, on the other – is effectively a global phenomenon, the new policy climate has taken on different inflections in different national settings (Maguire 2009). For example, although the trends might be similar, teachers working in the 'developing' economies of South America or Africa are obviously faced with very different kinds of demands and challenges from those working in Australia, New Zealand, Europe or the US (Day and Sachs 2004), and the scope for teachers to influence policy and shape their own practice also varies from region to region and from country to country. As Lipman has put it: 'global neo-liberal restructuring is "path-dependent" – taking different forms in different contexts shaped by specific histories, ideologies, and relations of social forces' (2009: 68).

This point can be illustrated by considering the relatively circum- scribed field of European national systems. For example, Jones's comparative study of the 'remaking of education in Europe' has drawn attention to stark differences in the capacity for trade unions and other social movements to influence policy. Jones distinguishes between 'societies – France, Italy – where [counter-hegemonic social or ideological] blocs exist in a form strong enough still to present major obstacles to neo-liberal policy, and other societies – Spain, Germany, England – in which . . . such blocs have been weaker or have been dispersed' (Jones 2005: 231; see also Stevenson 2007; Weis and Compton 2007). Thus, for example, whilst in England the privatization of educational services 'is already a set of accom- plished facts', in France 'privatisation is in most aspects only an imagined future'. The explanation for the 'French "exception" to the neo-liberal rule', according to Jones,

> lies in the fact that [in France] schooling has always been deeply inscribed in the political space of the republic . . . Public services [in France] are not only a technical mode of delivering goods to citizens, but a bond of social solidarity . . . Thus the policies of expansion and equalising opportunity pursued by educational reform in the 1970s and 1980s were underwritten by an ideology of political citizenship that greatly augmented their political force and social implantation . . . [T]he bloc of forces allied around an idea of the republican school has at the political level proved resilient enough to remain an obstacle to neo-liberal projects. The school of the republic has not (yet) been subjected to a comprehensive programme of change. (Jones 2005: 234)

England's historic trajectory is very different. It is characterized, in particular, Jones (2009) argues, by a longstanding and persistent neo-conservative anti-egalitarianism; a 'New' Labour party intent on shedding its 'Old' Labour, anti-'developmental' image; and a teacher trade union movement that has, since the 1980s (and unlike its Scottish counterpart), pursued a narrowly economistic strategy centred on teachers' pay at the cost of winning wider public support for an alternative vision of education based on ideas of equality and the nurturing of the 'democratic intellect' (McPherson and Raab 1988). All of this, according to Jones, helps to explain why the contemporary international policy orthodoxy that seeks to 'modernize' the teaching profession via discourses of efficiency and effectiveness, processes of marketization and central regulation, and a marginalization of teacher unionism has been so successful in England, and why it is that in England 'the most comprehensive programme of reform in Western Europe has been greeted with the most pliant response' (Jones 2009: 63).

Even within the apparently very similar Nordic countries there is considerable diversity in the ways in which governments have approached the restructuring of their education systems (Hudson 2007), with diverse implications for teachers' professional and personal identities and autonomy. For instance, in Norway the day-to-day working lives of teachers are tightly regulated by a prescriptive national curriculum, whilst in Sweden much 'softer' forms of central regulation of their work are achieved via a 'goal-oriented' national curriculum. As a consequence, the *individual* autonomy that teachers have over their work is arguably much weaker in Norway than in Sweden, where teachers are expected 'individually [to] interpret education aims, develop local syllabuses and decide on which methods are to be used' (Helgøy and Homme 2007: 244). In Norway, individual teacher autonomy is far more limited by a detailed mandatory curriculum, which includes the specification of teaching methods and a policy of enforced collaboration between teachers. Yet, according to Helgøy and Homme (ibid.), who interviewed seventy teachers and headteachers in two Swedish and two Norwegian cities, Norwegian teachers have 'a relatively strong *collective* professional identity', whilst Swedish teachers 'rely on a more personalized type of professionalism emphasizing teachers' knowledge, competence and performance as individual properties' (Helgøy et al. 2007: 200).

In Norway, Helgøy and Homme found, teachers opposed the new 'transparency policies' which involved increased standardization, monitoring and management of their work. They interpreted these 'as a breach of trust and as degrading their professional status' (2007: 245), and they collectively expressed their dissatisfaction by, for example, informally supporting a student boycott of national tests and vetoing the introduction of inspections and performance-related pay. The Swedish teachers, in contrast, 'rarely shared a common voice about teacher professional issues' (ibid.: 245) and did not oppose the introduction of individual teacher pay. Moreover, the Swedish teachers tended to experience national testing as a positive means of getting feedback on the quality of their individual teaching rather than as a threat to their classroom autonomy.

Autonomy-control: conceptual and normative complexities

Although we have not done justice to the full range and richness of the considerable literature on the restructuring of teachers' work, it is clear from the examples that we have considered that there is no single or simple story to tell here, and that something of the contestability and ambivalence that we have noted is characteristic of sociology is evident. For instance, it seems that neo-liberal reforms do not everywhere and at all levels necessarily lead to reductions in autonomy but can in some senses and in some instances be read as enhancing autonomy. Clearly, the work we have reviewed in the previous section, as with other work we have reviewed in this book, cannot be seen as purely descriptive, in that much of it has value judgements built into it and involves an element of more or less explicit critique – in many cases based on the reading that something valuable about teacher professionalism and collective and individual teacher autonomy has been eroded or is at risk. Neither does this work seem to be just academic in the sense of detached 'ivory tower' observations. It is work focused on the very real effects of contemporary policy change and, on the face of it, has practical relevance for anyone who wishes to deliberate about what kinds of policies should or should not be pursued with regard to teachers' work.

In what follows, we will argue that this kind of 'practical relevance' can be enhanced if the normative judgements embodied in sociology are taken seriously and carefully scrutinized, and, in doing so, we will further develop our argument that taking normative judgements seriously has the potential to strengthen sociology. Taking normative judgements seriously here, in short, means getting clear about what things are deemed to be bad or wrong and why this is the case. It is only to the extent that policy sociologists make these things clear that we can extract any action-guiding potential from their work. Indeed, it is the normative dimension of this work that in our view makes it important and interesting and which gives it practical relevance. As we hope is clear from the publications we have looked at, many authors do take this normative task seriously and go to some trouble to spell out why the phenomena they study trouble them. Nonetheless, there is a danger that the normative dimension is not always well attended to, and we would suggest that, to the extent that it is neglected, policy sociology is diminished in its descriptive, critical and constructive power.

In this instance, what we are saying is that the quality and relevance of sociological critiques of policies that impact on teacher

autonomy depend in part on policy sociologists being prepared to
ask questions about why teacher autonomy matters. This obviously
involves being clear about what kind or conception of autonomy is
under consideration. In this section of this chapter, therefore, we
want to unpack some of the conceptual complexities and normative
arguments surrounding questions of autonomy, before returning to
our argument about their implications for doing policy-oriented sociology. In some ways, this section might be seen as an excursion from
the main business of sociology of education, and this reading might
be reinforced by noting the shift in genre between the more strictly
sociological flavour of the first section of the chapter and the tone
of this section. However, we think it is important not to exaggerate
the distinction between the concerns underlying the policy sociology work we have just reviewed and those underlying the following
discussion of conceptual and normative complexity. Indeed, as we
have tried to indicate in earlier chapters, sociology of education can
make, and has made, a substantial contribution to illuminating the
norms and categories through which we make sense of educational
and social worlds.

Conceptualizing autonomy-control

The linked concepts of autonomy and control refer to very broad
– indeed loose – categories, and in mentioning either autonomy or
control people can be talking about a very wide range of different
things. In order to unpack and debate these issues in more depth,
it is helpful to distinguish between three dimensions of autonomy-
control: loci and modes of autonomy, domains of autonomy-control
and loci and modes of control.

Loci and modes of autonomy   This first dimension relates to whose
autonomy is in question and how it is being exercised. To talk about
autonomy presupposes the existence of agents, but obviously these
do not exist as an undifferentiated mass. There is a range of individual, collective and institutional agents to consider in the educational arena. Examples of individual agents are individual parents,
students and teachers (themselves differentiated, of course, by their
location in relation to axes of social differentiation relating to race,
class and gender, etc.). Collective agents include teachers acting in
teams within schools or politically – for example, through trade union
activity or lobbying at a national policy level – and parent or student
associations. And institutional agents include central government

agencies, local authorities, professional bodies and schools. It is important to spell out these distinctions because it is often the case that increasing one agent's autonomy decreases that of another. Indeed, social and political life is characterized by constant shifts in, and negotiations and conflicts around, the degrees of autonomy that are attached to different agents. Hence, if we want to evaluate the effects on autonomy of new modes of regulation consequent upon policy change, we need to consider a range of agents and be sensitive to the differential impact of policies on different agents, including the way in which one agent's autonomy can foster or inhibit the autonomy of other agents. We also need to be sensitive to the different ways in which agents can exercise their autonomy. An individual agent can exercise their autonomy as an individual, as part of a collectivity, or on behalf of an institution, and greater autonomy with respect to one of these dimensions can result in a reduction of autonomy in relation to another. For example, the Norwegian policy of enforcing teacher collaboration was introduced precisely in order to encourage a move away from that country's traditional emphasis on individual teachers acting autonomously within their individual classrooms.

Domains of autonomy-control   This second dimension relates to the spheres over which autonomy or control is being exercised. Whilst the first dimension relates to the question *'whose autonomy?'*, this dimension relates to the question *'autonomy/control over what?'* A classic way of conceptualizing different domains of autonomy-control relates to the relative freedom classroom teachers have to make decisions about curriculum, pedagogy and assessment, respectively. It is quite possible for one or two of these domains to be highly prescribed whilst, in relation to the other one or two domains, relative freedom is allowed for teachers to exercise their autonomy (although there are of course important interconnections between these three domains – see below). But there are countless other ways in which this notion of domains of autonomy-control has relevance. For example, in many countries quite a high priority has been attached to policies that encourage parental autonomy with respect to choice of school, but there is little priority attached to the idea that parental autonomy is important in relation to decisions about school selection policies, where states, local authorities or schools themselves have tended to retain control. This example, however, may be misleading because it refers to two domains of action (choice of school and school selection policies) which are relatively well insulated from one another. In other cases it is difficult to insulate domains in this way. For example, as is well known, because to some degree curriculum and pedagogy are constructed with the demands of assessment in mind, those agents who play a determining role in constructing models of assessment are necessarily influential in shaping the curriculum and pedagogy. Thus, as well as distinguishing conceptually between domains of autonomy, we need to be aware of how they interconnect and of the extent to which they are either insulated from one another or mutually constitutive.

Loci and modes of control   This final dimension relates to the questions *'who are the agents of control?'* and *'how is their agency exercised?'* The different kinds of individual, collective and institutional agents identified above, as well as being subject to control, have the potential to exercise control. Sometimes it is not clear where the locus of control lies. For example, control is not always exercised self-consciously and deliberately by specific agents. It can also be the product of apparently impersonal processes (e.g. markets, consumer cultures). But, insofar as we are interested in 'control' as opposed to 'constraint', then we are likely to be focusing on who lies or could lie behind these processes. As the example of markets indicates, control is also exercised in very different ways using different forms and mechanisms of influence. For example, as noted above, contemporary governments are employing a combination of 'input' controls (e.g. targeting of resources on specific initiatives) and 'output' controls (e.g. performance measurement). It is also possible to distinguish between different styles of control – for example, how far the forms of influence that 'control agents' use are bluntly coercive as opposed to gently persuasive. Some of these distinctions about different forms of influence are well illustrated by Hudson's analysis of different kinds and degrees of prescription and guidance that exist in relation to curriculum, pedagogy and inspection in different national systems. These can be more or less rigid, direct, closed or crude. For example, Hudson contrasts the 'in-your-eye' direct control style of the English inspection system with 'the much more subtle, indirect control' that characterizes the Finnish system (2007: 271).

These three dimensions, of loci and modes of autonomy, domains of autonomy-control and loci and modes of control, each complex in its own right, when put together, provide a highly complex multi-celled matrix, and the ways in which we understand or evaluate changing patterns of autonomy-control will depend crucially on which configuration of cells we are looking at. We will discuss this complexity further later in the chapter.

In order to appraise or critique policies, it is clearly important to grapple with the conceptual complexities that we have just outlined, but, in addition, as we have already argued, it is also necessary to get to grips with normative complexity. In brief, the reason for this is that, if we want to state or imply that some aspect of policy change is a good or a bad thing – e.g. if we want to suggest that performativity is inherently a 'terror' or that it is a bad thing that teachers are treated as 'recipe followers' – we can only do so from within a conception of what things matter and why these things matter.

Some normative arguments around autonomy-control

Here we will briefly set out some normative arguments about autonomy-control that help to illustrate why changes to models of teacher professionalism and, in particular, to forms of teacher autonomy matter to people. Because these arguments are purely illustrative, we will confine our discussion to one locus of teacher autonomy, namely individual teacher autonomy. We will begin by setting out some of the arguments for individual autonomy before going on to set out some of the arguments for limiting it.

The value of autonomy for individual teachers   Autonomy is important in teaching in large part because of the nature of teachers' professional expertise. In addition to subject knowledge, good teaching requires a combination of technical knowledge and practical wisdom. That is, as well as being concerned with how to teach effectively, teachers need to be able to make judgements about the kinds of attributes, dispositions and values they want to inculcate in their students and the kinds of formal and informal curricula, pedagogies and forms of assessment that are worthwhile. This judgement-making process cannot be a once-and-for-all event because, as with technical knowledge, practical wisdom involves being responsive to changing circumstances and the specificities of the unique situations teachers encounter on a day-to-day basis. In short, teachers have to make technical *and* normative judgements – for example, will this approach work in this particular classroom *and* is the approach desirable and acceptable? In relation to the latter, teachers need to reflect on their educational ideals – i.e. their 'ideas about what is educationally worthwhile . . . about what it means to be an educated person[, and their] ideas about the good society and the good life' (Biesta 2009: 186). And, because teaching is not a narrowly technicist job, teachers often resent policies which try to specify what they should be doing and how (ibid.: 184).

For individual teachers, freedom to decide what to teach and how to teach it, and freedom to play an active part in making decisions about the conditions in which they teach, can also be seen as a vital source of job satisfaction and physical and mental wellbeing. There is indeed a growing research literature which suggests that the curtailment of teacher autonomy associated with new forms of accountability has resulted in an increase in stress and a decline in morale (see, for example, Troman 2000; Smyth et al. 2000; Gleeson and Husbands 2001; Lambert and McCarthy 2006; Valli and Buese 2007).

Autonomy can also be defended on the grounds that it is a condition for creativity, experimentation and variety. For example, some of the teachers in the work reported in Ball (2003) and Lipman (2009) are clearly grieving for the loss of opportunities to exercise creativity and imagination in their classrooms. A system that encourages variety of provision is to be preferred not simply because of the freedom of manoeuvre it gives teachers to deploy their full personal resources in all of their idiosyncrasy, but arguably also because the innovation and experimentation that is fostered through these means can open up new conceptions of good practice and generate ways for teachers to learn from one another, and in so doing extend their conception of teaching for the benefit of students.

Finally, teacher autonomy can be defended as a source of effectiveness. If autonomy makes teachers happier in their jobs and enables them to exercise their creativity, then creative individuals are more likely to see teaching as an attractive profession, and this, in turn, is good for recruitment and retention of talented teachers (e.g. see Smethem 2007). Also autonomy arguably promotes the qualities of adaptability, flexibility and responsiveness that we mentioned above in relation to the nature of teachers' expertise. That is to say, autonomy enables teachers to make context- and person-sensitive judgements and thereby to target resources, including their own attention, where they are most likely to be needed and to result in the greatest benefit. However, it is also possible to produce powerful arguments for limiting individual teacher autonomy, and it is to some of these that we now turn.

The value of limiting individual teacher autonomy   Perhaps the least contentious argument for curtailing the autonomy of teachers concerns the prevention of harm. Although the boundaries of acceptable behaviour are contestable, it is clear that there are limits to what teachers should be able to do. For example, it is hard to argue against the proposition that teachers should not be allowed to abuse, bully or wilfully neglect their students. Analogous considerations apply to the design of pedagogy, curriculum and assessment: that is, ideas or educational processes can in themselves be seen as sources of harm – for example, those that encourage sexist or heterosexist dispositions. In circumstances where there is a risk of more or less serious harm, most people would agree that the state has a responsibility at least to draw some limits which are designed to prohibit harmful practices.

Another major argument for limiting teacher autonomy, at least for those who are committed to social justice in education, is the need for the state to underpin equal access to a decent standard of educational provision, which would seem to necessitate a degree of state regulation. For example, the introduction of new academic standards-related accountability mechanisms across Europe has been supported not only for economic reasons but also on the grounds that provision should be 'fair for all and fully consistent' (Eurydice 2004: 2). As one of the Swedish teachers interviewed by Helgøy and Homme (2007: 241) put it, '[w]e need some kind of conformity in education and between schools, a standard everybody has to reach'. More generally, the Swedish teachers in Helgøy and Homme's sample expressed hostility towards moves to devolve responsibility for education to the municipalities precisely because they viewed central state control as necessary to enable common national standards. This argument echoes those made in defence of bureaucracy by those inspired by a Weberian perspective about the importance of bureaucratic forms of organization in underpinning both fairness and social order (e.g. Du Gay 2000).

It is also important to recognize and rehearse counter-arguments to those that link autonomy to personal wellbeing. Arguably, official institutional rules, guidance and norms play a very important role in framing and supporting the decisions that teachers have to make. The alternative is to imagine that, in having to respond to each contingency of day-to-day practice, every teacher would prefer to have to think through all of the possible ramifications of different policies for themselves and make a decision as if they were writing on a completely blank slate. Likewise, there are arguably limits to how fair or realistic it is to ask teachers to be continuously innovative and imaginative in the way they do their jobs. Innovation and imagination are highly demanding of time and energy, so, if constant imagination is to be a standard expectation, there is a danger of policies being punitive unless such calls are accompanied by massive reductions in very high workload pressures. Whilst, as we have already suggested, imagination and inspiration are important in good teaching, it is also essential to acknowledge that there are costs associated with them.

Finally, teacher autonomy can be limited on the grounds of promoting commonality and cohesion. This kind of argument lies behind the introduction of national curricula, which are defended on the basis of a commitment not just to equal access to education but also to access, at least in large measure, to a common educational experience (e.g. see Lawton 1975; Holt 1978). Similar arguments often lie behind the advocacy of the principles of comprehensive schooling (perhaps most famously exemplified by Dewey ([1916] 1966), but see also Halstead and Haydon (2007) for a more recent treatment of these arguments). If we accept that commonality and cohesion are desirable educational principles, then it follows that the parameters of teacher autonomy will need to be drawn in such as way as to protect these principles.

To repeat, the arguments that we have rehearsed for extending individual teacher autonomy and those for limiting it should be seen as merely indicative. There is, of course, a range of other possible arguments that could be explored for and against different kinds of autonomy. Before moving on to consider the implications of this normative complexity for policy analysis, we should also note that our review of arguments about individual teacher autonomy is not merely limited but is arguably somewhat artificial. This is because, as we indicated earlier, individual teachers frequently exercise their agency as part of some collective – for example, as a member of department, a school, a subject association or a trade union. Individual teachers are often not free to act on their own autonomously to make a difference to the things they think are worthwhile. Some of the examples we have considered, such as a concern about equal access or social cohesion, obviously require concerted and collective professional and political action. This means, amongst other things, that analyses of teacher autonomy must encompass the ways in which teachers' choices are constrained not only by state regulation but also by the values and actions of other teachers.

We hope that setting out some contrasts between these arguments begins to illustrate what is wrong with any blanket implication that teacher autonomy is a good thing and that limiting it is bad. Whilst there are good arguments for extending teacher autonomy, there are, as we have seen, also some very strong arguments for limiting it. The same arguments can be advanced for limiting or extending state control. Moreover, there are different modes and styles of state control, some of which are more productive and/or less harmful than others. Thus, in attempting to assess the value of a particular form of autonomy-control, we need to pay attention to its specific loci, modes and consequences in specific domains.

Addressing conceptual and normative complexity sociologically

The arguments for and against individual teacher autonomy that we have just rehearsed in predominantly abstract terms can only be fully appraised in conjunction with sociological accounts of what the various values mentioned can and do amount to in real social settings. Without the kind of detailed and dense readings of particular settings provided by sociology, it is difficult to know precisely what is meant by, or why we should really value, such things as 'teacher creativity' or 'experimentation', on the one hand, and 'equal access' or 'commonality', on the other. For instance, Lipman's case study of Chicago illuminates both the kinds of things that can be gained by providing the conditions needed for teacher creativity to flourish – e.g. innovative curriculum developments that attempt to realize the principles of critical multiculturalism – and some of the ways in which educational cultures can be damaged when equal access is undermined in a climate of 'naming and shaming'.

Sociology also makes an important contribution to understanding the meaning(s) of autonomy and, in particular, the inseparability of the closely related ideas of autonomy and control. Our account of sociological work on teacher autonomy in the first part of this chapter has illustrated that the relationship between autonomy and control is by no means a simple one and in particular should not be read in a zero-sum fashion – that is, as if increases in control are necessarily inversely proportionate to decreases in autonomy, or vice versa. There are also a variety of ways in which autonomy and control overlap, and, if anything, the conceptual interrelatedness of autonomy and control has been made particularly salient by new modes of regulation where control is exercised precisely through the uses of autonomy at various levels. Indeed, as we have seen, moves to fragment and decentralize authority have been accompanied by an increase in central government steering, leading some commentators to argue that devolved systems of governance actually require an intensification of central government control or, alternatively, that devolution in itself represents a central steering mechanism (Majone 1996; Bache 2003). For example, Hudson (2007: 276) suggests that moves towards more self-evaluation by schools, evident across the Nordic countries and in Britain, can be understood as 'a smart move on the part of the state as it effectively gets schools to regulate themselves in the way it wants'. Here Hudson is talking about the 'self-regulation' of schools, but one could equally talk about the self-regulation of individual teachers – i.e. teachers' subjectivity and agency being colonized by the imperatives and priorities of national and local policies such that there is no clear distinction between teachers 'being controlled' and their 'being autonomous'.

Yet sociological work in this area shows that, just as autonomy can be harnessed as a form of control or steering, so control can enable the exercise of autonomy. For example, as we indicated when discussing the costs of personal autonomy, there is a real sense in which rules and procedures can be facilitative. Indeed, by enabling teachers to process certain decisions efficiently and confidently, bureaucratic rules and procedures can even be seen, in some instances, as positively empowering. Behind this idea is a basic philosophical insight, namely that autonomy cannot exist in a vacuum but is always exercised within systems of constraints and conventions which, at one and the same time, both circumscribe action and make it possible. This interplay between control and autonomy is an inevitable and pervasive phenomenon – and parallels the oft-quoted Foucauldian notion of power as neither simply bad nor good, neither destructive nor productive:

> What makes power hold good, what makes it accepted is simply the fact that it doesn't only weigh on us as a force that says no but that it traverses and produces things, it induces pleasure, forms of knowledge, produces discourse. It needs to be considered a productive network which runs through the whole social body, much more than as a negative instance whose function is repression. (Foucault 1980: 119)

It is this productive property of control that has enabled proponents and defenders of the UK education reforms to present many of these reforms as empowering. The research assessment exercise (RAE) in HE will serve as an example. Whilst often interpreted as a coercive mechanism to require all academics to become research active, it can and has also been interpreted by some as liberatory. For example, Sikes (2006) has shown how, in the new university she studied, the RAE provided recognition and a legitimacy and stimulus for some academics to engage in research when previously this had not been encouraged.

The contribution that sociology makes to addressing normative and conceptual complexity is important for two reasons. First, as we will discuss at greater length in the next chapter, it is an important plank of rigour. Second, it adds to the potential practical relevance and usefulness of the discipline. It contributes to rigour because it is impossible to make careful normative judgements and differentiations without paying very close attention to the characteristics of the phenomena one is studying, and it is very difficult to make one's normative judgements plausible and broadly defensible without providing rich and detailed descriptive accounts of the different ways in which things matter, and why and for whom they matter. In other words, paying attention to normative judgements forces us to produce more precise, and thicker, descriptions. And, in turn, better descriptions provide the basis for more robust and contextually sensitive normative judgements. Of course, this way of making our point relies on the assumption that descriptions and normative judgements can be separated out. In practice, as we have noted before, this separation is often not possible because many of the social phenomena that sociologists are interested in describing are of interest precisely because of the value judgements built into the way we characterize them – e.g. professional autonomy, creativity and inclusion. However, to the extent that we accept that descriptions and normative judgements are inextricably intertwined, this only strengthens the point we are making – i.e. it becomes simply impossible to do thorough descriptive work without doing thorough normative work at the same time.

It is for broadly the same reasons that we are arguing that paying attention to normative as well as conceptual complexity enhances the potential 'use value' of sociology. To start with a simply analogy, we would not want to make use of a map that we thought was inherently unreliable. It is only to the extent that we judge a map to be an accurate and carefully drawn representation of some domain that we would accord it any action-guiding role. It should, therefore, be obvious that anyone who is interested in the practical relevance of work in the sociology of education should place a high premium on rigour and, therefore, as we have said, on addressing the kinds of conceptual and normative complexities inherent in producing credible accounts of the nature of the social world. For this reason, we would maintain that an interest in the policy relevance of sociology can provide a valuable spur to producing good quality sociological work. At the same time, however, it is important to recognize the different kinds of policy relevance that sociologists might pursue.

As we have seen, policy sociology frequently centres on the appraisal of real-world policies, researching and analysing their strengths and weaknesses and their effects on different social constituencies. This kind of work can play an important civic role in contributing to debates about the direction of education policies and in providing rich analytic resources for those who participate in such debates. Although they are closely allied, this interest in policy appraisal should nevertheless be distinguished from a direct interest in constructing policies or making policy recommendations, an interest to which some sociologists might also aspire. Whilst accepting that such policy evaluation can play a political role and can be used, for example, by those who wish to criticize governments and/or frame policy alternatives, policy evaluation itself still sits squarely in the academic domain. If and when sociologists seek to make specific policy recommendations on the basis of their work, they are arguably entering into significantly different territory, shifting from a primary orientation towards understanding what is happening to one towards influencing what is happening. Our own view is that this is not necessarily an illegitimate thing for sociologists to do, but we think it is important to signal that this possibly represents an extension of the role of sociology that some would see as illegitimate and one that is fraught with problems. (Again we will come back to this in the next chapter.) However, even if sociologists confine their attention to policy evaluation, there are significant challenges to overcome, to which we will now turn.

The challenges of policy evaluation

There is no doubt that the work we have reviewed in the first part of this chapter provides a powerful resource for anyone who wishes to evaluate the consequences of neo-liberal reform for teacher autonomy and the other 'goods' to which we have referred. But this leaves open the question about the extent to which sociologists can themselves provide evaluations of policy change. Indeed, the very power of sociology in illuminating both the complexity and the contestability of the issues that we have rehearsed might lead some people to conclude that sociologists should be extremely cautious before offering substantive and definitive-sounding evaluations of policies.

Those who are interested in systematically evaluating the consequences of new forms of regulation within specific settings face a daunting set of considerations. First of all, they need to examine the empirical effects of regulations in each cell of the matrix that we introduced in our discussion of conceptual complexities – i.e. what effects do different combinations of forms and styles of regulation have on the autonomy of different individual, institutional and collective agents, in relation to each of the different relevant domains? Doing this work just for one national setting is obviously complicated enough, but if we want to do comparative analysis the task is even more complex. This would involve looking at the similarities and differences in the effects of more or less similar forms of regulation in each of the cells. For example, as we have seen, the answer to the question of whether teacher autonomy has been more diminished by new forms of regulation in Norway or in Sweden cannot be answered in general terms but requires a differentiated analysis looking at the different cells in the matrix (with Swedish teachers experiencing stronger individual classroom autonomy and weaker collective autonomy with regard to policymaking than their Norwegian counterparts) (Helgøy and Homme 2007).

However, if we want to normatively evaluate the overall effects of policies in a systematic way and try to draw conclusions about whether on balance they are a good thing or a bad thing, or whether they are to be valued more in one national setting than another, the task becomes even more difficult, as at this point we need to grapple with the conceptual, empirical and normative complexities simultaneously: i.e. we need, in summary, (a) to include each cell of the matrix in the analysis, (b) to find out what is empirically going on in each cell, e.g. in what ways autonomy is being extended or limited, (c) to consider the respective value of the limits to autonomy that are evident in that particular cell and the value of the autonomy that is evident within it, and (d) to look across all the cells, trying to consider and weigh the value of all the different kinds of autonomy and limits to autonomy that are occurring across the matrix (in other words, to consider system-wide *patterns* of autonomy-control). This mapping of the methodological elements and difficulties of this kind could be extended and refined indefinitely, but even this relatively crude four-element map is enough to indicate the scale of the challenge.

We should stress that we are not imagining some kind of technical method here – perhaps involving some algorithm that aggregates a series of evaluative 'cost–benefit' analyses. We do not imagine that is possible to 'measure' the normative acceptability of patterns of autonomy-control. On the contrary, we take the view that these judgements are fundamentally non-technical because they are inherently practical, political and contested, and we will say more about that in a moment. Rather we are interested in opening up, and drawing attention to, the range of relevant considerations and in thereby resisting the temptation to make these judgements on unexamined normative assumptions or on very partial evidence. It is perhaps worth briefly summarizing and stressing four of the reasons why we take it that the making of comparative evaluative judgements about patterns of autonomy-control is an inherently inexact and contested business. First, and most obviously, these evaluations draw upon ethical and political value judgements which are, almost by definition, contentious. Second, they will involve 'swings and round-abouts' – i.e. they will involve judging trade-offs between different kinds of 'gains' and 'losses' (e.g. less individual versus more collec-tive autonomy for teachers) where there are plausible, but different, grounds for favouring both the competing patterns. Third, they will, to some extent, be context-sensitive – i.e. they will reflect the socio-economic and cultural histories and circumstances of particular systems. Hence, a pattern of autonomy-control that suits one system well may be seen as much less 'fitting' for another system. Fourth – and this might be viewed as a very specific example of context-sensitivity – there is no reason to suppose that patterns of autonomy-control are 'stable objects' that can be definitively identified by policy analysts or made to last by policymakers. It seems more plausible to see such patterns as, at best, in unstable equilibrium and embodying constantly evolving tensions and corrections. On this model, the job of policymakers is continuously to manage and 'correct for' what come to be seen as imbalances in autonomy-control, and the job of policy analysts is to make sense of these processes of adaptation and to produce analyses which capture this 'path dependency'. Hence, on this model, normative judgements about new forms of regulation need to reflect the very specific adaptations in play within the policy dynamics of particular systems.

Conclusion

The arguments we have rehearsed in this chapter, we suggest, mean that it makes sense for sociologists to be cautious about intervening directly in policy processes, especially if their interventions involve straightforward approvals, disapprovals or recommendations for alternatives. Although, in some cases, straightforward evaluations may be justifiable, many real-world education policies do not fall into this category, and therefore it makes sense for sociologists to appraise policies in ways which are cautiously expressed, nuanced and carefully qualified. Indeed, it is possible to argue that sociologists of education – in their role as sociologists – should deliberately resist the temptation to intervene in the policy process in order to signal clearly the limits of their province and expertise. This stance involves an unambiguous division of labour between sociologists and practical actors, with the former confined to the business of justifying claims about the nature of the social world and the latter having sole responsibility for questions about what ought to be done. We will return to this argument in the next chapter, but what we have tried to show in this part of the book is that, even were we to accept an absolute division of labour of this kind, it does not follow that sociologists should not be closely engaged with practical contexts and the specific dilemmas facing policymakers and practitioners in specific historical settings or with the evaluation of policies. On the contrary, we would argue, there is everything to be gained from such engagement, because it 'concentrates the mind' of the sociologist on the extent of the empirical, conceptual and normative complexity that has to be addressed to understand educational settings and in this way contributes to the depth, sensitivity and rigour of analyses in sociology of education.

It seems that sociology of education has to steer a course between disciplinary purity and practical relevance, and that it may not be possible to have both of these things. The remarks we have just been making highlight the great difficulties, and therefore the dangers, of sociologists taking a close interest in practical judgements about what ought to happen. But, to conclude the chapter, we would like also to draw attention to the opposite danger – that is, the danger of sociologists disregarding specific questions about what ought to be done. In this latter case the danger is that those working in sociology of education will soon find themselves 'floating above' the phenomena they are purportedly dealing with and losing a feel for what these phenomena are and why they matter 'on the ground'.

PART III

Conclusion

8
Extending Reflexivity in Sociology of Education

This book has been organized around two main strands. The first is a review of substantive themes within sociology of education, including some of the developments and trends that have characterized the evolution of the field. The second is an argument about the central importance for sociology of education of normative questions. This chapter completes this second strand of work and specifically makes a case for what we call 'ethical reflexivity' and its relevance for policy-oriented sociology. In doing so, it marks a break with the tenor of previous chapters in that we will not be using it to map and review substantive scholarship in sociology of education; rather, we will be placing almost all our emphasis on questions about its purposes and related methodological considerations. Our central concern in this chapter is, therefore, the role and purposes of sociology of education. In particular, we are interested in consolidating and concluding our arguments about the question of how sociology deals with, and could deal with, value judgements and the different, but partly overlapping, question of how far sociology can and should be policy-oriented – that is, operate as an applied rather than a pure discipline.

Throughout the book we have sought to demonstrate that sociology has an important normative – i.e. ethical and political – dimension. In many cases, most obviously within expressly critical currents, such as Marxism, feminism and CRT, this dimension is deliberately and self-consciously pursued and 'owned'. In other cases, normativity is more implicit. That is, there is a range of ways in which value judgements are embedded in, or implied by, work that is presented as essentially descriptive or explanatory in nature. We have suggested that – and tried to illustrate the ways in which

– both kinds of work make a substantial, although not always recognized, contribution to analysing and understanding educational and social values.

As we hope we have shown, the rationale of much of the work in sociology of education cannot be understood except on the premise that sociologists are interested in the many different kinds of individual and collective goods and harms in which education is implicated. We have used the concept of value fields to indicate the complexity, breadth and diversity of the value concerns lying behind sociology of education. As we indicated in chapter 1, the issue of relative disadvantage is the central normative axis that runs through work in the discipline, and thus the discipline makes the most substantial contribution to understanding the value field of equality and the manifold ways in which various kinds of inequality are reproduced in and through educational processes. However, as we have also seen, the value field of equality interacts with a number of other value fields that sociological work illuminates, including those that have formed the themes of the previous three chapters – knowledge, identity and autonomy. Sociological work on these values and value fields is vital because it moves beyond the processing of conceptual abstractions by engaging with a detailed consideration of what these values can and might mean in specific contexts, the various forms in which they can be socially realized or frustrated, and the continual struggles over how value and worth are allocated.

However, whilst we would maintain that sociology has made and can make an important contribution in this area, we also have to acknowledge that, for very good reasons, there is a very real controversy about how far and in what ways the making of ethical and political judgements can or ought to be seen as part of the job of sociology. What we have said so far is that normative judgements are bound up in sociological work and that sociological work can make a large contribution to understanding the normative dimension of education. It does not follow from these assertions that the making of normative judgements about education (or indeed any other social phenomena) should be embraced as a core task of sociology. That is to say, we can accept (a) that value judgements are inevitable in sociological work and (b) that sociological work is useful in illuminating social values[1] without accepting (c) that sociology has the making of value judgements as a central focus or goal. Indeed, in this book we have highlighted the fundamental ambivalence of much contemporary sociology with regard to values – on the one hand, producing work that is organized around and saturated with the making of value judgements and, on the other, expressing great caution about the possibility of defending value judgements. This ambivalence, we have suggested, has come increasingly to a head as the discipline has developed over the past sixty years and is most conspicuously associated with poststructuralist scepticism – a scepticism which has led, as we said in chapter 4, to a tendency to portray normative complexity but to shy away from directly making normative judgements.

We will spend most of this chapter exploring the relationship between concerns about descriptive and explanatory rigour, on the one hand, and concerns about rigour in the treatment of ethical and political judgements, on the other. Concern for descriptive and explanatory rigour is a well-known component of sociological work. Our central argument is that normative reflexivity, by contrast, is not recognized as a mainstream component of sociological practice,[2] and, in particular, we want to suggest that the intractability of the problem of values in sociology can best be explained by a persistent failure to acknowledge that, in practice, concerns about descriptive/explanatory and ethical/political rigour are inseparable. Hence, we argue, sociologists must find ways of self-consciously addressing these two aspects of rigour together, and we make some suggestions about what might be involved in doing this systematically. In large part we build our argument by engaging with the contrasting position that Hammersley has elaborated and defended in various writings. We begin by using one final example to underline and elucidate further the inextricable links between description/explanation and the evaluative nature of the sociology of education. This example returns us to a number of issues we have previously introduced, including the linkages between explanation and the attribution of responsibility which we introduced in chapter 1, the discussion in chapter 3 about how implicit normativity is produced through the focus and framing of sociological work, and the reflections in that chapter on the ethics and politics of colour-blindness. It also serves as a reminder of the core problematic of structure and agency which pervades the discipline and was the organizing theme of chapter 2. We then go on to make a case for what we call ethical reflexivity through comparison and contrast with Hammersley's arguments and reflect on some of the challenges generated by our position.

In the final section of the chapter we will return to the question with which we began the book, namely that of the nature and purposes of sociology, and summarize our conclusions about the possibilities for and advantages of a policy-oriented sociology of education.

Explanation and responsibility in sociological research

Our example relates to research around inequalities in the attainment of students in schools. In the UK, boys in general, and black boys in particular, have been singled out for special concern in recent public debates around attainment, and it is frequently said that black boys are more likely than other categories of student to be excluded from school or to leave school with low or no formal academic qualifications. The academic debate on this issue – rather like the wider public debate – tends to be somewhat polarized. Broadly speaking – and at the risk of oversimplification[3] – there is, on the one hand, the view represented by researchers such as Gillborn (1990; Gillborn and Youdell 2000). These researchers tend to focus on institutional racism in schools, drawing attention to the ways in which school processes systematically produce the failure and exclusion of a disproportionate number of black boys. By making racism their primary locus of concern, they tend to locate responsibility for the low academic attainment of black boys firmly in the hands of the schooling system. On the other hand, there is the less conventional view, most closely associated in the UK with the work of Sewell, whose primary locus of concern is students' identities and peer-group processes (Sewell 1997; Sewell and Majors 2001). Sewell does write about racism in schools, but his analysis focuses particularly on the need to tackle an anti-school peer-group culture. Whilst, for Gillborn, the solution lies in eradicating racist practices, for Sewell, it consists, to a significant extent, in helping boys who are anti-school both to change their attitudes and behaviour and to navigate the mainstream culture successfully.[4] One of the many analytical difficulties in arbitrating between these competing positions is that of applying competing conceptions of agency and structure and the relationships between them. For example, how far do teachers and black boys have room for manoeuvre to work around and challenge institutional racism, or is the possibility of agency so constrained that it is more valid and politically useful to see teacher and student 'agency' as essentially a product (i.e. explained by) persistent structures of domination and oppression?

There is clearly persuasive evidence supporting both peer-level and institution-level explanations – i.e. that some black boys do get caught up in an anti-school culture and that there are deeply entrenched racist practices in operation in schools which contribute to the academic failure of many black boys. However, the work of Gillborn, Sewell and other specialists in this area shows that the interaction between peer-group cultures and school processes in the production of failure is complicated. There is no mathematical formula that could tell us how much can be explained by institution-level effects and how much by peer-level effects, or indeed how the two kinds of effects interrelate. The analyst therefore has to make a choice about where to place the explanatory emphasis. He or she can emphasize one or the other or both. But whatever choice of explanatory framing the analyst makes has implications for the way in which responsibility for the problem is constructed and thereby has political implications. From Sewell's perspective, the political implication of overstating the extent of institutional racism is the risk of promoting a victim culture where boys can let themselves off the hook if they fail at school by blaming racist schools and teachers. Presumably, for Gillborn, the political implication of locating responsibility with the boys is to allow the schools and the education system to be let off the hook and to help legitimate the arguments of right-wing groups who want us to believe that institutional racism is a myth. An alternative stance is to emphasize both institutional- and peer-group-level explanations. Such a stance also has political implications in that it can be seen as challenging the dualistic either/or terms of the contest and therefore demanding more complex policy solutions. In addition, pointing to different and complementary sources of explanation does not get around the issue of attributing responsibility. It simply ascribes it to both institutional and peer-group levels in some more or less specified combination.

Another key concern that sociologists working in this area have raised is that the whole way in which the debate is often framed – the way in which the supposed problem of the under-attainment of black boys has been identified and the manner in which the question has been asked in the first place – may have potentially damaging ethical or political implications. There are several aspects to this concern. First, as Keddie and Mills, amongst others, have argued (see chapter 4), the emphasis on test performance can contribute to a narrowing of conceptions of what constitutes educational success. Second, placing a strong emphasis on a racialized reading of differences in attainment can obscure other readings of attainment differences, e.g. those that give emphasis to class as an explanatory factor (which some commentators argue are in some measure the 'real' issue). Third, this racialized reading may itself create or reinforce deficit and demeaning representations of black boys which may themselves produce precisely the forms of inequality that are of concern here. Yet, on the other hand, the avoidance of racialized readings risks leaving racist practices intact and could be argued to suffer the same epistemological and political defects of the forms of colour-blindness rejected by critical race theorists. Once again, it is clear that the range of readings open to us are deeply intertwined with fundamental ethical and political dilemmas. In addition, it is worth noting that, in presenting such readings, sociology can be seen as a form of action which can have real effects in the social world, and hence it is a mistake to see the question of focus and framing as purely an academic one.

In short, sociological research is unavoidably bound up with ethical and political considerations. In the rest of the chapter we want to address the question of what sociologists should do about it. In other words, how should sociologists deal with ethical and political considerations and commitments?

There is a longstanding debate in sociology about this very issue. On the one hand, there are those who argue that sociologists should strive to be value neutral and, on the other, those who argue for politically committed or partisan research. The first position is classically represented by Weber (1949) and the second by Gouldner (1962). There is not space here to rehearse and review the history of these debates, so we are going to take as our starting point a sophisticated articulation of the Weberian line presented by Hammersley (2000; Foster et al. 1996). Hammersley's position is useful, not only because it sets out many of the key issues about the relationship between sociology and social values, but also because it represents a plausible and well-defended alternative to the position we are advocating, and we will use his arguments as a way of introducing and elaborating our own central concerns. Whilst there is much in Hammersley's position that we agree with, we are also critical of some aspects of his position. In what follows, we will review what we see as the strengths and weaknesses of Hammersley's line and use this review as a springboard for proposing an alternative approach.

The Hammersley line

The crux of Hammersley's position is that politically committed research is incompatible with academic rigour. The task of sociology, as Hammersley sees it, even when it is related to important public policy debates, should be confined to the production of factual knowledge which is relevant to such debates. As he puts it, '[w]hat is crucial is that as researchers we treat the production of knowledge about some matter as the exclusive immediate goal' (Hammersley 2004). Hammersley's point here is strongly analogous to the point that we considered in chapter 5 about 'cognitive interests' (Schmaus 1994) being separable from political interests. Although Hammersley acknowledges that value judgements are unavoidable in the research process, like Weber, he argues that sociologists should strive to maintain a separation between facts and values and to prevent their values from distorting the facts. Hammersley is not arguing that sociologists should not think about or be influenced by values. Indeed, he maintains that there are at least three ways in which values enter into research. First, he notes that the commitment to the goal of producing knowledge is itself a value commitment. Second, he accepts that a researcher's personal values, including their beliefs about what is of benefit to society, should influence their selection of research topics and questions. Third, he asserts that researchers need to conduct research in ways that protect the interests and welfare of those they are studying, and that this involves them making a series of value and ethical judgements whilst collecting, analysing and writing about data.

So what is it that Hammersley is opposed to? There seem to be at least three main things he is against. First, he is against researchers letting their values shape the way data is collected and analysed, and he argues that establishing the facts about the topic should not be effected by political considerations. However, his call for value-neutral research is not based on a naïve view that this is wholly achievable. His point is simply that '[t]he closer we can approximate to [value neutrality], the less the danger of our political or practical values biasing our results' (Hammersley 2000: 33).[5] Second, Hammersley argues that, in framing their research questions, researchers should avoid making evaluative assumptions and judgements without acknowledging that this is what they are doing and/or without defending their evaluative stance. Third, he is opposed to researchers making policy prescriptions. The exact way he makes this point seems to vary, but he gives a number of reasons for his scepticism here. In particular, he is against any assumption on the part of researchers that they are better qualified to make the everyday moral decisions of the people they are studying than those people themselves. He is also opposed to the tendency for researchers to recommend courses of action which are impractical or which risk making matters worse rather than better. Above all, Hammersley is opposed to researchers prescribing courses of action as if they follow from their research findings rather than from their prior political or ethical beliefs.

According to Hammersley, research cannot provide an adequate basis for policy or practice for two reasons: first, because policy and

practice depend upon making value judgements, which he believes
are outside the scope of research; and, second, because the decisions
made by policymakers and practitioners rely on practical judgements
which are based on local knowledge and experience – knowledge and
experience, for instance, of what is possible or likely to be effective in
the specific circumstances in which they are working.

As we indicated earlier, there is much in Hammersley's position
that we agree with. In particular, we agree that researchers need to
be self-conscious about the way in which their value judgements
shape their research, that researchers need to be especially wary of
the danger of their value judgements preventing them from actively
seeking out and taking account of evidence that might challenge their
prior beliefs and values (although, as Hammersley notes, some value
commitments can help to eliminate error), and that, where necessary, they should be prepared to articulate and defend the evaluative
stances that inform their work. Where we depart from Hammersley
is in relation to the very strong distinction he wants to draw between
knowledge production and knowledge use. As we noted earlier, it is
crucial for Hammersley that research has as its exclusive immediate
goal the production of knowledge, and this means that, when they get
involved in writing about practical or policy implications, researchers
are stepping outside the proper boundaries of research. Maintaining
this strong distinction plays a very important role in Hammersley's
argument in that it helps to underline his emphasis on descriptive and
explanatory rigour in knowledge production by separating off knowledge production from debates about what ought to happen. However,
we are sceptical about how far it is possible or even meaningful to distinguish between the researcher as a producer of knowledge and the
researcher as a citizen with an interest in how knowledge is used, and
it seems to us that Hammersley's emphasis on insulating knowledge
production from knowledge use closes off from scrutiny and consideration issues which should be of vital concern for sociologists.[6] In
particular, Hammersley's position closes off from discussion some of
the practical dilemmas of actors who have to make decisions.[7] Here
we are referring to the practical dilemmas of both researchers and the
people being researched.

To take the situation of researchers first, they are part of the world
they are researching and their work is inevitably bound up with
countless ethical and political choices. Examples of the practical-
ethical issues that concern researchers operating within the real world
are – from whom do we take money to fund our research? What constraints do we allow funders to place on the questions that we ask, the

data that we collect and the way we write about our research? With whom do we collaborate? Above all, how does the way we conduct our research or the focus and framing that we give to it produce real-world effects of the kind we illustrated above in the discussion of black boys' attainment? Hammersley is not denying that these concerns exist. But it seems that he is arguing that they need to be addressed *outside* the domain of research practice and not *within* it.

Hammersley's position also seems to close off from discussion questions about how the people we are researching do and should navigate the political and ethical terrain in which *they* are operating. For Hammersley, the job of the researcher is to produce factual knowledge. Then it is up to practitioners or policymakers to decide what to do with that knowledge. So, arguably, the most crucial and difficult questions relating to what should be done are left to policymakers or practitioners or citizens. Now Hammersley recognizes that researchers are citizens as well as researchers, but he argues for a clear demarcation between these roles. It is only as citizens, he believes, that researchers should concern themselves with the question of what should be done, not as researchers. Hence, once again, these questions about what is to be done are located outside rather than within the domain of research practice. Indeed, it is central to Hammersley's argument that the practical dilemmas of researchers and the people they are studying, although important, should not be allowed to interfere with the goal of knowledge production.

So, if we return to the example we started with, for Hammersley, sociologists, as sociologists, should not concern themselves with what policymakers or teachers should do with the knowledge they have about the causes of the disproportionate numbers of black boys getting low examination grades and being excluded from school. If practical judgements are outside the domain of research, then we have to leave policymakers and teachers to get on with the difficult task of evaluating what is practically desirable and possible in the particular national or local contexts within which they are working. As sociologists, according to Hammersley's model, we should do our fieldwork and write it up on its own terms, detached from vested interests and the pressures of practice, and resist the temptation to interfere with the decisions about what should be done in specific circumstances.

In contrast to Hammersley, who wants to keep the messy world of policy and practice and questions about what should be done at arm's length, we want to argue that engaging with that world should be a central task of sociology. There are two reasons for this. First, whilst accepting the risks to descriptive and explanatory rigour that

Hammersley stresses, we are not convinced that sociologists as sociologists can and should exempt themselves from participating in discussions about what should be done. Although we would not want to overplay the usefulness of sociological expertise in practical and political decision-making, it seems unnecessarily restrictive to rule out the possibility of the sociologist, as sociologist, making any contribution to public life other than the production of knowledge. In short, we would argue that sociologists are not only citizens as well as sociologists but that they are partly citizens *as* sociologists. Second, it seems to us that the distinction between knowledge production and knowledge use is an abstraction that cannot ultimately be sustained in practice. Whether or not sociologists explicitly address or set out the policy and practical implications of their work, practical implications are very frequently either implied by the work or 'read into' it. This is because the way in which accounts are constructed, the language that is used, the factors that are fore-grounded, and the models of explanation that are invoked are all entangled with judgements about what is feasible and desirable. We are using the expression 'entangled with' here to indicate that, although some sociological accounts may directly state or clearly imply normative conclusions, in other cases it is more correct to say that normative claims are practically 'tied up with' the descriptive/explanatory claims made. The descriptive and the normative dimensions of sociological work are knotted together, and often in ways that sociologists 'resist' unknotting.[8] In other words, socio-logical analyses may not *state* practical or policy implications but they often to some degree *point to* them. In addition, as we noted above, our accounts can also have real-world effects. These things being the case, we would argue that sociologists have no choice but to accept responsibility for the practical implications of their work. The example we gave earlier about the discursive framing of the supposed problem of black boys' under-attainment will serve as an illustration of this point. Simply talking in terms of such a 'problem' implies that something should and can be done to address it. Yet questions of whether something should or can be done, let alone of whether there is a problem in the first place, are morally and politically contentious ones. The point we are making here is an echo of the point we made in chapter 3 about the importance of 'hidden premises' in sociological writing, the hidden premise in this case being that something should and can be done to address black boys' under-attainment. It is not easy to get around the operation of hidden premises. We could, for example, simply try to avoid talking about the under-attainment of black boys as a 'problem' at all. But, if we make it an object of study and write about it as if it is a locus of concern, the hidden premise is that it is a problem.

For these reasons, grappling with the practical demands, ethical dilemmas and political considerations embedded in policy and practice forms a central element in the stance we want to advocate here – the stance that we referred to earlier as an ethically reflexive one. We will now set out the elements of what such an ethically reflexive sociology of education might involve.

An ethically reflexive sociology of education

In what follows we are using the term 'ethical reflexivity' as shorthand for political and ethical reflexivity – that is, for reflexivity about the normative dimension of sociological work. In advocating an ethically reflexive sociology of education we are using the concept of reflexivity in a way that reflects, but also extends, fairly common usage in sociology – that is, that one element of rigour involves sociologists being ready to give an account of the way in which their personal involvement in social and fieldwork relations shapes their data collection, analysis and writing. By talking about ethical reflexivity we are emphasizing that it is not just researchers' social relationships in the field that determine the direction and products of their research but also their ethical and political beliefs.[9]

We do not wish to contend that ethical reflexivity demands a particular approach, style or set of methods, or even a self-conscious attachment to the idea of ethical reflexivity. At the end of chapter 3 we identified three broad approaches to managing the normative dimension of sociology of education, and we would like our notion of ethical reflexivity to be seen as sufficiently elastic to have some application within each of these three approaches. The first approach is broadly the one that Hammersley defends, which attempts the highest possible level of value neutrality within the conduct of sociological research. The second approach is the one adopted by critical sociologists who are happy to take normative stances. And the third approach is the poststructuralist one of working with but simultaneously problematizing value judgements. Our contention is that sociologists working within each of these three currents can be more or less ethically reflexive. However, to offer a general account of possible approaches to ethical reflexivity, we would suggest that it could encompass the following elements:

- first, being explicit, as far as is possible, about the value assumptions and judgements that inform or are embedded in every stage of our research
- second, being prepared to deliberate about – and offer an elucidation and defence of – our assumptions and judgements, to the extent that either they might not be shared by others or, conversely, that they are not sufficiently problematized by others[10]
- third, acknowledging, and where possible responding to, tensions between the various values that are embedded in our research
- fourth, taking seriously the practical judgements and dilemmas of the people we are researching[11]
- and, finally, taking responsibility for the political and ethical implications of our research.

Some of these elements echo the line that Hammersley embraces and some take issue with what we have just identified as the limitations of his position. In particular, the first three elements can be seen as a summary of the kind of line that Hammersley adopts about the importance of acknowledging the influence of values on social research, whereas the fourth and fifth elements explicitly give weight to the value dimensions of knowledge use which Hammersley places outside the domain of social research.

What we should stress at this point is that, in arguing for more ethical reflexivity in sociological research, we are not assuming that nobody does it. Nor are we suggesting that everyone should be doing sociology like this all of the time. Furthermore, even for those people who are committed to producing an ethically reflexive account of their work, there are important practical limits to how far one can stand back from and explicate the range of value commitments and judgements inherent in this work.[12] Nevertheless, what we are arguing is that, collectively as sociologists, we need to be more ethically reflexive.

It is worth distinguishing between what we are calling ethical reflexivity and a more general reflexivity about values that is common in critical sociology, especially feminist and poststructuralist work. This general reflexivity about values, which is a key element of methodological rigour, typically involves reflections on the identity of the researcher as a way of indicating the socially constructed nature of the research process and the partiality and contingency of the research account. Ethical reflexivity, on the other hand, in the fullest sense in which it is being advocated here, requires that the researcher links these reflections to an attempt to deliberate about, clarify and justify the value positions that are adopted and to take seriously the feasibilities and practicalities of realizing any alternative, more desirable possible worlds that are implied in those value positions.

The problem we are trying to address here is what we see as a tendency within sociology of education not to take ethical reflexivity seriously enough. In the case of those who adhere to the Hammersley model, reflexivity about values is encouraged in relation to knowledge production but not in relation to knowledge use (a distinction that we have argued above is hard to maintain in practice). Thus, whilst such sociologists might do well in terms of the first three elements that we have outlined, they tend to neglect the other two. For critical sociologists, on the other hand, political commitments and values are central to the research process. Such researchers often seek to defend the values that they espouse and are self-conscious about the political implications of their work (the first, second and fifth elements). However, there is, we would argue, some tendency within this critical genre to ignore or gloss over the tensions between the different values espoused[13] and not to focus upon the practical dilemmas of the people who are being researched[14] (the third and fourth elements). Critical sociologists sometimes write, for example, as if policymakers and practitioners should be able to ameliorate every kind of injustice at once, without addressing the fact that the different facets of justice they are espousing in their research might in practice be incompatible. A typical example of this is where such sociologists promote the values of cultural recognition and associative democracy both at the same time. To put this more concretely, critical sociologists might, for instance, imply that schools ought to respect and validate the cultural identities of students and parents whilst simultaneously implying that school decision-making processes should give more voice to students and parents. Now, of course, these two values are not necessarily incompatible, but they may be – for example, where some of the parents and students in question are sexist, racist, homophobic or disabilist, or a combination of all of these things. In such a situation, practitioners need to decide which value to favour, i.e. voice or recognition – and indeed what the limits to recognition are.[15] For them, there are no means of evading these choices. Typically, the failure of critical sociologists to acknowledge and discuss the implications of tensions between different values arises from a tendency towards doing 'sociology from above' (Cribb and Gewirtz 2003) – that is, a failure to engage with the real-world demands of how the values that they are assuming or espousing might actually be realized. Hence the third and fourth elements of ethical reflexivity are in practice often bound up together.

As we noted in chapter 7, and is also clear from the example that we have drawn upon in this chapter, the issue of 'value tensions' referred to in the third element of ethical reflexivity – given the inextricable linkages between explanations and evaluations for which we have been arguing – is of general epistemological importance for the conduct of sociology. Faced with multiple and often competing readings of the same social phenomena, we could just treat this multiplicity as an interesting assemblage of contrasting 'stories' and leave the various tensions between these stories as unresolved or even unarticulated. We could, in principle, go so far as to affirm that various competing stories (e.g. that to focus on black boys produces racism, on the one hand, and helps combat racism, on the other) are equally true, and indeed this is, as we have signalled before, sometimes a tendency within poststructuralism. In some ways, as we have also indicated, this tendency towards 'relativity' can be productive in that it highlights the different senses and respects in which apparently contradictory statements can be affirmed. However, to the extent to which sociologists are committed to producing valid descriptions and explanations about the nature of the social world, they also need to be prepared to do their best to discriminate between stories where these compete with or contradict one another. The alternative, as we argued in chapter 5, is to embrace (overtly or covertly) a form of wholesale relativism which rules out the possibility of being able either to defend descriptions or to defend ethical and political judgements about how things could and ought to be.

We have argued that there are contrasting 'ethical hazards' attached both to a value-neutral model of sociology – even the heavily qualified and sophisticated version advanced by Hammersley – and to a critical stance. For the former, there is a danger of failing to acknowledge the extent to which sociological analyses are practically entangled with particular ethical and political positions within debates about policy and practice, and hence of sociologists failing to take responsibility for their influence and role as potential social and political agents. For the critical sociologist, on the other hand, there is a danger of relying on a more or less explicit political commitment, often accompanied by an implication that things ought to be done differently, with insufficient attention being given either to debating, clarifying or defending the value judgements made or – even when that is done – to working through the feasibility of, and practical dilemmas associated with, implied alternatives (Sayer 2000).

As we have stressed, what we are advocating as ethical reflexivity is intended to be compatible with a range of approaches and emphases, and we are not suggesting that it is an agenda that everyone should want to embrace in the same way or to the same degree. At a minimum, what we are saying is that the rigour of sociology of education as a discipline is enhanced by some sociologists spending time being explicitly reflexive about educational and social values as well as about the other elements of their work. However, we have also been underlining the potential for stronger and richer versions of ethical reflexivity in sociological scholarship. In particular, in highlighting what we have called 'the fullest sense' of ethical reflexivity – which requires us to deliberate and defend claims about both our value positions and the practicalities of socially realizing them – we are partly reimagining the boundaries and purposes of sociology. According to this 'strong version' of our thesis, the point is not simply that sociologists are necessarily implicated in normative thinking and that they can and should be allowed to take some responsibility for this thinking but that, to put things optimistically, sociologists are in a position to make an important contribution to normative as well as descriptive and explanatory forms of knowledge. In short, on this account, it is not only that ethics contributes to sociology but also that sociology contributes to ethics.

Although we do not have the space here to extend this discussion on the role of sociology within ethical scholarship – and nor would it be appropriate to do so – it is worth noting its significance briefly. Moral and political philosophy has become increasingly preoccupied with the complex relationships, and potential complementarities, between 'ideal theory' (theory which sets aside 'real world' complications), 'nonideal theory' (theory which is responsive to 'real world' complications) and scholarship on 'action design' (Robeyns 2008), and many applied philosophers are looking to form interdisciplinary partnerships with social scientists in order to advance these debates. We believe that, in this sense, sociologists can be 'ethicists' and that they have a very important contribution to make in relation to these debates about the practical realization of ethics.

Key challenges for ethically reflexive sociology

Whilst we have argued that more ethical reflexivity is necessary, we do not want to give the impression that we think that doing it is easy. In the course of this chapter a number of complexities and problems associated with ethical reflexivity have emerged, and in this section we would like to return to what we see as the three main challenges involved.

The first challenge is how to respond to the apparent boundlessness of ethical reflexivity. There are two aspects to this challenge: the question of how far to go and the question of who should do it. There is no obvious limit to how far sociologists can unpack, reflect upon, analyse, debate and defend the value judgements implicit in their work, and, if this process of reflection were taken to extremes, it seems that all research would collapse into a process of value analysis at the expense of the substantive issues that are the focus of the research. Whilst acknowledging that this is a problem in principle, we would suggest that, in essence, it is no different from other aspects of reflexivity that most sociologists now take for granted. For example, the influence of fieldwork and other social relationships upon data collection and analysis could equally well be unpacked and reflected on indefinitely; and, just as with these other forms of reflexivity, the solution to the problem of open-endedness lies in making judgements about what it is significant to focus on and what it is practical to do in the time and space available. Exactly what is significant will obviously depend upon the nature and purposes of the research being undertaken and the social, political and organizational contexts in which the researcher is working. Here we just want to underline the two general criteria of significance that we have indicated in our formulation of the second element of ethical reflexivity: that is, 'being prepared to deliberate about – and offer an elucidation and defence of – our assumptions and judgements, to the extent that either they might not be shared by others or, conversely, that they are not sufficiently problematized by others'. In other words, within any particular research community there will be values that are known to be contentious and controversial and that, as a consequence, stand in need of some clarification and justification. However, it is equally important that, at least some of the time, researchers are prepared to debate – and strive to make explicit and scrutinize – those value commitments which form part of the taken-for-granted world view of the research community of which they are a part.

As regards the question of who should 'do' ethical reflexivity, in practical terms, it is clear that not everyone can be doing it all of the time. Just as some sociologists pay attention to scrutinizing the methodological principles, procedures or instruments that others will relatively unreflexively use as 'tools of the trade', it is also necessary for some to take it upon themselves to scrutinize the often unproblematized ethical judgements that inform sociological analysis. For these sociologists, specific kinds of interdisciplinarity will be invaluable. This will include, as noted above, engaging with scholars in moral and political philosophy or legal theory who are centrally focused on normative questions and engaged in both elucidating normative categories and distinctions and interrogating the basis of normative claims (e.g. Fraser and Honneth 2003). Likewise, we would hope that all sociologists would be prepared to take seriously the importance of this work even if they are not doing it themselves to any significant degree. Indeed, we would see a strong analogy, and even continuity, here between ethical reflexivity as a mode of rigour and what is more conventionally understood as methodological reflexivity as a mode of rigour.

The second challenge is how to respond to the need to combine reflexivity about values and value tensions in the abstract with a concern about the practical realization of values. For, from an ethically reflexive perspective, making visible one's value stances and judgements is not simply an abstract matter of sorting out what one believes to be desirable and why. In deciding what it is we believe, we need to bear in mind the relevance of our beliefs for the practical contexts we are researching. Doing this is much harder than doing 'sociology from above', where values tend to be articulated in the abstract regardless of whether they can feasibly be realized. In concrete terms, an ethically reflexive perspective involves sociologists being prepared to develop their value judgements in a way that is responsive to, and learns from, the practical dilemmas faced by those operating in the social contexts being studied (Cribb and Gewirtz 2005). Responding to this challenge means that sociologists sometimes have to get their hands dirty and possibly be seen to retreat from abstract 'ideals' that are important to them or those around them. Although this attention to practical implications may appear to be asking a lot of them, it only really involves sociologists assuming the same burden of responsibility for their value judgements that practitioners routinely have to take on in deciding what to do on a daily basis.

The final challenge we are going to consider here is arguably the most important upshot of taking the Hammersley model seriously. That is, how can sociologists who have a sense of responsibility for the practical implications of their writing avoid this sense of responsibility from compromising other aspects of methodological rigour – in particular, an openness to falsification claims or to alternative readings of data? It is this challenge that lies behind what we earlier called the intractability of the problem of values in sociology. The problem is how sociologists can let their value commitments fuel their research and, at the same time, be scrupulous about not simply discovering what it is they would like to find out. In relation to this challenge, Hammersley (2004) warns of the danger of 'self-censorship or even the reconstruction of findings to make them more appropriate'. Hammersley's solution to this problem, as we have discussed above, is to make a clear separation between knowledge production and knowledge use, with the sociologist, as sociologist, having responsibility only for the former and seeking to avoid any engagement with the latter. However, as we have also argued above, we do not believe such a clear separation is possible, because every formulation of knowledge will use categories and have emphases that are full of practical import and, in addition, carry potential real-world effects. Hence, a degree of self-censorship in our writing, whether or not we are conscious of it, is inevitable. We cannot negate this fact simply by not paying attention to it. However, recognizing the inextricable practical links between knowledge production and knowledge use does not take away the concern that underpins Hammersley's desire to separate the two. We would acknowledge that there can be a real problem of sociological researchers adopting a deliberately or carelessly partisan approach to the collection and analysis of data in which data is sought and used selectively to support prior commitments or political goals. The challenge, as we see it, entails the researcher being ready to take responsibility for the practical import and effects of their work but doing so in a way that minimizes the kinds of threats to rigour that Hammersley is concerned about.

In fact, we would argue that taking responsibility for the practical implications of our work represents an extension of those concerns with rigour that Hammersley himself stresses. If we are concerned to explicate the way in which our values help to shape fieldwork practices and analysis in the production of knowledge, then as part of that we need to be self-conscious about the way our interests in, or concerns about, potential applications or readings of our research influence the process and products of that research. It is in this way that the imperatives behind Hammersley's position and the partisan model come together: that is to say, the goal of insulating the research process from 'value bias', on the one hand, and the goal of contributing to political and social change through research, on the other. Furthermore, such self-consciousness about the influence of values in the production of knowledge will enable us to signal any potential influences to the reader. It will also demand from us more careful differentiation in the way we write. In particular, we need to differentiate between those recommendations and prescriptions that we believe are based at least in part on our research analyses and those which flow from our prior beliefs and commitments. Although we accept that these processes of explication and differentiation will inevitably be limited and partial, the discipline these involve can only help to enhance rigour. In short, we believe that the need for rigour is best served not by trying to put interests in knowledge use on one side – because this is simply not possible – but rather by incorporating reflexivity about knowledge use into our model of methodological rigour.

The principal concern we have been addressing so far in this chapter is that of sociologists not taking values seriously enough, either because their work is based on a model of value neutrality or because it does not sufficiently interrogate the relationships between their value positions and the ways in which they conduct and write about their research. Our response to this concern is to argue for more of what we are calling ethical reflexivity. Throughout we have elaborated our position by comparing and contrasting it with that of Hammersley. Hammersley's position can itself be seen as a thoughtful and credible response to this need to take values seriously, and we would be happy to see his position labelled as a form of ethical reflexivity. His response, like ours, attempts to avoid the pitfalls of naïve value neutrality and the potential weaknesses of unreflexive partisanship in sociology. His position is based on a careful articulation of the value-laden nature of research and places a particular stress on knowledge as the core value that is constitutive of sociology and one that needs 'safeguarding' from other values which might undermine its centrality. Our response to the question of taking values seriously is based on a different analysis of the relationship between knowledge production and knowledge use and of the role of the sociological researcher, and is one which has more sympathy with the project of partisan research. We see no reason, in principle, why someone cannot do good, rigorous sociology which is informed by a commitment to bringing about social and political change (although we readily acknowledge there are a number of hazards on this path). In fact, we have argued that sociologists have a responsibility to think about the role their work plays or might play in the ethical and political contexts and contests in which it is located.

In summary, we want to agree with Hammersley that we must be careful that our value commitments do not undermine the rigour and independence of our work. But we also want to align ourselves with those within critical sociology traditions who see their research work as politically committed. The task, as we see it, is to pay attention both to rigour and to values, and that means – amongst other things

– aiming for rigour in the way we handle values in our research. In fact, what we are arguing is that paying attention to values needs to become a taken-for-granted component of methodological rigour.

Conclusion

To conclude, we will return to the question of the purposes of sociology, which is closely allied to the questions about values we have been debating in this chapter. To reiterate the point we made in chapter 1, the core raison d'être of sociology of education is to contribute to knowledge. Hammersley's robust defence of the central importance of knowledge production to sociology is a useful reminder of this. However, as we have just been suggesting, we do not see this as ruling out the possibility or benefits of a more policy-oriented sociology, and, as we have seen through a broad range of examples reviewed in this book, there are many examples of sociologists whose work revolves around issues of contemporary social concern and which has a strong applied dimension. The field we have been reviewing in this book is, therefore, not purely an academic discipline and is in large part a sociology *for* education as well as a sociology *of* education.

As we noted at the end of chapter 4, the evolution of the discipline can be seen as a story of proliferating perspectives in which confidence about the practical usefulness of the discipline is gradually lost as theoretical sophistication is gained. It is a story of an increasing awareness of normative complexity accompanied by an increasing wariness about the making of normative judgements. Given that the policy-oriented role depends upon a willingness to take some kind of stand on political and ethical matters, then this wariness about normativity easily translates into a kind of extremely elaborate and sophisticated agnosticism about policy and practice. However, our view is that sociologists, in their role as sociologists (and not just as non-sociological citizens), should not feel debarred from making interventions in either ethical debates or policy processes, although doing so should entail a high degree of reflexivity and should, of course, be subject to the same level of public and political scrutiny as any other element of their work. Furthermore, as Hammersley (2008) readily acknowledges, many people who call themselves researchers do see it as their role to participate in debates about knowledge use. Whilst we wholeheartedly agree with Hammersley that policy prescriptions 'are not logically derived from research evidence', and that, therefore, the contribution of researchers to knowledge use should not be in this form and should, in any event, be treated with a very sceptical eye, this is precisely why we are advocating ethical reflexivity. Our point is that the fudges about the boundaries between knowledge production and knowledge use that Hammersley is concerned about will not be eliminated simply by refusing to label certain activities as research or by asserting that certain things fall outside the researcher's role. Collective ethical reflexivity would, we believe, help to expose the very fudges that Hammersley is exercised about.

In addition, for the reasons that we explored in this and the previous chapter, there are good reasons for sociologists to feel more hesitant about making specific policy recommendations than about setting out broad critiques and recommendations concerning policy directions. But, above all, and this is the crux of what we have been arguing, we believe that a policy orientation can be of intrinsic value to sociology. Specifically, we are saying that the kind of epistemological orientation that takes policy relevance seriously fosters useful analytic and theoretical dispositions (including those relating to ethical reflexivity), which can lead to more defensible and 'thicker' descriptions of educational phenomena, and thereby contributes to the health of the discipline and not just to practical agendas.

Finally, we wish to question whether the stress that we have placed upon sociologists and practical actors being differently positioned might not, after all, be overdone. Poststructuralist perspectives, for example, can be seen as a way of articulating the problems and limitations of what Taylor calls 'the epistemological standpoint' (Taylor 1997: 2) – i.e. the modernist conception of knowledge as a detached neutral representational account of an external, stable social world. As Taylor puts it, 'our understanding of the world is grounded in our dealings with it' (ibid.: 12). It is not just that the social world is complex and in flux. It is that we can ultimately only make sense of it from, so to speak, within the midst of it. This insight subverts the traditional distinction between detached, context-independent theory, on the one hand, and situated, context-constituted practical agency, on the other. There is no context-independent vantage point, no 'view from nowhere' (Nagel 1986), from which it is possible to understand social agents. Rather, if they wish to understand social agents, sociologists have to be prepared to take seriously and engage with the practical choices these agents face – i.e. what to do in specific contexts and how to ethically appraise the processes in which one is implicated. If we accept this, then it becomes imperative for sociologists to close the gap between 'theory' and 'situated life-worlds', and to build bridges between theoretical judgement and practical judgement.

Notes

Preface

1 Here we are using the term 'normative' in a different sense from the one that is common in sociology. In the latter sense normative means normalizing, i.e. presenting certain things (e.g. certain identities or forms of behaviour) as 'normal', and thereby positioning those who do not share these 'normal' identities and forms of behaviour as 'other', aberrant or deficient. In the sense we are using it here, 'normative' means embodying political and ethical value judgements – that is, more or less explicit judgements that certain things are ethically 'bad' or 'wrong' and ought to be different in respects that may be more or less specified.

Chapter 1   Understanding Education

1 Here the term 'normative' is being used in the more conventional socio-logical sense (see note 1 above)

Chapter 2   Understanding Structure and Agency

1 It is perhaps worth noting that this view of education as serving an integrative function is still prevalent in some sectors of society, if not in sociology, as illustrated by the case of the Bedouin girls that we discussed in chapter 1, where it is presumed, at least in official policy discourses, that the integration of the girls into the 'mainstream' values of Israeli society is a good thing.

2 Sometimes this contrast is made by reference to a broader tradition such as 'interpretivism', which encompasses other influential currents of work with different philosophical roots, notably phenomenology and hermeneutics, which has entered sociology through the work of figures such as Schutz, Berger and Luckman.

3 Although it must be noted that Bourdieu and Bernstein are, in many ways, drawing on a 'different' Durkheim from the Durkheim who

appears in the American structural functionalism of Parsons and his acolytes. The version upon which Bernstein and Bourdieu tend to draw (evident particularly in Durkheim's work on religion and primitive classification) is the one more often associated with the French anthropological tradition of structuralist and poststructuralist thought (Bernstein 1974; Atkinson 1985), which focuses on the way in which subjectivity is shaped by categories of thought and language.

4 Political arithmetic is an important tradition of work in sociology of education. However, we have not focused on it in this chapter because it is arguably more a practical tradition than a theoretical perspective. Its central concern is the deployment of 'hard' data with the intention of influencing policymaking. It typically focuses on class inequalities in access to education at various levels and, in the UK, was influential at key points in the twentieth century, most famously influencing the move away from selective schooling from the late 1960s onwards. Work in the political arithmetic tradition tends to be largely atheoretical and is not allied to any particular theoretical paradigm (Heath 2000).

5 For an excellent review of the new sociology and its contributions to understandings of the curriculum, see Whitty (1985).

Chapter 3   Varieties of Critique

1 Later in the book (see chapter 6) we distinguish between shallower and deeper forms of multicultural education. What Ladson-Billings and Tate are analysing and critiquing here is broadly what we refer to as the shallower version of multicultural education. One way of producing deeper versions of multicultural education is precisely to take into account the lessons of CRT.

2 Here Walkerdine is drawing attention to a fundamental aspect of what we introduced above as intersectionality, namely the need to think simultaneously about class and gender (and indeed about the manifold social processes through which women's identities and positions are produced).

3 Here we are using this vague expression 'carried by', rather than the expression 'embedded in' that we have used in other places, because there are a range of ways in which value judgements may 'attach' to sociological analyses (and we will provide further clarification of this in chapter 8). However, a useful indication of what we mean is provided by the 'hidden premise' model which will be presented shortly. 'Carried by' indicates that, although some sociological claims may directly entail normative conclusions, in other cases it is more correct to say that descriptive claims and normative claims are entangled with one another.

Chapter 4   Social Reproduction

1 While he does not discuss Bernstein here, Giroux's characterization

and critique of Bourdieu's approach could arguably equally be taken to apply to Bernstein's work on classification and framing (see chapter 2). Although he offers a far more fine-grained and sophisticated analysis of the relationship between social relations of power, knowledge and individual consciousness than that provided by the radical left theories Giroux is criticizing, ultimately Bernstein seems to give far more emphasis to the role of social structures and systems in shaping individual consciousness than the other way round.

2 Again this is a criticism that could equally be applied to Bernstein's work at the time.

3 There are echoes here of Walkerdine's arguments about the limits that the materiality of the body places on the range of available subject positions (see chapter 3).

Chapter 5   Knowledge and the Curriculum

1 We are using politics here as shorthand to represent what might more accurately be described as political, economic and social interests. And we are using the term curriculum to refer to both the formal or official curriculum and the hidden curriculum (and thereby to encompass those aspects of pedagogy and assessment that co-constitute the curriculum).

Chapter 6   Identity

1 In drawing attention to the role of discourse in the construction of identities, we are not adopting a strong social constructionist stance. Specifically, we are not claiming that there is no objective reality that is being represented by these discourses, but only that it is through discourse that certain features of the objective reality are made significant. For example, in our society it is common for people to identify themselves in terms of their ethnicity, but it is rare for people to identify themselves in terms of eye colour or foot size, even though these are equally part of the objective reality.

2 Shain is referring here to disturbances in the English northern towns of Bradford, Oldham, Leeds, Burnley and Stoke-on-Trent in the spring and summer of 2001. These disturbances were the culmination of long-standing inter-ethnic tensions in these areas, fuelled by the racist activities of the National Front and the British National Party. They prompted a series of commissions and reports on community cohesion.

Chapter 8   Extending Reflexivity in Sociology of Education

1 There are a whole lot of interesting and important questions that fall within a domain that might be labelled 'sociology of ethics and values', which concerns amongst other things the social construction of value judgements, the social explanation of the construction of value positions and the social

effects of value judgements – in short, a sociology about ethics. The central concerns of this chapter overlap with this domain but are rather different. Here we are interested primarily in values and ethics within the practice of sociology itself but also, as we will go on to suggest, in the potential contribution of sociology to ethics as an interdisciplinary field.

2 For example, when reviewing articles that have been submitted for publication, sociologists will routinely ask questions such as – How solid is the evidence base upon which the claims are made? Are the interpretations of the evidence plausible? Have alternative interpretations been overlooked? Does the author show an appreciation of the subtleties of the processes he or she is describing or explaining? There is no similar expectation that analogous questions will be asked about the defensibility of the normative assumptions, reasoning or judgements in the work being reviewed.

3 We recognize that the authors we go on to cite, and others working in this area, have positions that are more nuanced and complex than we can do justice to here, but our primary concern is to illustrate the kinds of value positions that are embedded in sociological research rather than to capture the exact value positions of specific authors. Nonetheless, it is important to see that, however nuanced positions are, some degree of polarization persists, to the extent that authors place emphasis upon or foreground some explanatory readings over others.

4 As we will see, it can be argued that neither Gillborn nor Sewell should be offering solutions and that, in doing so, they are leaving behind the proper business of sociology. By contrast, we are maintaining that the teasing out of practical implications should be an important part of sociology. But, in any case, for the purpose of our argument here, what matters is that work such as that of Gillborn and Sewell has practical implications that point in certain directions, whether or not these implications are explicitly spelled out or advocated. We return to this point below as part of our debate with Hammersley.

5 It should be noted, though, that Hammersley also acknowledges 'that non-epistemic values and commitments' can contribute to more defensible sociological claims, as 'sometimes they may enable us to recognise things and draw inferences that others, with different values and commitments, would have overlooked or seen wrongly' (2008: 553). The argument that values can help to strengthen sociology is also advanced by Abraham (1996: 84), who argues, amongst other things, that 'political commitments … may further [the pursuit of truth] because committed researchers may investigate their problems more relentlessly and thoroughly than their counterparts who are socially indifferent'.

6 Other authors (e.g. Abraham 1995, 1996; Connolly 2001) have made analogous points to the ones we are making here. In particular, Connolly (2001), in his own critique of Hammersley's position, has set out what he sees as the basis and the practical implications of researchers' political

responsibility for their work. Like us, he is also happy to endorse the Hammersley line on the importance of methodological rigour, and quite properly points out that methodological rigour is a necessary component of political responsibility, and hence that partisanship in research, without rigour, is likely to be self-defeating. We should also reinforce the point, made above, that the line that Connolly takes and that we are taking here stands in a tradition of work in defence of partisan research (Gouldner 1962).

7 It also closes off from discussion the way in which knowledge production is shaped through collective action in practical contexts. That is, researchers produce knowledge not on their own but by drawing on insights derived from their engagement with others outside formalized research practices (Jones 2004). This is another respect in which we would suggest the distinction between knowledge production and knowledge use can be overstated.

8 We are talking about the *entanglement* of the normative and the descriptive rather than wanting to suggest that the descriptive directly *entails* the normative because of what Hammersley (2008: 551) calls 'the contingent relationship between facts and value conclusions'. We are grateful to Hammersley for reminding us so forcefully of this contingent relationship.

9 Perhaps we should make clear that our advocacy of reflexivity does not imply an attachment to what Hammersley calls an 'expressivist epistemology, whereby any account of the world produced by research simply reflects the personal and social characteristics of the person who produced it and therefore can never be said objectively to represent the relevant aspects of reality' (Hammersley 2004). We see reflexivity not as a manifestation of a person-relative conception of knowledge, but as a dimension of rigour in the context of a realist conception of knowledge.

10 Such deliberation is important because, although values are inherently contestable, it is important for sociologists to acknowledge that they are nevertheless rationally debatable (Abraham 2008; Gewirtz and Cribb 2008b).

11 This approach of placing the making of practical judgements at the heart of social science research is an example of what Flyvbjerg (2001), drawing upon the Aristotelean tradition, calls *phronetic* social science, and what he furthermore suggests ought to be the *raison d'être* for *all* social science research. *Phronetic* social science involves finely textured description and analysis of practical activity and the ways in which practical knowledge is used in everyday situations, with the specific purposes of understanding what is happening in a particular instance, in whose interests it is happening, whether it is desirable and what can be done to improve things.

12 A good example of this is Walford's (1994) account of the evaluative judgements made in an ethnographic study of Kingshurst City

Technology College (Walford and Miller 1991), in which just a few brief examples from the data set generate several pages of ethical reflection, thereby illustrating how the process could be extended indefinitely.

13 In critical poststructuralist work there is even a tendency to make a virtue of presenting unresolved tensions and contradictions as part of one's account.

14 Focusing on the practical dilemmas of the people we are researching might mean a number of things, ranging from involving them in the design and conduct of the research (as in recent moves towards greater 'user engagement' or more radical movements around democratic research) to somehow putting ourselves 'in their shoes'.

15 Of course, in cases, for example, where the views voiced by parents and students diverge, they may also need to decide whose voices to listen to.

References

Abraham, J. (1995) *Divide and School: gender and class dynamics in comprehensive education*, London: Falmer.

Abraham, J. (1996) Positivism, prejudice and progress in the sociology of education, *British Journal of Sociology of Education*, 17 (1): 81–6.

Abraham, J. (2008) Politics, knowledge and objectivity in sociology of education: a response to the case for 'ethical reflexivity' by Gewirtz and Cribb, *British Journal of Sociology of Education*, 29 (5): 549–58.

Abu-Rabia-Queder, S. (2006) Between tradition and modernization: understanding the problem of Bedouin female dropout, *British Journal of Sociology of Education*, 27 (1): 3–19.

Adams, M. (2006) Hybridizing habitus and reflexivity: towards an understanding of contemporary identity? *Sociology*, 40 (3): 511–28.

Ahmad, F. (2001) Modern traditions? British Muslim women and academic achievement, *Gender and Education*, 13 (2): 137–52.

Althusser, L. (1971) Ideology and the ideological state apparatuses, in L. Althusser, *Lenin and Philosophy, and Other Essays*, trans. B. Brewster, New York: Monthly Review Press.

Apple, M. W. (1982) Reproduction and contradiction in education: an introduction, in M. W. Apple (ed.), *Cultural and Economic Reproduction in Education*, London: Routledge & Kegan Paul.

Apple, M. W. (2004) *Ideology and Curriculum*, New York: Routledge.

Archer, L. (2003) *Race, Masculinity and Schooling: Muslim boys and education*, Buckingham: Open University Press.

Archer, L. (2008) The impossibility of minority ethnic educational 'success'? An examination of the discourses of teachers and pupils in British secondary schools, *European Educational Research Journal*, 7 (1): 89–107.

Archer, L., and Francis, B. (2007) *Understanding Minority Achievement in Schools: race, gender, class and 'success'*, London: Routledge.

Archer, L., Hollingworth, S., and Halsall, A. (2007) 'University's not for me – I'm a Nike person': urban, working-class young people's negotiations of 'style', identity and educational engagement, *Sociology*, 41 (2): 219–38.

Aronowitz, S., and Giroux, H. (1991) *Postmodern Education: politics, culture and social criticism*, Minneapolis: University of Minnesota Press.

Atkinson, D. (1998) The production of the pupil as a subject within the art curriculum, *Journal of Curriculum Studies*, 30 (1): 27–42.

Atkinson, P. (1985) *Language, Structure and Reproduction: an introduction to the sociology of Basil Bernstein*, London: Methuen.

Bache, I. (2003) Governing through governance: education policy control under New Labour, *Political Studies*, 51 (2): 300–14.

Back, L. (1996) *New Ethnicities and Urban Culture: racisms and multiculture in young lives*, London: UCL Press.

Ball, S. J. (1994) Education policy, power relations and teachers' work, in S. J. Ball, *Education Reform: a critical and post-structural approach*, Buckingham: Open University Press.

Ball, S. J. (2003) The teacher's soul and the terrors of performativity, *Journal of Education Policy*, 18 (2): 215–28.

Ball, S. J. (2007) *Education plc: understanding private sector participation in public sector education*, London and New York: Routledge.

Banks, J. A. (1993) Multicultural education: development, dimensions, and challenges, *Phi Delta Kappan*, 75: 22–8.

Barnes, R. D. (1990) Race consciousness: the thematic content of racial distinctiveness in critical race scholarship, *Harvard Law Review*, 103: 1864–71.

Barry, B. (2001) *Culture and Equality*, Cambridge: Polity.

Basit, T. (1997) *Eastern Values, Western Milieu: identities and aspirations of adolescent British Muslim girls*, Aldershot: Ashgate.

Bauman, Z. (2004) *Identity*, Cambridge: Polity.

Becher, T., and Trowler, P. (2001) *Academic Tribes and Territories*, Buckingham: Open University Press.

Beck, J., and Young, M. (2005) The assault on the professions and the restructuring of academic and professional identities: a Bernsteinian analysis, *British Journal of Sociology of Education*, 26 (2): 183–97.

Becker, H. S. (1952a) Social class variations in the teacher–pupil relationship, *Journal of Educational Sociology*, 25: 451–65.

Becker, H. S. (1952b) The career of the Chicago public school teacher, *American Journal of Sociology*, 57: 470–7.

Becker, H. S. (1953) The teacher in the authority system of the public school, *Journal of Educational Sociology*, 27: 128–41.

Bell, D. (1979) Bakke, minority admissions, and the usual price of racial remedies, *California Law Review*, 76: 3–19.

Bell, D. (1987) *And We are Still Not Saved: the elusive quest for racial justice*, New York: Basic Books.

Bell, D. (2004) *Silent Covenants: Brown vs. Board of Education and the unfulfilled hopes for racial reform*, New York: Oxford University Press.

Benjamin, S., Nind, M., Hall, K., Collins, J., and Sheehy, K. (2003) Moments of inclusion and exclusion: pupils negotiating classroom contexts, *British Journal of Sociology of Education*, 24 (5): 547–58.

Bernstein, B. (1971) On the classification and framing of educational knowledge, in M. Young (ed.), *Knowledge and Control: new directions for the sociology of education*, London: Collier-Macmillan.

Bernstein, B. (1974) *Class, Codes and Control*, London: Routledge & Kegan Paul.

Biesta, G. (2009) The role of educational ideals in teachers' professional work, in S. Gewirtz, P. Mahony, I. Hextall and A. Cribb (eds), *Changing Teacher Professionalism: international trends, challenges and ways forward*, London and New York: Routledge.

Bottomore, T. (1977) Foreword to P. Bourdieu and J.-C. Passeron, *Reproduction in Education, Society and Culture*, London and Beverly Hills: Sage.

Bourdieu, P. (1972) *Outline of a Theory of Practice*, Cambridge: Cambridge University Press.

Bourdieu, P., and Passeron, J.-C. (1977) *Reproduction in Education, Society and Culture*, London and Beverly Hills: Sage.

Bowles, S., and Gintis, H. (1976) *Schooling in Capitalist America: educational reform and the contradictions of economic life*, New York: Basic Books.

Bowles, S., and Gintis, H. (1988) Reply to our critics, in M. Cole (ed.), *Bowles and Gintis Revisited: correspondence and contradiction in educational theory*, London and New York: Falmer Press.

Brah, A. (1992) Difference, diversity and differentiation, in J. Donald and A. Rattansi (eds), *'Race', Culture and Difference*, London: Sage.

Brewster, P. (1988) School days, school days, in D. Spender and E. Sarah (eds), *Learning to Lose: sexism and education*, London: Women's Press.

Bryan, B., Dadzie, S., and Scafe, S. (1985) Learning to resist: black women in education, in B. Bryan, S. Dadzie and S. Scafe (eds), *The Heart of the Race: black women's lives in Britain*, London: Virago.

Butler, J. (1990) *Gender Trouble: feminism and the subversion of identity*, London: Routledge.

Butler, J. (1993) *Bodies that Matter*, New York: Routledge.

Butler Kahle, J., Parker, L., Rennie, L., and Riley, D. (1993) Gender differences in science education: building a model, *Educational Psychologist*, 4: 379–404.

Burr, V. (1995) *An Introduction to Social Constructionism*, London: Routledge.

Byfield, C. (2008) *Black Boys Can Make It: how they overcome the obstacles to university in the UK and USA*, Stoke-on-Trent: Trentham.

Byrne, E. (1978) *Women and Education*, London: Routledge & Kegan Paul.

Castells, M. (2004) *The Information Age: economy, society and culture*, Vol. 2: *The Power of Identity*, 2nd edn, Oxford: Blackwell.

Christensen, C. (1996) Disabled, handicapped or disorordered: 'what's in a name?', in C. Christensen and F. Rizvi (eds), *Disability and the Dilemmas of Education and Justice*, Buckingham: Open University Press.

Clarke, J., and Newman, J. (2009) The rise of the citizen-consumer: implications for public service professionalism, in S. Gewirtz, P. Mahony, I. Hextall and A. Cribb, (eds), *Changing Teacher Professionalism: international trends, challenges and ways forward*, London and New York: Routledge.

Cohen, P. (1968) *Modern Social Theory*, London: Heinemann.

Connolly, P. (2001) Review symposium: taking sides in social research: essays on partisanship and bias, *British Journal of Sociology of Education*, 22 (1): 164–9.

Connolly, P. (2003) The development of young children's ethnic identities, in C. Vincent (ed.), *Social Justice, Education and Identity*, London: Routledge/Falmer.

Corrigan, P. (1979) *Schooling and the Smash Street Kids*, Macmillan: London.

Crenshaw, K., Gotanda, N., Peller, G., and Thomas, K. (1995) Introduction to K. Crenshaw, N. Gotanda, G. Peller, and K. Thomas (eds), *Words that Wound: critical race theory, assaultive speech, and the First Amendment*, Boulder, CO: Westview Press.

Cribb, A., and Gewirtz, S. (2003) Towards a sociology of just practices: an analysis of plural conceptions of justice, in C. Vincent (ed.), *Social Justice, Education and Identity*, London: Routledge/Falmer.

Cribb, A., and Gewirtz, S. (2005) Navigating justice in practice: an exercise in grounding ethical theory, *Theory and Research in Education*, 3 (3): 327–42.

Cribb, A. and Gewirtz, S. (2007) Unpacking autonomy and control in education: some conceptual and normative groundwork for a comparative analysis, *European Educational Research Journal*, 6 (4): 203-13.

Dale, R. (1981) Control, accountability and William Tyndale, in R. Dale, G. Esland, R. Fergusson and M. McDonald (eds), *Education and the State*, Vol. 2: *Politics, Patriarchy and Practice*, Lewes: Falmer.

Dale, R. (1982) Education and the capitalist state: contributions and contradictions, in M. W. Apple (ed.), *Cultural and Economic Reproduction in Education*, London: Routledge & Kegan Paul.

Davies, B. (1989) *Frogs and Snails and Feminist Tales: preschool children and gender*, Sydney: Allen & Unwin.

Davies, B. (1993) *Shards of Glass: children reading and writing beyond gendered identities*, Cresskill, NJ: Hampton Press.

Day, C., and Sachs, J. (2004) *International Handbook on the Continuing Professional Development of Teachers*, Maidenhead: Open University Press.

De Wolfe, P. (1988) Women's studies: the contradictions for students, in D. Spender and E. Sarah (eds), *Learning to Lose: sexism and education*, London: Women's Press.

Delamont, S. (1989) *Knowledgeable Women: structuralism and the reproduction of elites*, London: Routledge.

Delgado, R., and Stefancic, J. (2000) Introduction to R. Delgado and J. Stefancic (eds), *Critical Race Theory: the cutting edge*, 2nd edn, Philadelphia: Temple University Press.

Dewey, J. ([1916] 1966) *Democracy and Education*, New York: Free Press.

DfEE (Department of Education and Employment) (2000) *Sex and Relationship: education guidance*, London: DfEE.

Dixson, A. D., and Rousseau, C. K. (2005) And still we are not saved: critical race theory and education ten years later, *Race, Ethnicity and Education*, 8 (1): 7–27.

Du Gay, P. (2000) *In Praise of Bureaucracy: Weber, organization, ethics*, London: Sage.

Duncan, G. (2002) Beyond love: a critical race ethnography of the schooling of adolescent black males, *Equity and Excellence in Education*, 35 (2): 131–43.

Durkheim, E. (1961) *Moral Education*, New York: Free Press.

Eurydice (2004) *Evaluation of Schools providing Compulsory Education in Europe*, Brussels: Eurydice, Directorate-General for Education and Culture, European Commission.

Evans, G. (1988) 'Those loud black girls', in D. Spender and E. Sarah (eds), *Learning to Lose: sexism and education*, London: Women's Press.

Fernandez, L. (2002) Telling stories about school: using critical race theory and Latino critical theories to document Latina/Latino education and resistance, *Qualitative Inquiry*, 8 (1): 45–65.

Fisher, P., and Fisher, R. (2007) The 'autodidact', the pursuit of subversive knowledge and the politics of change, *Discourse: Studies in the Cultural Politics of Education*, 28 (4): 515–29.

Flyvbjerg, B. (2001) *Making Social Science Matter: why social inquiry fails and how it can succeed again*, Cambridge: Cambridge University Press.

Foster, P., Gomm, R., and Hammersley, M. (1996) *Constructing Educational Research: an assessment of research on school processes*, London: Falmer.

Foucault, M. (1980) *Power/knowledge*, ed. C. Gordon, Harlow: Prentice-Hall.

Fraser, N. (1989) *Unruly Practices: power, discourse and gender in contemporary social theory*, Cambridge: Polity.

Fraser, N. (1997) *Justice Interruptus: critical reflections on the 'postsocialist' condition*, New York: Routledge.

Fraser, N., and Honneth, A. (2003) *Redistribution or Recognition? A political-philosophical exchange*, London and New York: Verso.

Gellner, E. (1974) The new idealism, in A. Giddens (ed.), *Positivism and Sociology*, London: Heinemann.

Gellner, E. (1992) *Postmodernism, Reason and Religion*, London: Routledge.

Gewirtz, S. (2002) *The Managerial School: postwelfarism and social justice in education*, London: Routledge.

Gewirtz, S. and Cribb, A. (2003) Recent Readings of Social Reproduction: four fundamental problematics, *International Studies in Sociology of Education*, 13 (3): 243–260.

Gewirtz, S. and Cribb, A. (2006) What to do about values in social research: the case for ethical reflexivity in the sociology of education, *British Journal of Sociology of Education*, 27 (2): 141-155.

Gewirtz, S. and Cribb, A. (2008a) Identity, diversity and equality in education: mapping the normative terrain, *European Educational Research Journal*, 7 (1): 39-49.

Gewirtz, S., and Cribb, A. (2008b) Differing to agree: a reply to Hammersley and Abraham, *British Journal of Sociology of Education*, 29 (5): 559–62.

Gibson, M. A. (1988) *Accommodation without Assimilation: Sikh immigrants in an American high school*, New York: Cornell University Press.

Giddens, A. (1991) *Modernity and Self-Identity: self and society in the late modern age*, Cambridge: Polity.

Gillborn, D. (1990) *'Race', ethnicity and education: teaching and learning in multi-ethnic schools*, London: Unwin Hyman.

Gillborn, D. (2005) Education policy as an act of white supremacy: whiteness, critical race theory and education reform, *Journal of Education Policy*, 20 (4): 484–505.

Gillborn, D. (2008) *Racism and Education: coincidence or conspiracy?* Abingdon & New York: Routledge.

Gillborn, D., and Mirza, H. (2000) *Educational Inequality: mapping race, class and gender*, London: Ofsted.

Gillborn, D., and Youdell, D. (2000) *Rationing Education: policy, practice, reform and equity*, Buckingham: Open University Press.

Giroux, H. (1983) Theories of reproduction and resistance in the new sociology of education: a critical analysis, *Harvard Educational Review*, 53 (3): 257–93.

Gitlin, T. (1995) *The Twilight of Common Dreams: why America is wracked by culture wars*, New York: Henry Holt.

Gleeson, D., and Husbands, C. (2001) *The Performing School: managing, teaching, and learning in a performance culture*, London: Routledge/Falmer.

Goldrick-Rab, S. (2006) Following their every move: an investigation of social-class differences in college pathways, *Sociology of Education*, 79 (1): 61–79.

Gouldner, A. (1962) Anti-minotaur: the myth of value-free sociology, *Social Problems*, 9: 199–213.

Gramsci, A. (1971) *Selections from the Prison Notebooks*, London: Lawrence & Wishart.

Hall, S. (1996) Who needs 'identity'?, in S. Hall and P. Du Gay (eds), *Questions of Cultural Identity*, London: Sage.

Halsey, A. H., Floud, J., and Anderson, C. A. (eds) (1961) *Education, Economy and Society: a reader in the sociology of education*, New York: Free Press.

Halstead, M., and Haydon, G. (2007) *The Common School and the Comprehensive Ideal: a defence by Richard Pring with complementary essays*, Chichester: Wiley-Blackwell.

Hammersley, M. (2000) *Taking Sides in Social Research: essays on partisanship and bias*, London and New York: Routledge.

Hammersley, M. (2004) Personal communication, 22 March.

Hammersley, M. (2008) Reflexivity for what? A response to Gewirtz and Cribb on the role of values in the sociology of education, *British Journal of Sociology of Education*, 29 (5): 549–58.

Harding, S. (1986) *The Science Question in Feminism*, Milton Keynes: Open University Press.

Harding, S. (1991) *Whose Science? Whose Knowledge? Thinking from women's lives*, Milton Keynes: Open University Press.

Harker, R., and May, S. A. (1993) 'Code and habitus': comparing accounts of Bernstein and Bourdieu, *British Journal of Sociology of Education*, 14 (2): 160–78.

Harris, C. (1993) Whiteness as property, *Harvard Law Review*, 106: 1707–91.

Harris, R. (2006) *New Ethnicities and Language Use*, Basingstoke: Palgrave Macmillan.

Hayes, D. (2003) Mapping transformations in educational subjectivities: working within and against discourse, *International Journal of Inclusive Education*, 7 (3): 7–18.

Heath, A. (2000) The political arithmetic tradition in the sociology of education, *Oxford Review of Education*, 26 (3–4): 313–31.

Hebdige, D. (1979) *Subculture: the meaning of style*, London: Methuen.

Helgøy, I., and Homme, A. (2007) Towards a new professionalism in school: a comparative study of teacher autonomy in Norway and Sweden, *European Educational Research Journal*, 6 (3): 232–49.

Helgøy, I., Homme, A., and Gewirtz, S. (2007) Local autonomy or state control? Exploring the effects of new forms of regulation in education, *European Educational Research Journal*, 6 (3): 198–202.

Hildebrand, G. (1996) Redefining achievement, in C. Gipps and P. Murphy (eds), *Equity in the Classroom: towards effective pedagogy for girls and boys*, London: Falmer.

Holt, M. (1978) *The Common Curriculum: its structure and style in the comprehensive school*, London: Routledge & Kegan Paul.

hooks, b. (1994) *Teaching to Transgress: education as the practice of freedom*, New York: Routledge.

Hudson, C. (2007) Governing the governance of education: the state strikes back, *European Educational Research Journal*, 6 (3): 266–82.

Hughes, E. C. (1942) The study of institutions, *Social Forces*, 20: 307–10.

Hughes, G. (2001) Exploring the availability of student scientist identities within curriculum discourse: an anti-essentialist approach to gender-inclusive science, *Gender and Education*, 13 (3): 275–90.

Humm, M. (1991) *Border Traffic: strategies of contemporary women writers*, Manchester: Manchester University Press.

Jackson, S. (1988) Girls and sexual knowledge, in D. Spender and E. Sarah (eds), *Learning to Lose: sexism and education*, London: Women's Press.

Jay, M. (2003) Critical race theory, multicultural education, and the hidden curriculum of hegemony, *Multicultural Perspectives*, 5 (4): 3–9.

Jenkins, R. (1992) *Pierre Bourdieu*, London: Routledge.

Jones, K. (2004) In the destructive element immerse? Research/activism. Paper presented in the 'Really Useful Knowledge? Qualitative research, policy and practice' Seminar Series, Centre for Public Policy Research, King's College London, 9 February.

Jones, K. (2005) Remaking education in Western Europe, *European Educational Research Journal*, 4 (3): 228–42.

Jones, K. (2009) Peculiarities of the English? International policy orthodoxy and 'national cultures' of teaching, in S. Gewirtz, P. Mahony, I. Hextall and A. Cribb (eds), *Changing Teacher Professionalism: international trends, challenges and ways forward*, London and New York: Routledge.

Katz, Y. (1998) *Report of the Investigating Committee on the Bedouin Education System in the Negev*, Jerusalem: Ministry of Education [in Hebrew].

Keddie, A., and Mills, M. (2007) Teaching for gender justice, *Australian Journal of Education*, 51 (2): 205–19.

Kelly, A. (1987) The construction of masculine science, in A. Kelly (ed.), *Science for Girls*, Milton Keynes: Open University Press.

Kincheloe, J., and Steinberg, S. (1997) *Changing Multiculturalism*, Buckingham: Open University Press.

Kozol, J. (1991) *Savage Inequalities*, New York: Crown.

Ladson-Billings, G. (1998) Just what is critical race theory and what's it doing in a nice field like education? *International Journal of Qualitative Studies in Education*, 11 (1): 7–24.

Ladson-Billings, G. (1999) Preparing teachers for diverse student populations: a critical race theory perspective, *Review of Research in Education*, 24: 211–47.

Ladson-Billings, G., and Tate, W. F. (1995) Toward a critical race theory of education, *Teachers College Record*, 97 (1): 47–68.

Lambert, R., and McCarthy, C. (eds) (2006) *Understanding Teacher Stress in an Age of Accountability*, Greenwich, CT: Information Age.

Lather, P. (1991) *Getting Smart: feminist research and pedagogy with/in the postmodern*, New York: Routledge.

Lawton, D. (1975) *Class, Culture and the Curriculum*, London: Routledge & Kegan Paul.

Lingard, B., Martino, W., Mills, M., and Bahr, M. (2002) *Addressing the Educational Needs of Boys: strategies for schools*, Canberra: Commonwealth Department of Education, Science and Training.

Lipman, P. (2009) Neo-liberal reform and teachers' work: the case of Chicago, in S. Gewirtz, P. Mahony, I. Hextall and A. Cribb (eds), *Changing Teacher Professionalism: international trends, challenges and ways forward*, London and New York: Routledge.

Lobban, G. (1977) Sexist bias in reading schemes, in M. Hoyles (ed.), *The Politics of Literacy*, London: Writers and Readers Publishing Cooperative.

Mac an Ghaill, M. (1988) *Young, Gifted and Black*, Milton Keynes: Open University Press.

Mac an Ghaill, M. (1994) *The Making of Men: masculinities, sexualities and schooling*, Buckingham: Open University Press.

Mac an Ghaill, M. (2000) The cultural production of English masculinities in late modernity, *Canadian Journal of Education*, 23 (2): 88–101.

McLaren, P. (1995) *Critical Pedagogy and Predatory Culture*, London and New York: Routledge.

MacNaughton, G. (1997) Feminist praxis and the gaze in the early childhood curriculum, *Gender and Education*, 9 (3): 317–26.

McPherson, A., and Raab, C. (1988) *Governing Education: a sociology of policy since 1945*, Edinburgh: Edinburgh University Press.

McRobbie, A., and McCabe, T. (1981) *Feminism for Girls*, London: Routledge & Kegan Paul.

Maguire, M. (2009) Towards a sociology of the global teacher, in M. W. Apple, S. J. Ball and L. A. Gandin (eds), *The Routledge International Handbook of the Sociology of Education*, London: Routledge.

Mahony, P. (1988) Introduction, in D. Spender and E. Sarah (eds), *Learning to Lose: sexism in education*, London: Women's Press.

Mahony, P., and Hextall, I. (1998) Effective teachers for effective schools, in R. Slee, G. Weiner and S. Tomlinson (eds), *School Effectiveness for Whom? Challenges to the school effectiveness and school improvement movements*, London: Routledge.

Majone, G. (ed.) (1996) *Regulating Europe*, London: Routledge.

Marx, K. ([1867] 1969) *Capital*, vol. I, Moscow: Progress.

Marx, K., and Engels, F. ([1848] 2002) *The Communist Manifesto*, New York: Penguin.

May, S. (ed.) (1999) *Critical Multiculturalism: rethinking multicultural and anti-racist education*, London: Falmer.

Middleton, S. (1993) *Educating Feminists: life histories and pedagogy*, New York: Teachers College Press.

Middleton, S. (1995) Doing feminist theory: a post-modernist perspective, *Gender and Education*, 7 (1): 87–100.

Miller, J. (1990) *Creating Spaces and Finding Voices: teachers collaborating for empowerment*, New York: SUNY Press.

Mills, C. W. (1959) *The Sociological Imagination*, Harmondsworth: Penguin.

Mirza, H. (1992) *Young, Female and Black*, London: Routledge.

Mirza, H. (2008) *Race, Gender and Educational Desire: why black women succeed and fail*, London: Routledge.

Molnar, A. (1996) *Giving Kids the Business: the commercialization of America's schools*, Dunmore, PA: Westview Press.

Molnar, A. (2005) *School Commercialism: from democratic ideal to market commodity*, New York: Routledge.

Moore, R., and Young, M. (2001) Knowledge and the curriculum in the sociology of education: towards a reconceptualisation, *British Journal of Sociology of Education*, 22 (4): 445–61.

Moore, R., Arnot, M., Beck, J., and Daniels, H. (eds) (2006) *Knowledge, Power and Educational Reform: applying the sociology of Basil Bernstein*, London: Routledge.

Morais, A., Neves, I., Davies, B., and Daniels, H. (eds) (2001) *Towards a Sociology of Pedagogy: the contribution of Basil Bernstein to research*, New York: Peter Lang.

Muller, J., Davies, B., and Morais, A. (eds) (2004) *Reading Bernstein, Researching Bernstein*, London: Routledge/Falmer.

Nagel, T. (1986) *The View from Nowhere*, Oxford: Oxford University Press.

Nash, R. (1999) *School Learning: conversations with the sociology of education*, Palmerston North, NZ: Delta.

Nash, R. (2004) Can the arbitrary and the necessary be reconciled? Scientific realism and the school curriculum, *Journal of Curriculum Studies*, 36 (5): 605–23.

Ozga, J. (1987) Studying educational policy through the lives of policy makers: an attempt to close the macro–micro gap, in S. Walker and L. Barton (eds), *Changing Policies, Changing Teachers*, Milton Keynes: Open University Press.

Ozga, J. (1988) *Schoolwork: approaches to the labour process of teaching*, Milton Keynes: Open University Press.

Parsons, T. (1961) The school class as a social system, in A. H. Halsey, J. Floud and C. A. Anderson (eds), *Education, Economy and Society: a reader in the sociology of education*, New York: Free Press.

Payne, I. (1988) Sexist ideology and education, in D. Spender and E. Sarah (eds), *Learning to Lose: sexism and education*, London: Women's Press.

Pinson, H. (2008) The excluded citizenship identity: Palestinian/Arab Israeli young people negotiating their political identities, *British Journal of Sociology of Education*, 29 (2): 201–12.

Power, S., Edwards, T., Whitty, G., and Wigfall, V. (2003) *Education and the Middle Class*, Buckingham: Open University Press.

Rattansi, A. (1992) Changing the subject: racism, culture and education, in J. Donald and A. Rattansi (eds), *'Race', Culture and Difference*, London: Sage.

Reay, D. (2005) Beyond consciousness? The psychic landscape of social class, *Sociology*, 39 (5): 911–28.

Renold, E. (2005) *Girls, Boys and Junior Sexualities: exploring children's gender and sexual relations in the primary school*, London: Routledge/Falmer.

Renold, E. (2006) 'They won't let us play unless you're going out with one of them': girls, boys and Butler's 'heterosexual matrix' in the primary years, *British Journal of Sociology of Education*, 27 (4): 489–509.

Rich, A. (1983) Compulsory heterosexuality and lesbian existence, *Signs*, 5 (4): 631–60.

Robertson, S. (2000) *A Class Act: changing teachers' work, the state, and globalisation*, New York: Falmer.

Robertson, S. (2008) 'Remaking the world': neo-liberalism and the transformation of education and teachers' labour, in L. Weis and M. Compton (eds), *The Global Assault on Teachers, Teaching and their Unions*, New York: Palgrave.

Robeyns, I. (2008) Ideal theory in theory and practice, *Social Theory and Practice*, 34 (3): 341–61.

Robins, D., and Cohen, P. (1978) *Knuckle Sandwich: growing up in a working-class city*, Harmondsworth: Penguin.

Rousseau, C., and Tate, W. (2003) No time like the present: reflecting on equity in school mathematics, *Theory into Practice*, 42 (3): 210–16.

Sarah, E. (1988) Teachers and students in the classroom: an examination of classroom interaction, in D. Spender and E. Sarah (eds), *Learning to Lose: sexism and education*, London: Women's Press.

Sarah, E., Scott, M., and Spender, D. (1988) The education of feminists: the case for single-sex schools, in D. Spender and E. Sarah (eds), *Learning to Lose: sexism and education*, London: Women's Press.

Sarup, M. (1978) *Marxism and Education*, New York: John Wiley.

Sayer, A. (2000) *Realism and Social Science*, London: Sage.

Schmaus, W. (1994) *Durkheim's Philosophy of Science and the Sociology of Knowledge*, Chicago: University of Chicago Press.

Scott, M. (1988) Teach her a lesson: sexist curriculum in patriarchal education, in D. Spender and E. Sarah (eds), *Learning to Lose: sexism and education*, London: Women's Press.

Scott, M. (2005) Writing the history of humanity: the role of museums in defining origins and ancestors in a transnational world, *Curator*, 48 (1): 74–85.

Sewell, T. (1997) *Black Masculinities and Schooling: how black boys survive modern schooling*, Stoke-on-Trent: Trentham.

Sewell, T., and Majors, R. (2001) Black boys and schooling: an intervention framework for understanding the dilemmas of masculinity, identity and underachievement, in R. Majors (ed.), *Educating our Black Children: new directions and radical approaches*, London: Routledge/Falmer.

Seymour, E. (1995) The loss of women from science, mathematics, and engineering undergraduate majors: an explanatory account, *Science Education*, 4: 437–73.

Shain, F. (2003) *The Schooling and Identity of Asian Girls*, Stoke-on-Trent: Trentham.

Sikes, P. (2006) In the shadow of the research assessment exercise? Working in a 'new' university, *Studies in Higher Education*, 31 (5): 555–68.

Skeggs, B. (2004) *Class, Self, Culture*, London: Routledge.

Skelton, C., and Francis, B. (2005) *A Feminist Critique of Education*, London: Routledge.

Smethem, L. (2007) Retention and intention in teaching careers: will the new generation stay? *Teachers and Teaching*, 13 (5): 465–80.

Smith, E. (2003) Failing boys and moral panics: perspectives on the underachievement debate, *British Journal of Educational Studies*, 51 (3): 282–95.

Smyth, J., Dow, A., Hattam, R., Reid, A., and Shacklock, G. (2000) *Teachers' Work in a Globalizing Economy*, London and New York: Routledge.

Solorzano, D. (2001) Critical race theory, racial microagressions, and campus racial climate: the experiences of African-American college students, *Journal of Negro Education*, 69: 60–73.

Solorzano, D., and Yosso, T. (2002) Critical race methodology: counter-storytelling as an analytical framework for education research, *Qualitative Inquiry*, 8: 23–44.

Spender, D. (1988) Education or indoctrination, in D. Spender and E. Sarah (eds), *Learning to Lose: sexism and education*, London: Women's Press.

Spender, D. and Sarah, E. (eds) ([1980] 1988) *Learning to Lose: sexism in education*, London: Women's Press.

Stevenson, H. (2007) Guest editorial: changes in teachers' work and the challenges facing teacher unions, *International Electronic Journal for Leadership in Learning*, 11 (13), http://www.ucalgary.ca/~iejll/volume11/editorial.htm (accessed 18 March 2008).

Tate, W. F. (1994) From inner city to ivory tower: does my voice matter in the academy? *Urban Education*, 29 (3): 245–69.

Tate, W. F. (1997) Critical race theory and education: history, theory and implications, *Review of Research in Education*, 22: 195–247.

Taylor, C. (1997) *Philosophical Arguments*, Cambridge, MA: Harvard University Press.

Teranishi, R. (2002) Asian Pacific Americans and critical race theory: an examination of school racial climate, *Equity and Excellence in Education*, 35 (2): 144–54.

Trenchard, L. (1988) Young lesbians in school, in D. Spender and E. Sarah (eds), *Learning to Lose: sexism and education*, London: Women's Press.

Troman, G. (2000) Teacher stress in the low-trust society, *British Journal of Sociology of Education*, 21 (3): 331–53.

Troyna, B., and Carrington, B. (1990) *Education, Racism and Reform*, London and New York: Routledge.

Valli, L., and Buese, D. (2007) The changing roles of teachers in an era of high-stakes accountability, *American Educational Research Journal*, 44 (3): 519–58.

Vlaeminke, M., McKeon, F., and Comber, C. (1997) *Breaking the Mould: an assessment of successful strategies for attracting girls into science, engineering and technology*, London: Department of Trade and Industry.

Walford, G. (1994) Political commitment in the study of the City Technology College, Kinghurst, in D. Halpin and B. Troyna (eds), *Researching Education Policy: ethical and methodological issues*, London: Falmer.

Walford, G., and Miller, H. (1991) *City Technology College*, Milton Keynes: Open University Press.

Walkerdine, V. ([1981] 1990) Sex, power and pedagogy, in V. Walkerdine, *Schoolgirl Fictions*, London: Verso.

Walkerdine, V., Lucey, H., and Melody, J. (2001) *Growing Up Girl: psychosocial explorations of gender and class*, Basingstoke: Palgrave.

Ward, S. (1996) *Reconfiguring Truth: post-modernism, science studies and the search for a new model of knowledge*, New York: Rowman & Littlefield.

Waters, M. C. (1994) Ethnic and racial identities of second-generation black immigrants in New York City, *International Migration Review*, 28: 795–820.

Weaver-Hightower, M. (2003) The 'boy turn' in research on gender and education, *Review of Educational Research*, 73 (4): 471–98.

Weber, M. (1949) *The Methodology of the Social Sciences*, New York: Free Press.

Weis, L., and Compton, M. (eds) (2007) *The Global Assault on Teachers, Teaching and their Unions*, New York: Palgrave.

Whitbread, A. (1988) Female teachers are women first: sexual harassment at work, in D. Spender and E. Sarah (eds), *Learning to Lose: sexism and education*, London: Women's Press.

Whitty, G. (1985) *Sociology and School Knowledge: curriculum theory, research and politics*, London: Methuen.

Whyte, J. (1985) Girl friendly science and the girl friendly school, in J. Whyte, R. Deem and M. Cruickshank (eds), *Girl Friendly Schooling*, London: Methuen.

Wilkinson, R. (2005) *The Impact of Inequality: how to make sick societies healthier*, London: Routledge.

Williams, P. (1997) *Seeing a Color-Blind Future: the paradox of race*, New York: Noonday Press.

Williams, R. (1981) *The Sociology of Culture*, Chicago: University of Chicago Press.

Willis, P. (1977) *Learning to Labour: how working class kids get working class jobs*, Farnborough: Saxon House.

Winch, C., and Foreman-Peck, L. (2005) Towards an applied theory of teaching. Paper presented in the 'Changing Teacher Roles, Identities and Professionalism' ESRC/TLRP Seminar Series, Seminar 3: Conceptions of Professionalism and Professional Knowledge, King's College London, 16 May; http://www.tlrp.org/dspace/handle/123456789/754 (accessed 21 November 2008).

Yates, L. (1997) Gender equity and the boys' debate: what sort of challenge is it? *British Journal of Sociology of Education*, 18 (8): 337–47.

Young, M. (ed.) (1971) *Knowledge and Control: new directions for the sociology of education*, London: Collier-Macmillan.

Young, M. (1973) Curricula and the social organization of knowledge, in R. Brown (ed.), *Knowledge, Education and Cultural Change*, London: Tavistock.

van Zanten, A. (2004) Education restructuring in France: middle-class parents and educational policy in metropolitan contexts, in S. Lindblad and T. Popkewitz (eds), *Educational Restructuring: international perspectives on travelling policies*, Greenwich, CT: Information Age.

Index